LITTLEPORT

LINE ART

JEAN SHAW

Littleport Line Art - Local Businesses and Landmarks

ISBN-13: 978-0955773693
ISBN-10: 0955773695

Disclaimer:

Note from Jean

We all lead busy lives, rushing from one thing to another with barely time to pause for breath, BUT sometimes we just have to slow down and be aware of our surroundings.

This book is a snapshot of some of the businesses you can find in Littleport, together with their telephone numbers where possible. However, I make no guarantees about their accuracy as nothing remains the same for ever.

The book is in three sections – businesses in the village, some of those on the outskirts, and churches, schools, etc.

I apologise in advance for those I've missed out.

All the drawings can be **lightly coloured** if you wish.

Mindful colouring is a relaxing pastime known to reduce stress, but I would suggest you use crayons as opposed to paints or felt tips.

They are more versatile and less likely to bleed through to the following pages.

(My youngest son (who has autism) helped me take the photos, usually early on Sunday mornings when there were few people around. We know they are not brilliant, but at least we didn't have our thumbs in any of them. Hopefully they are all recognisable.)

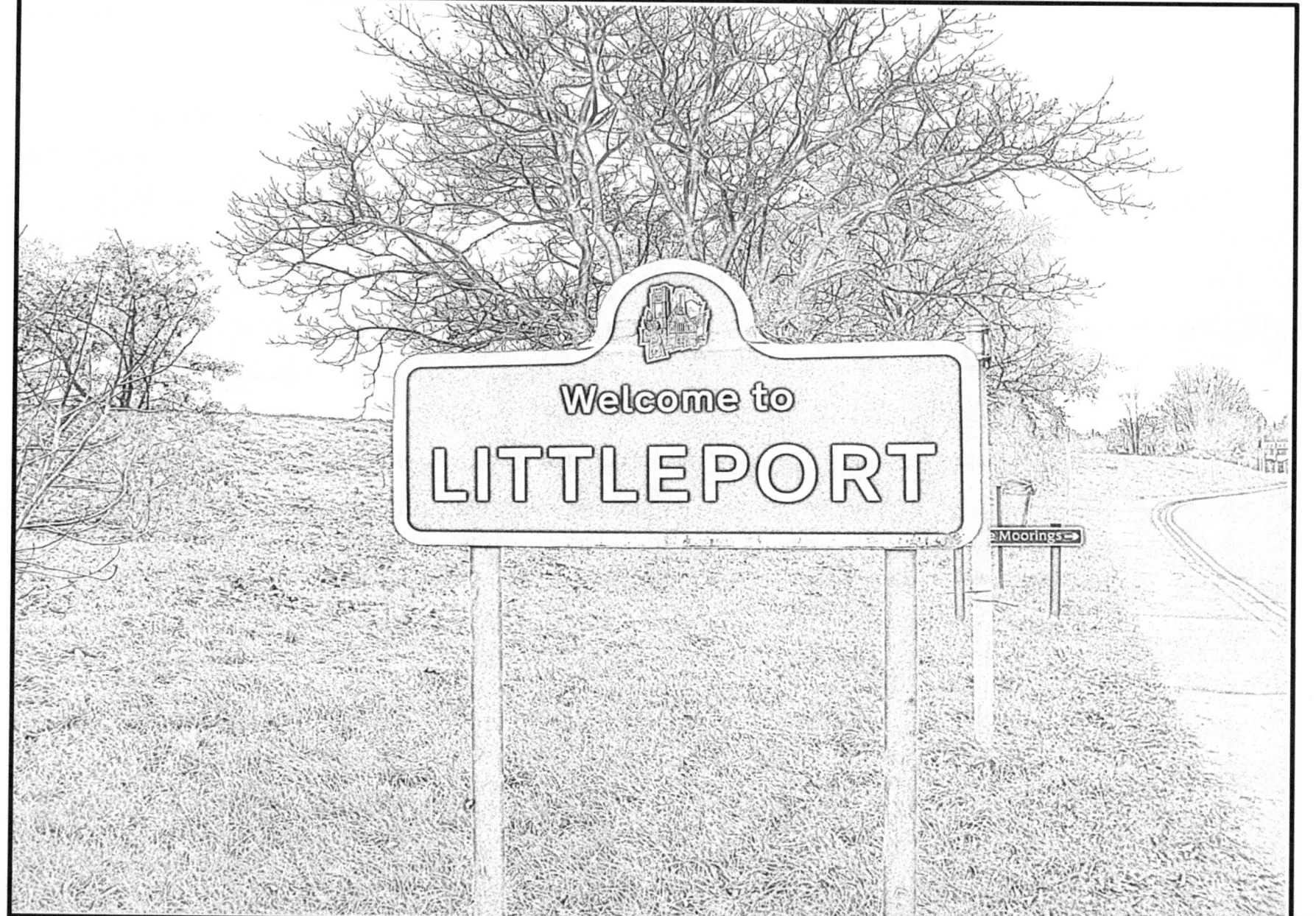

Here is a poem I wrote several years ago BEFORE we lost our butcher, baker, bank, estate agent, hardware store, wedding outfitter, and annual show, so I apologise for it no longer being accurate.

That's the nature of life though...

...nothing remains the same for ever.

Littleport

Set within the fenlands
Is the village I call home
Littleport's expanding fast
It certainly has grown

The locals are all friendly
And most will say "Hello"
They'll smile and pass the time of day
It wasn't always so

Back in the 1800's
That may not have been the case
For taxes led to riots
Causing havoc in the place

Some labourers went to prison
Five hung by their necks
Others went to New South Wales
Names changed to keep respect

Years have passed now senseless crime
Gives Littleport a name
Like vandalism, petty theft
By people with no shame

If punishments as years before
Were deportation, hanging, prison
These mindless individuals
Might have a different vision

Littleport's got a lot to offer
Has all the shops we need
Butcher, baker, grocer
Library for those who read

We have a new health centre
Optician, dentist too
Turf accountant if you want to bet
Tattoo parlour –yes that's true

We've a handy bank, Post Office
And a useful launderette
Sports centre, pubs and garages
And free parking don't forget

Two local schools and playgroups
A drop in centre too
Chapels, Halls, St. George's Church
To suit your point of view

If you're looking for a carpet
Hardware or DIY
Special gift or wedding suit
Main Street's the place to try

We've restaurants and takeaways
For all who like to eat
Hairdressers and chiropodist
For bad hair or troubled feet

There's an accountant if you need one
Solicitors as well
Even estate agents
If you've a house to rent or sell

We've a very pleasant river
Fire station that's just fine
And a useful railway station
Which serves the London line

As transport links get better
The employment's not just farming
Industrial parks are growing up
With a speed that's quite alarming

But still we have the rich fen soil
And dark and fertile means
Sugar beet, potatoes, wheat
Barley, oats and beans

Historically there's been an annual show
Where produce was displayed
But development's meant the site has gone
So locals are dismayed

For people came from miles around
To celebrate the day
Even Harley riders
From as far as USA

Littleport has quite a lot
As a village it's okay
It's where I chose to make my home
And where I'll likely stay

Section 1

- J H Adam & Son — (01353) 860222
- Alis Kebabs — (01353) 863862
- Baynurs Tattoos — (01353) 860552
- Bijou Kitchen — (01353) 860518
- Bizzie Lizzie — (01353) 860002
- Branching Out Charity Shop — (01353) 863561
- The Cod Father — (01353) 860362
- Co-op Main Street — (01353) 860234
- Co-op Wisbech Road — (01353) 864040
- The Copper Cup — (01353) 861317
- Cost Cutter — (01353) 967102
- The Crown — (01353) 862700
- Erika's Barbershop — (01353) 862429
- The Fen House Restaurant — (013530 860645
- Flowers by Chloe — (01353) 863200
- YPL Granby Businesses Café and Charity Shop — (01353) 864777
- Habis Café and Restaurant — 07445831648
- Happy House — (01353) 860064
- Hey Bendalls — (01353) 663581
- Holmes Furnishers and The Other Shop — (01353) 860985
- Hongs Fish and Chips and Chinese Takeaway — (01353) 968034
- The Indian Garden — (01353) 863642
- Inspire Hairdresser — (01353) 864664
- J & E Clothing Alterations and Repairs — 07550141953

- Kings Barbers — (01353) 967843
- Littleport Bargain Centre — (01353) 862242
- Littleport Dental Surgery — 08443756454
- Littleport Ex Servicemens Club — (01353) 860378
- Loach and Wade Optometrists — (01353) 862333
- McColls — (01353) 864780
- P J Medcalf Accountant — (01353) 861675
- Plough and Harrow — (01353) 863512
- Melly made Designs — 07979357844
- Ness & Ems Hairdressers — (01353) 860521
- Nik Nik's Unisex Hairdressers — (01353)967080
- R J Pepper Funeral Services — (01353) 860400
- Pizza Town — (01353) 860860
- Rimas Shop — 07599378885
- Rumble's Fish Bar — (01353) 860200
- SD Bookmakers — (01353) 860144
- S& J Accountancy Services — (01353) 864928
- Sigma Embroidery & Printing — (01353) 863049
- Spice Lounge — (01353) 864663
- Supermarket Cheap — 07572552930
- Swan on the River — (01353) 861677
- Tanya Constable Hair — (01353) 862586
- Angela Wilson — (01353) 862470
- Wok This Way — (01353) 860669
- YPL Performing Arts Studio — (01353) 864611

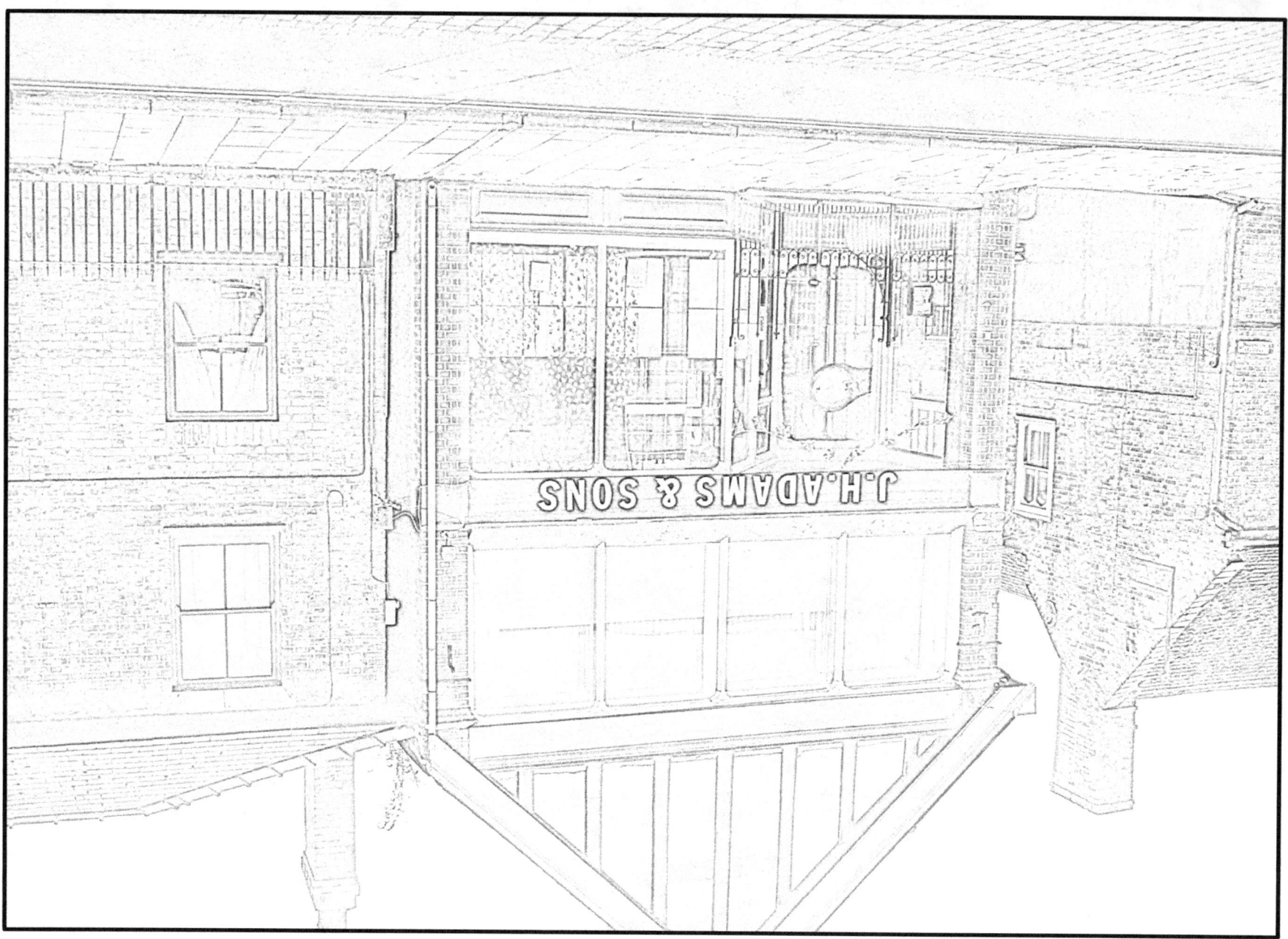

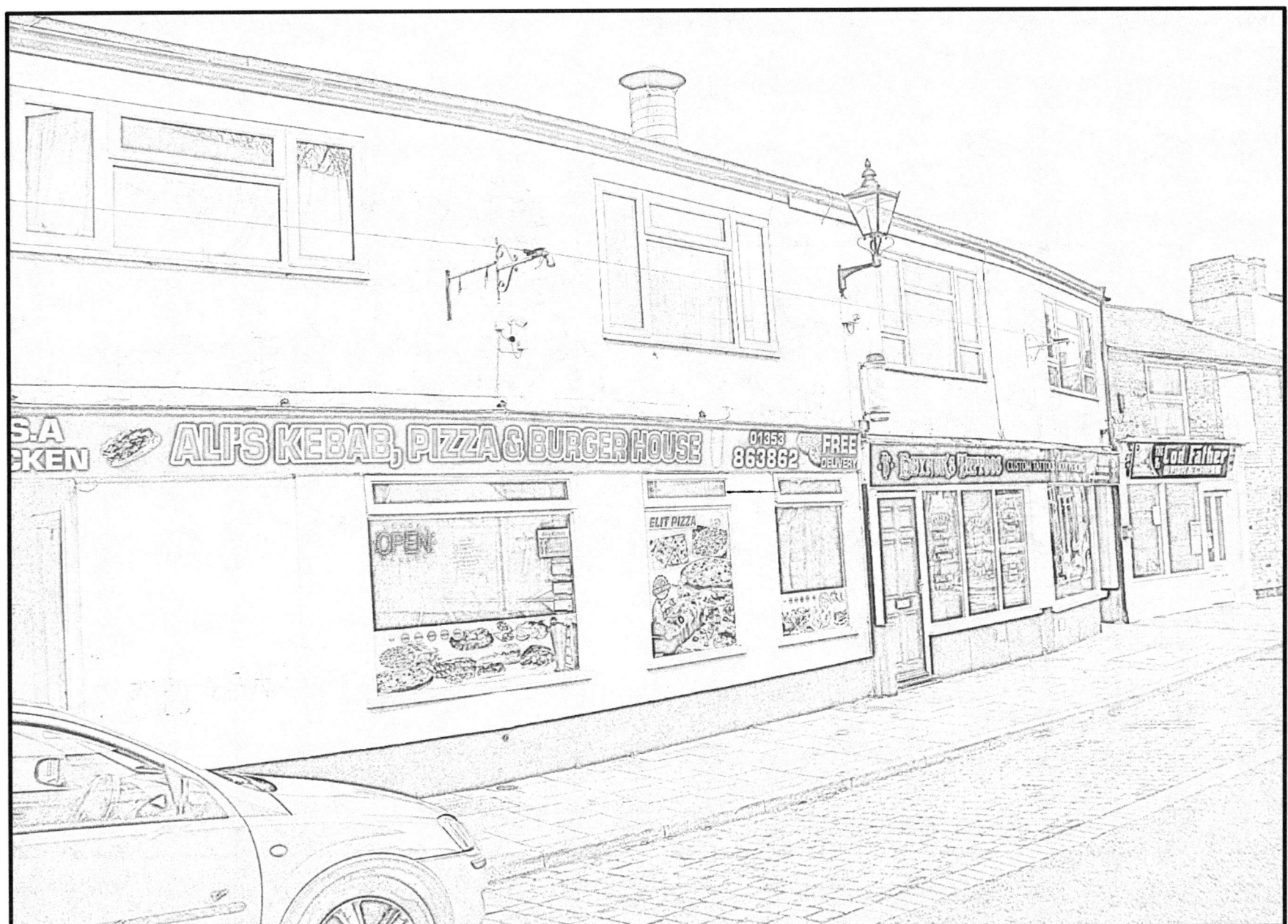

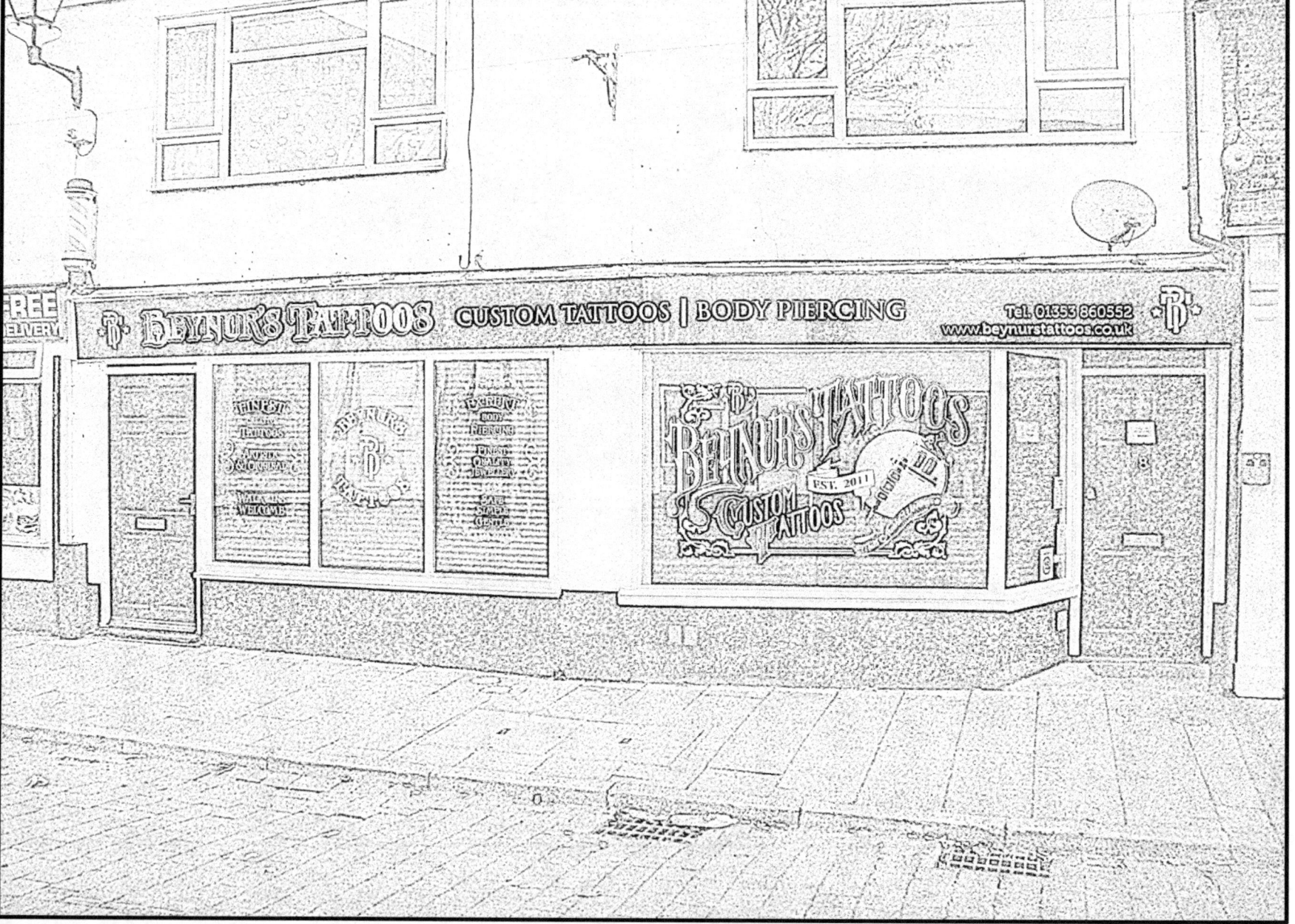

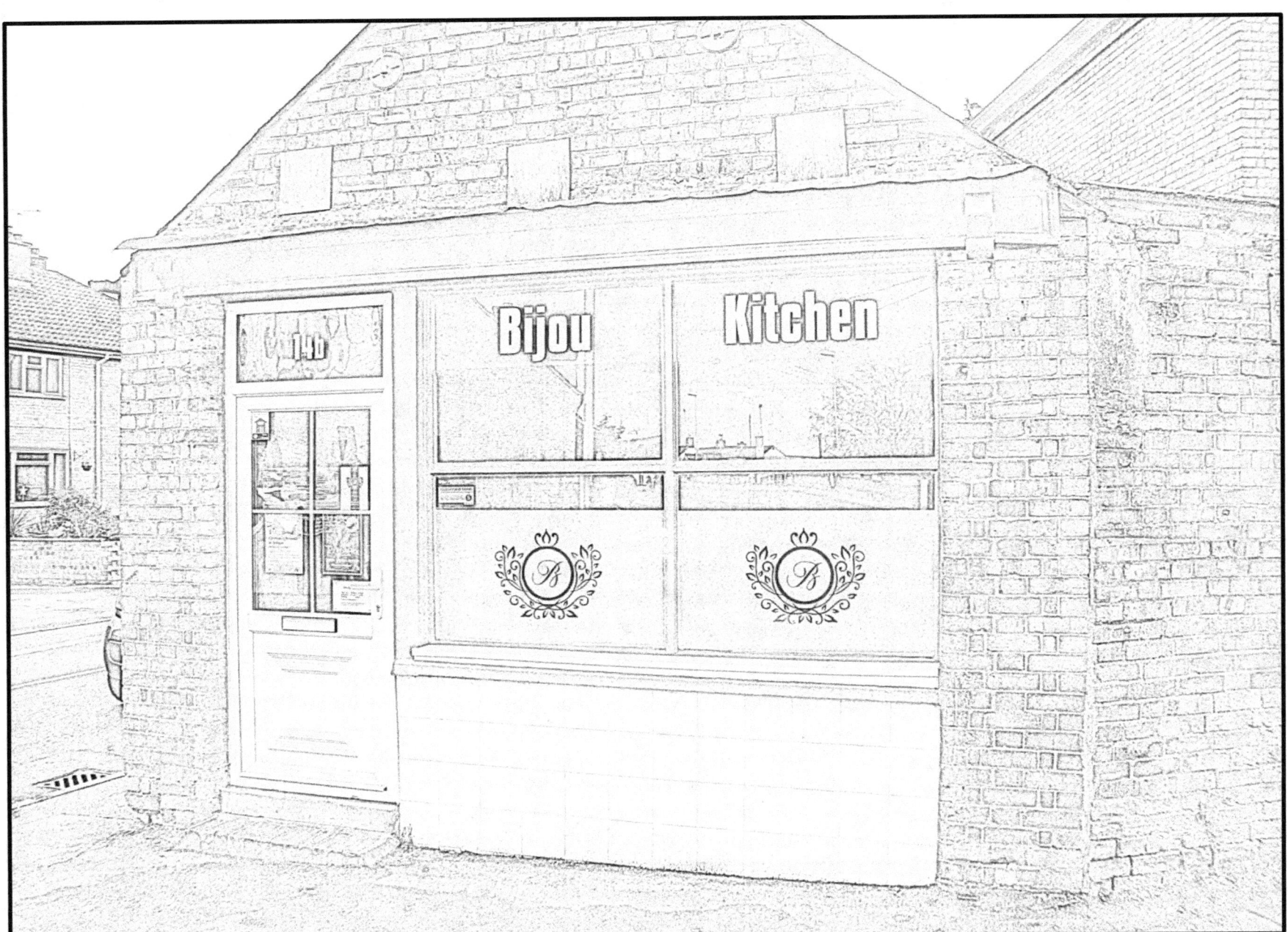

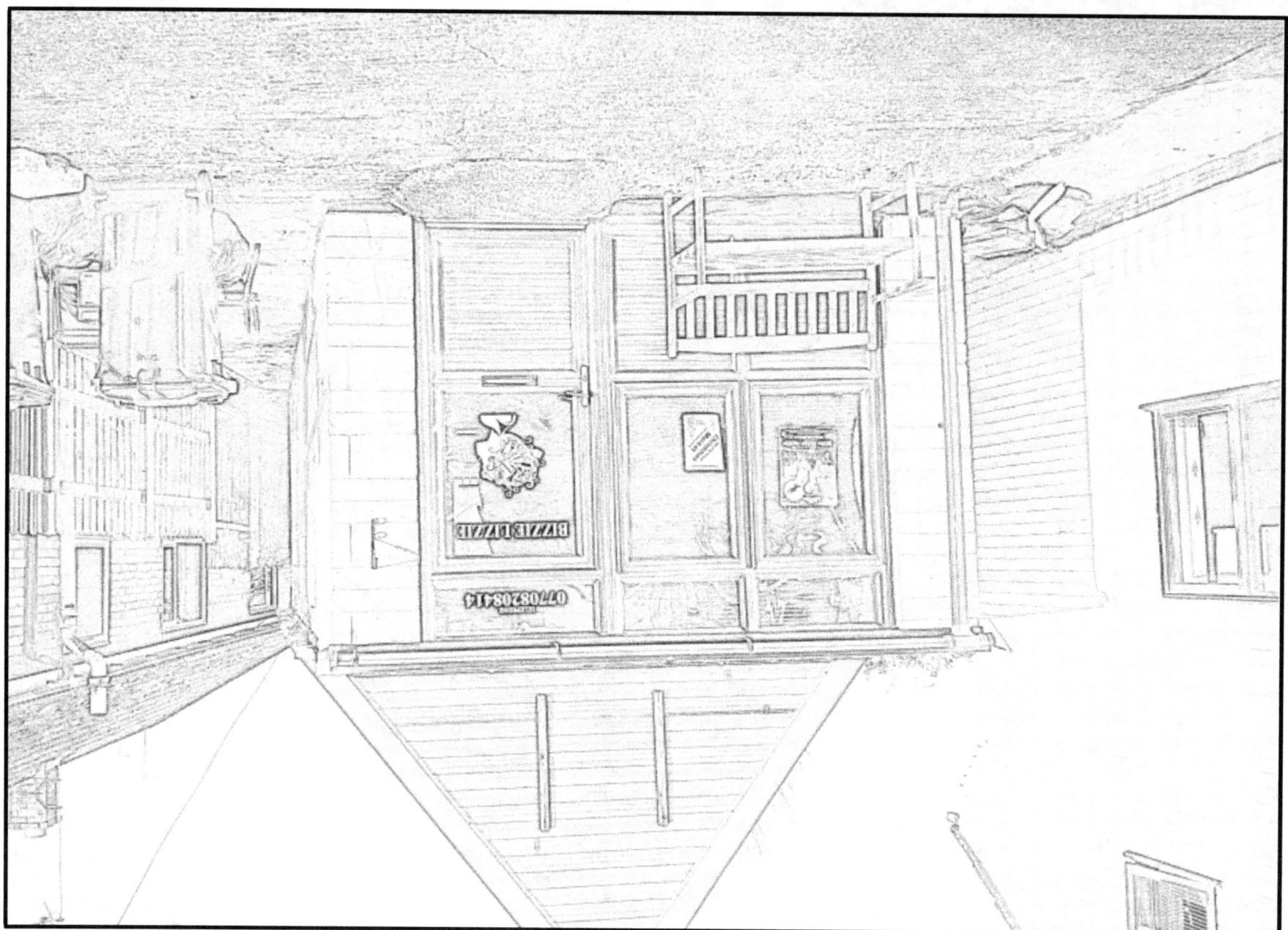

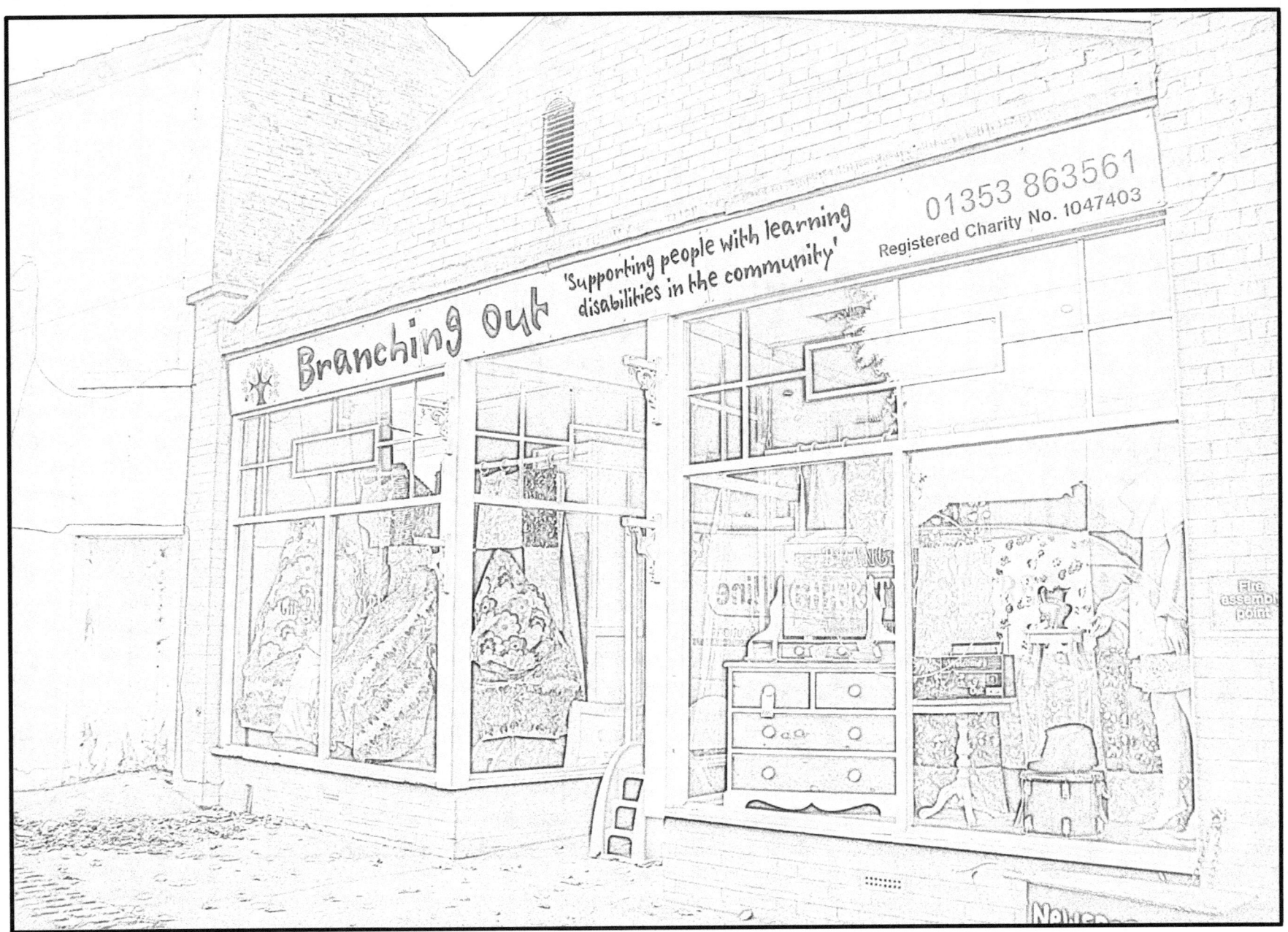

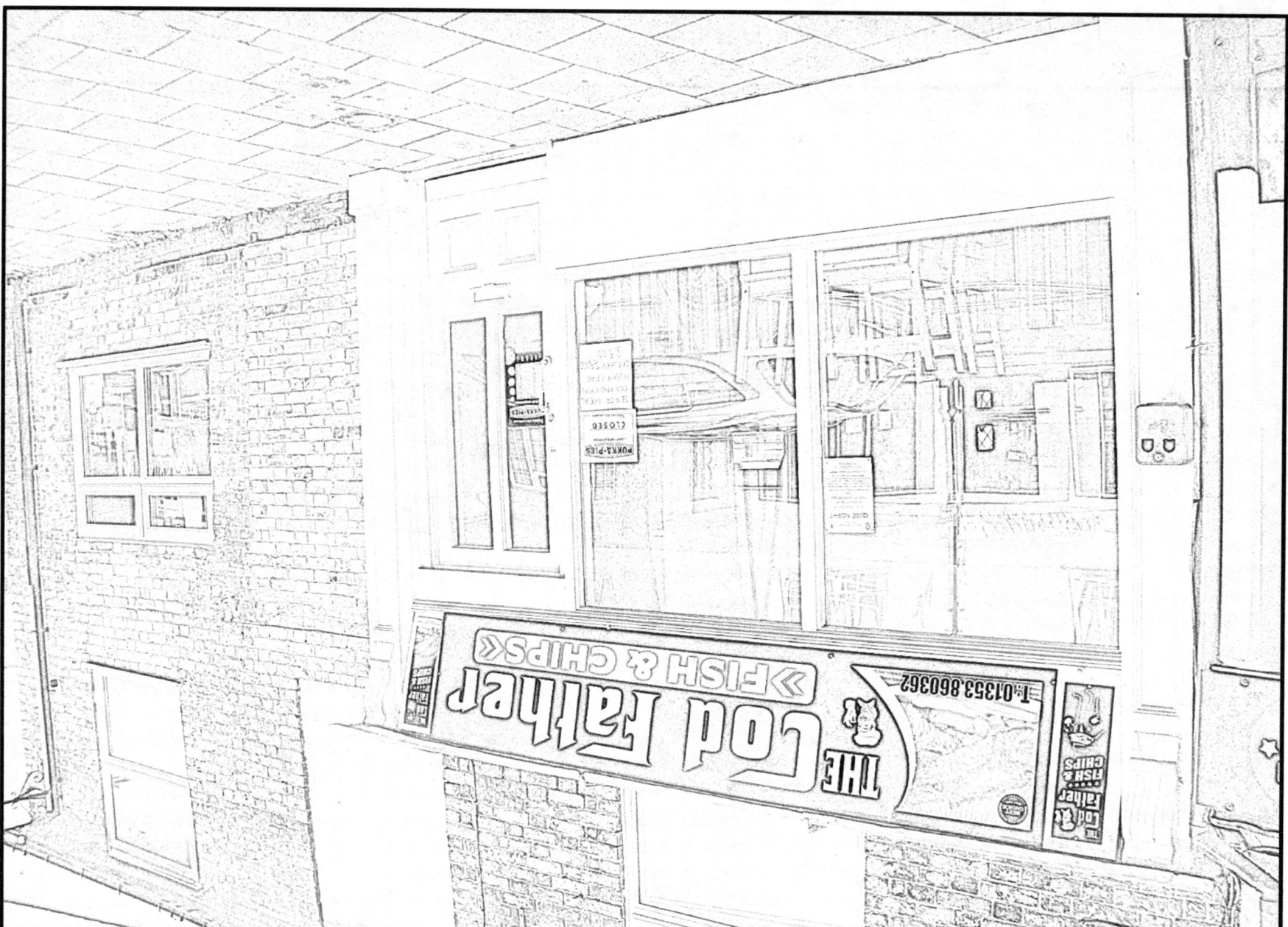

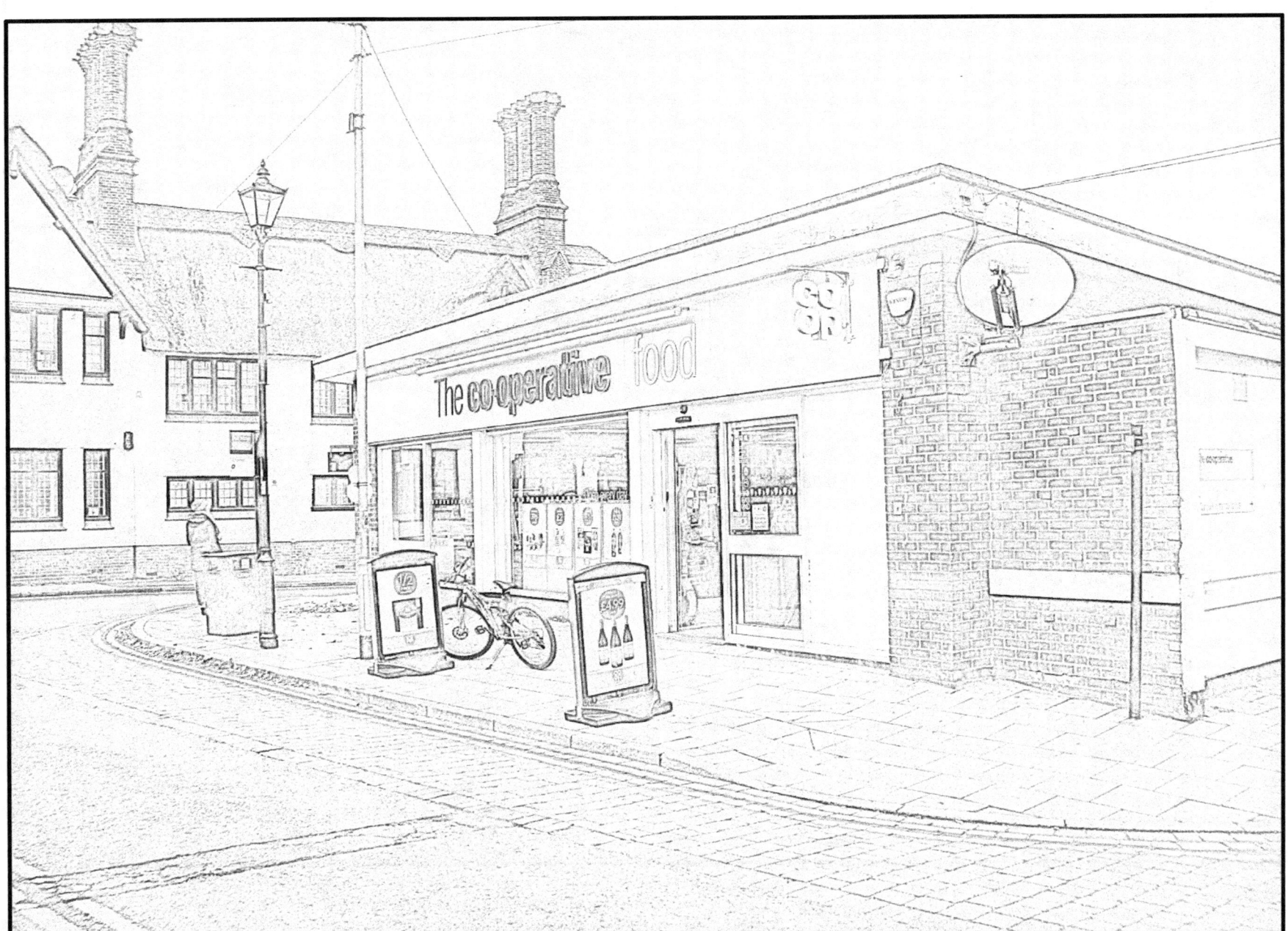

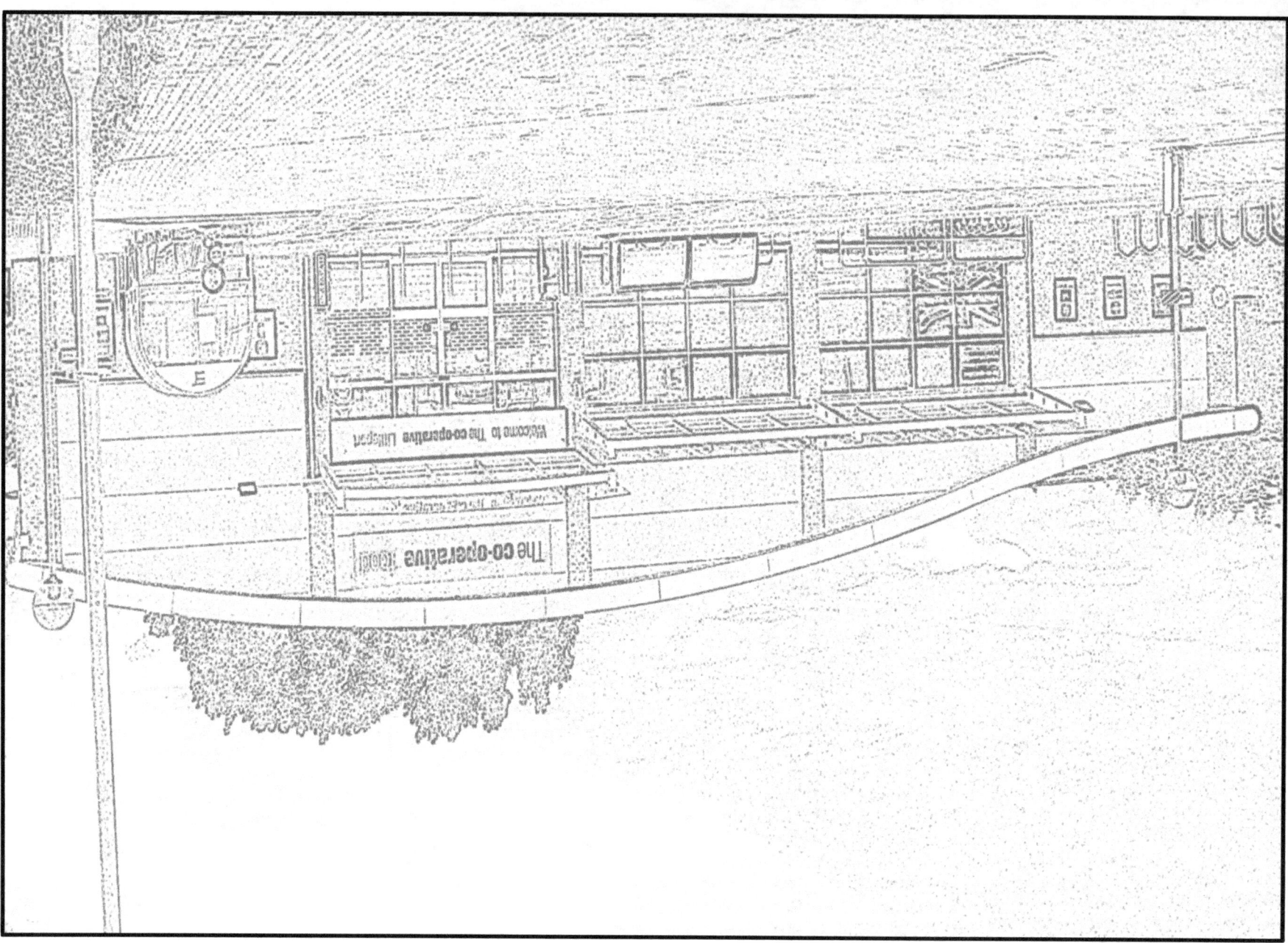

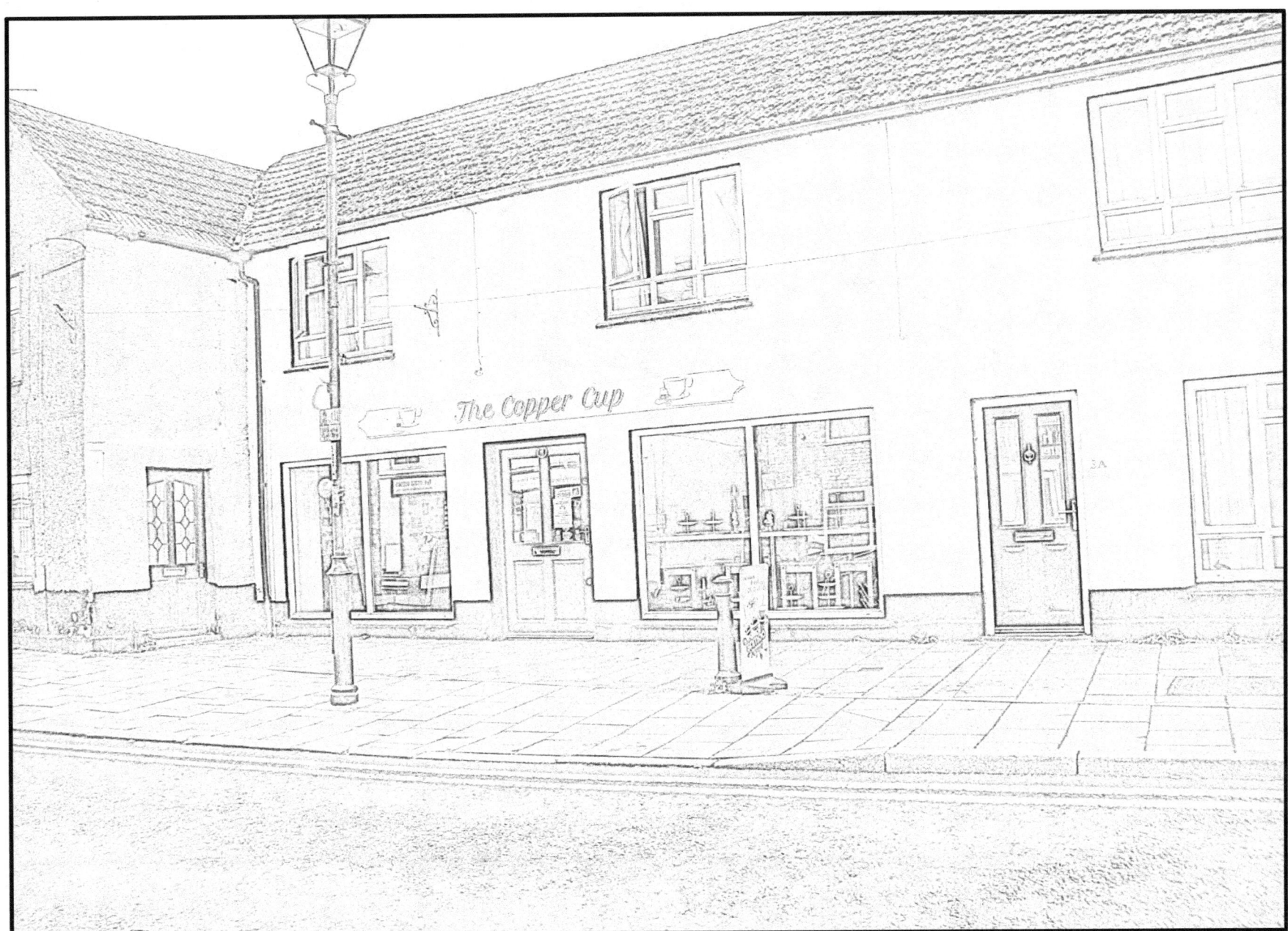

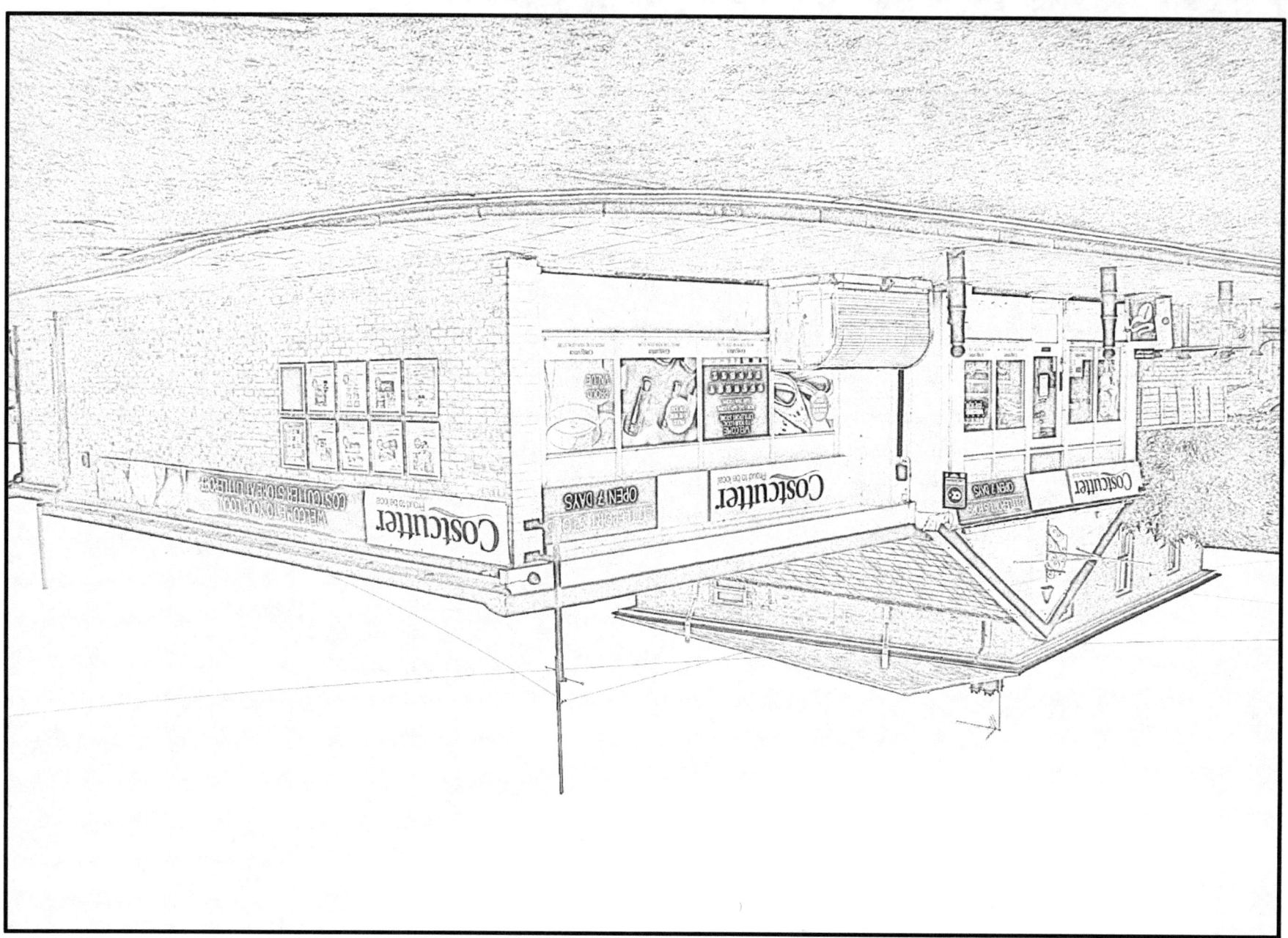

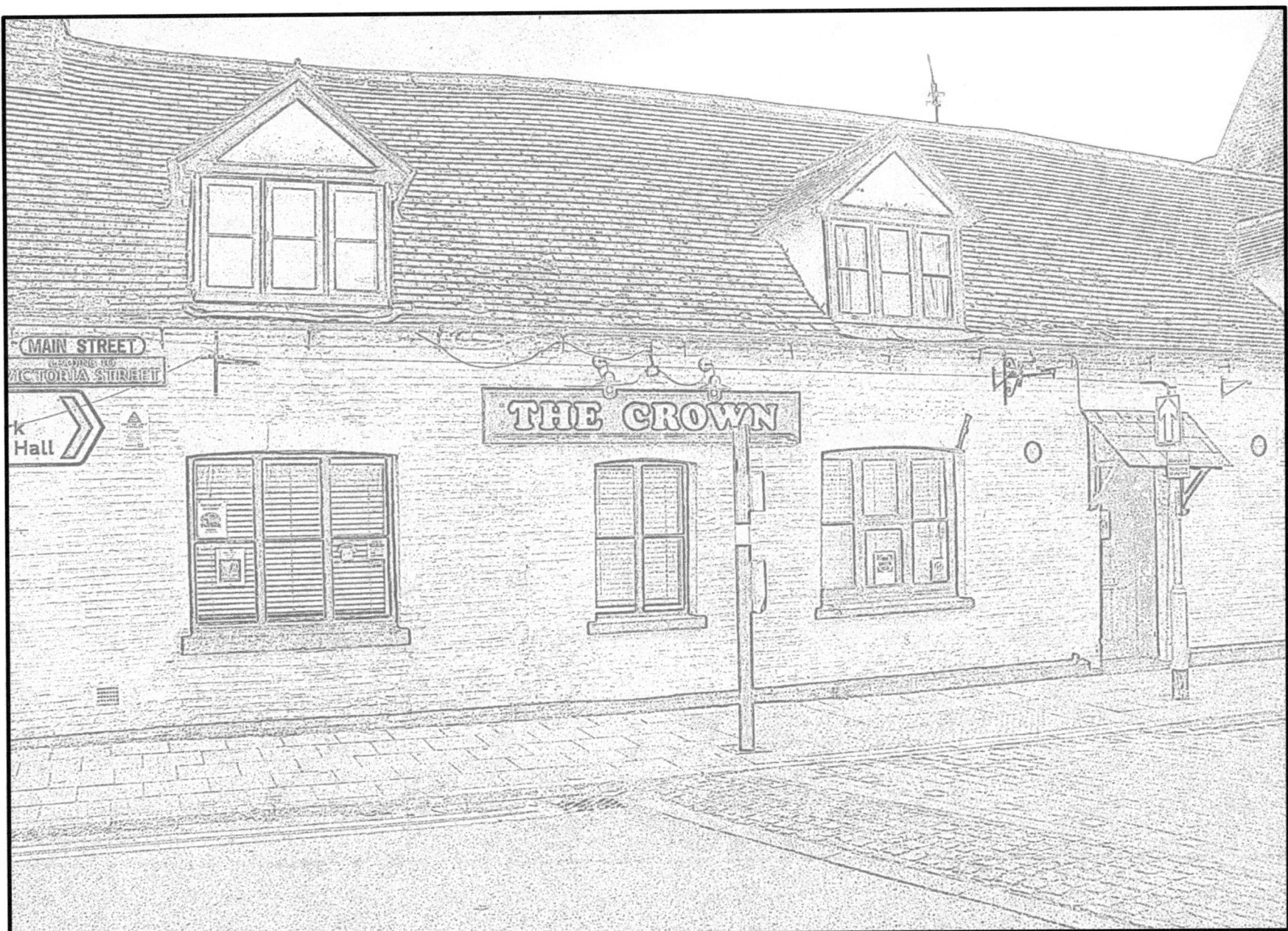

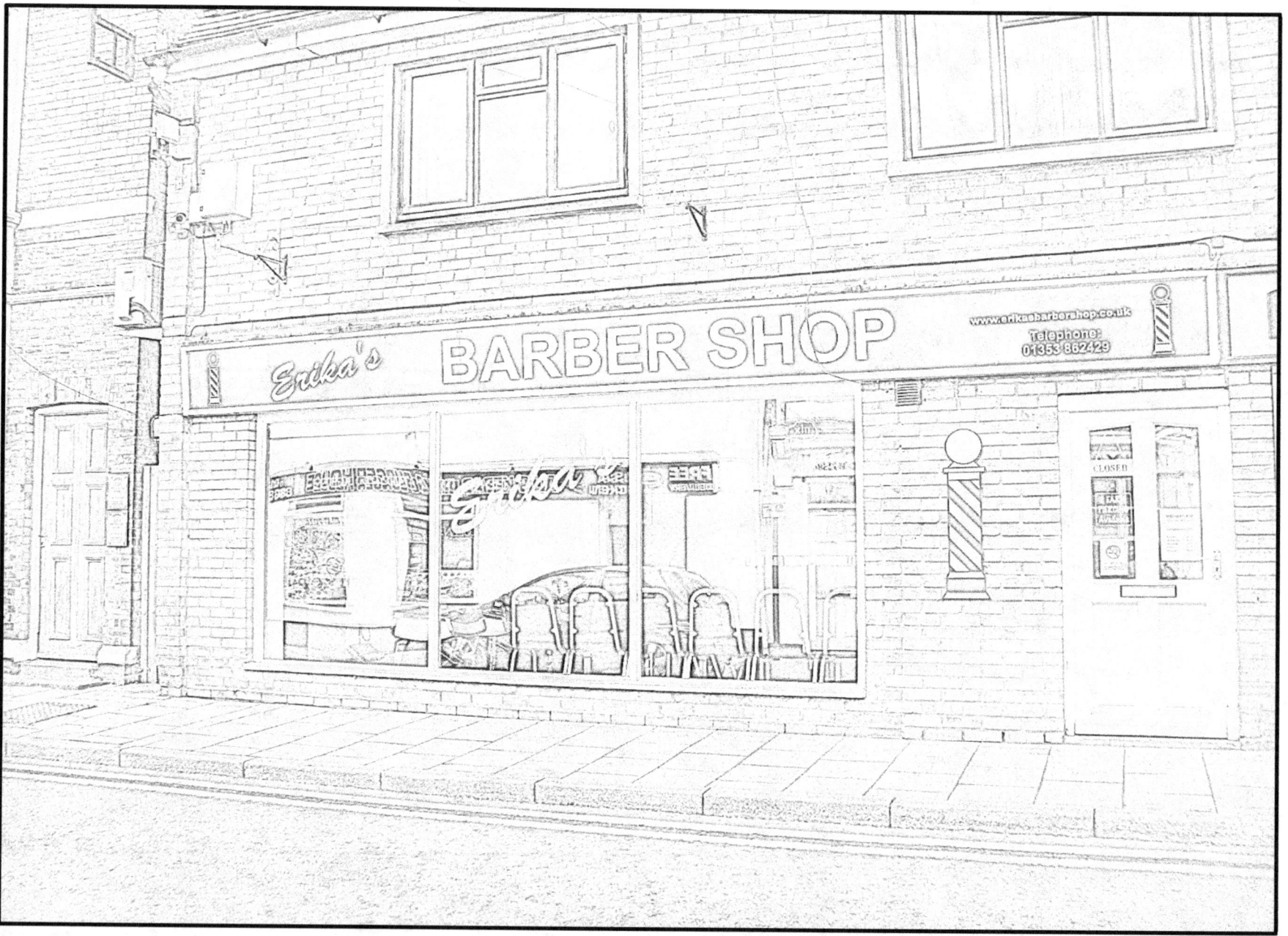

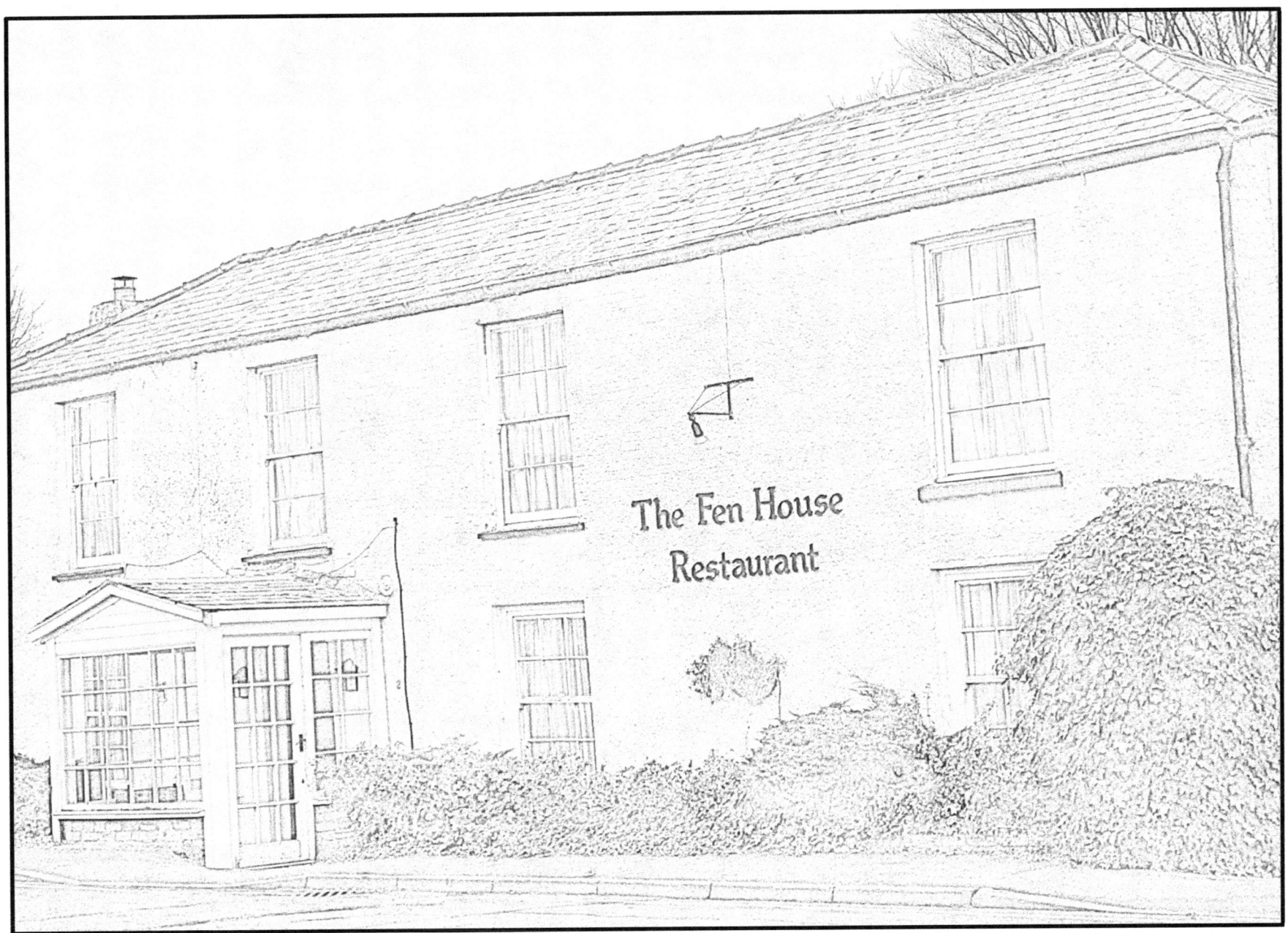

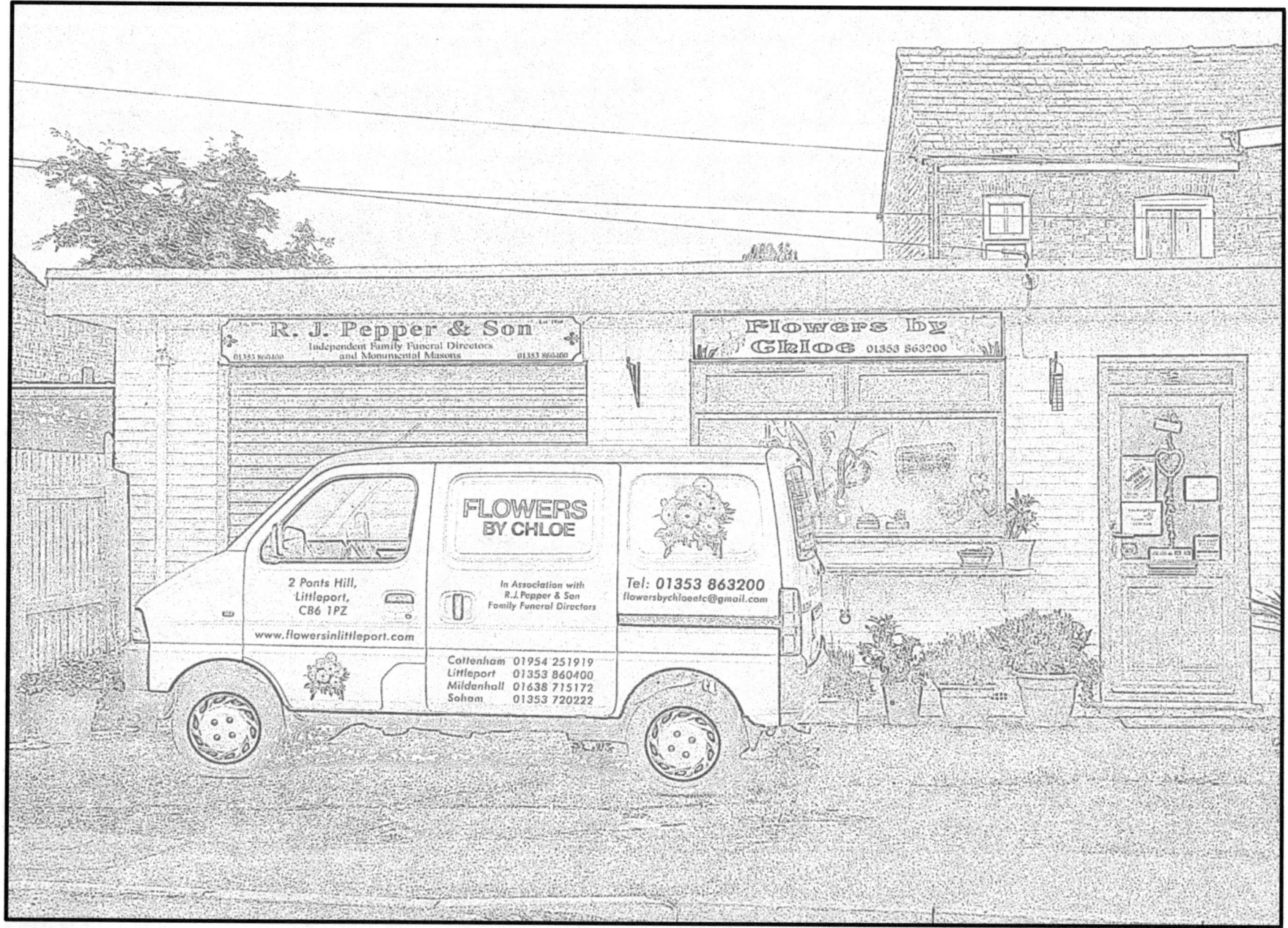

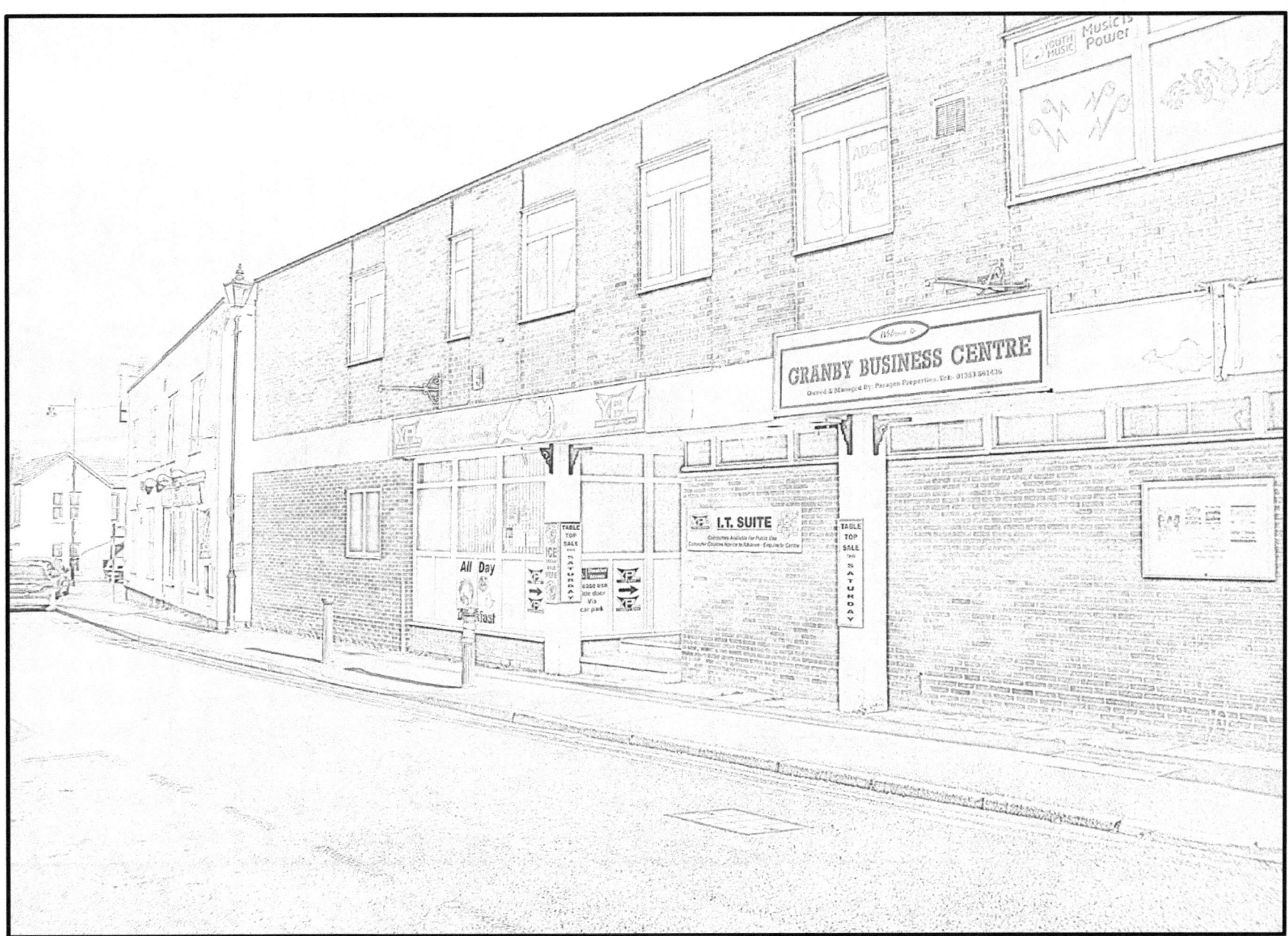

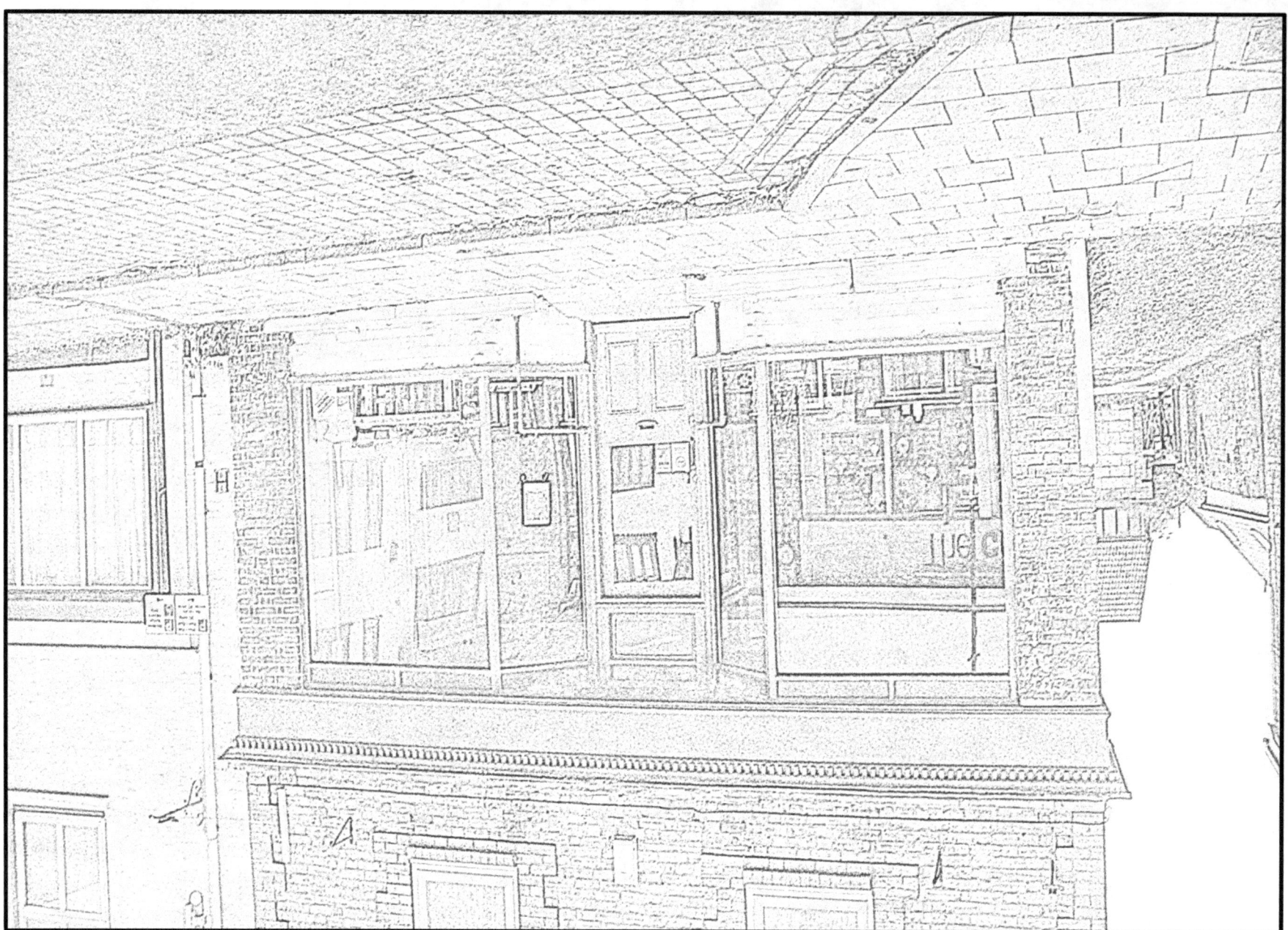

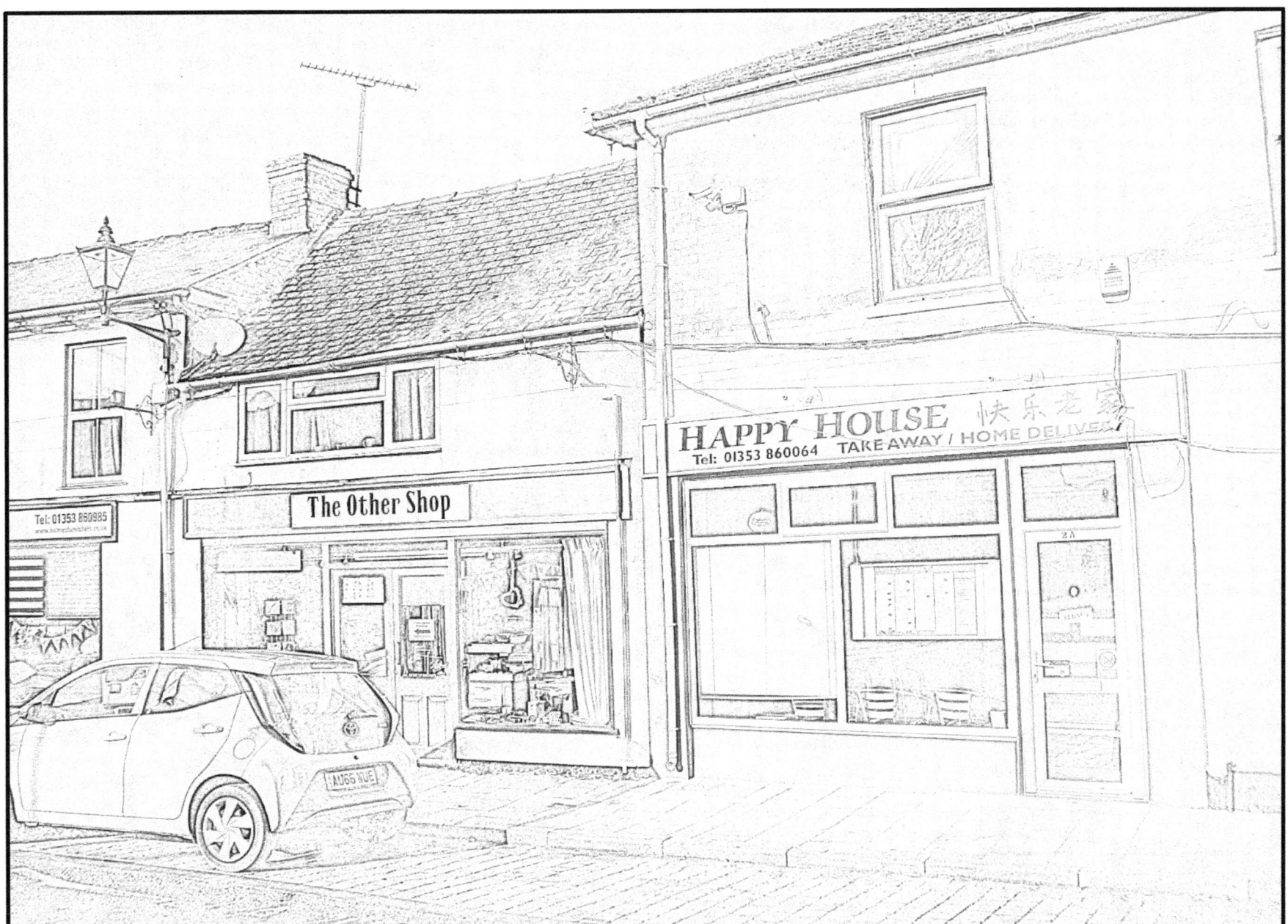

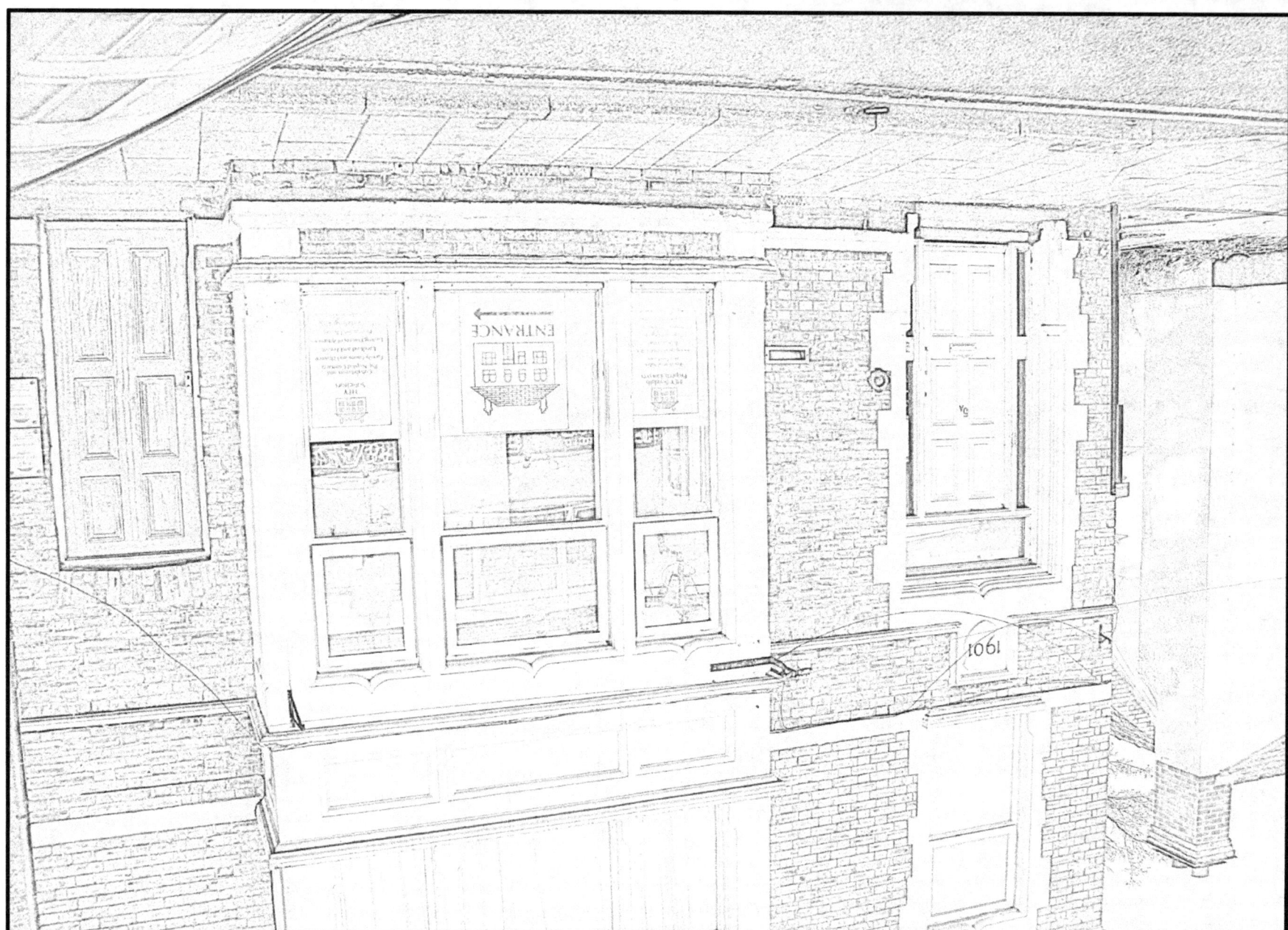

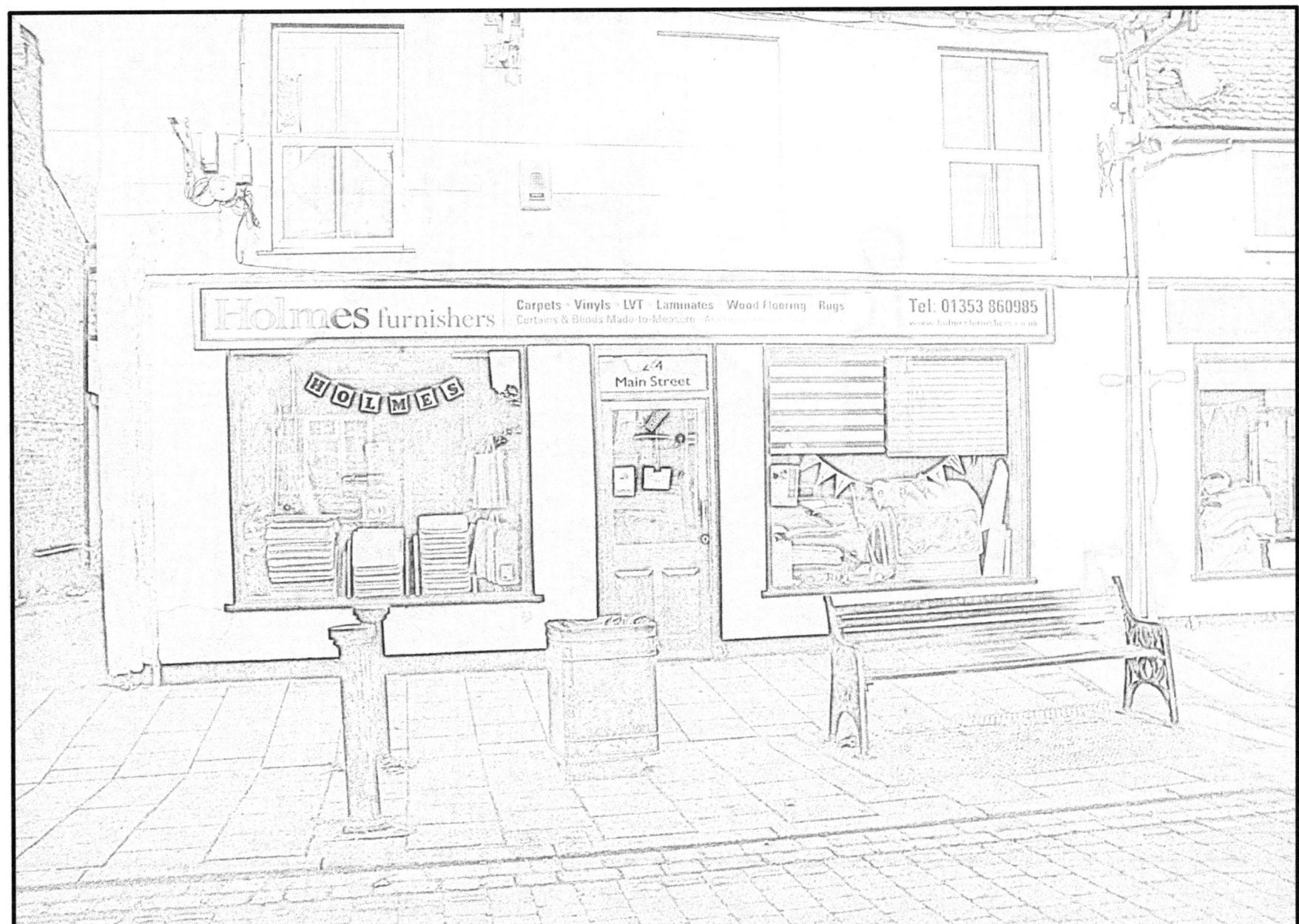

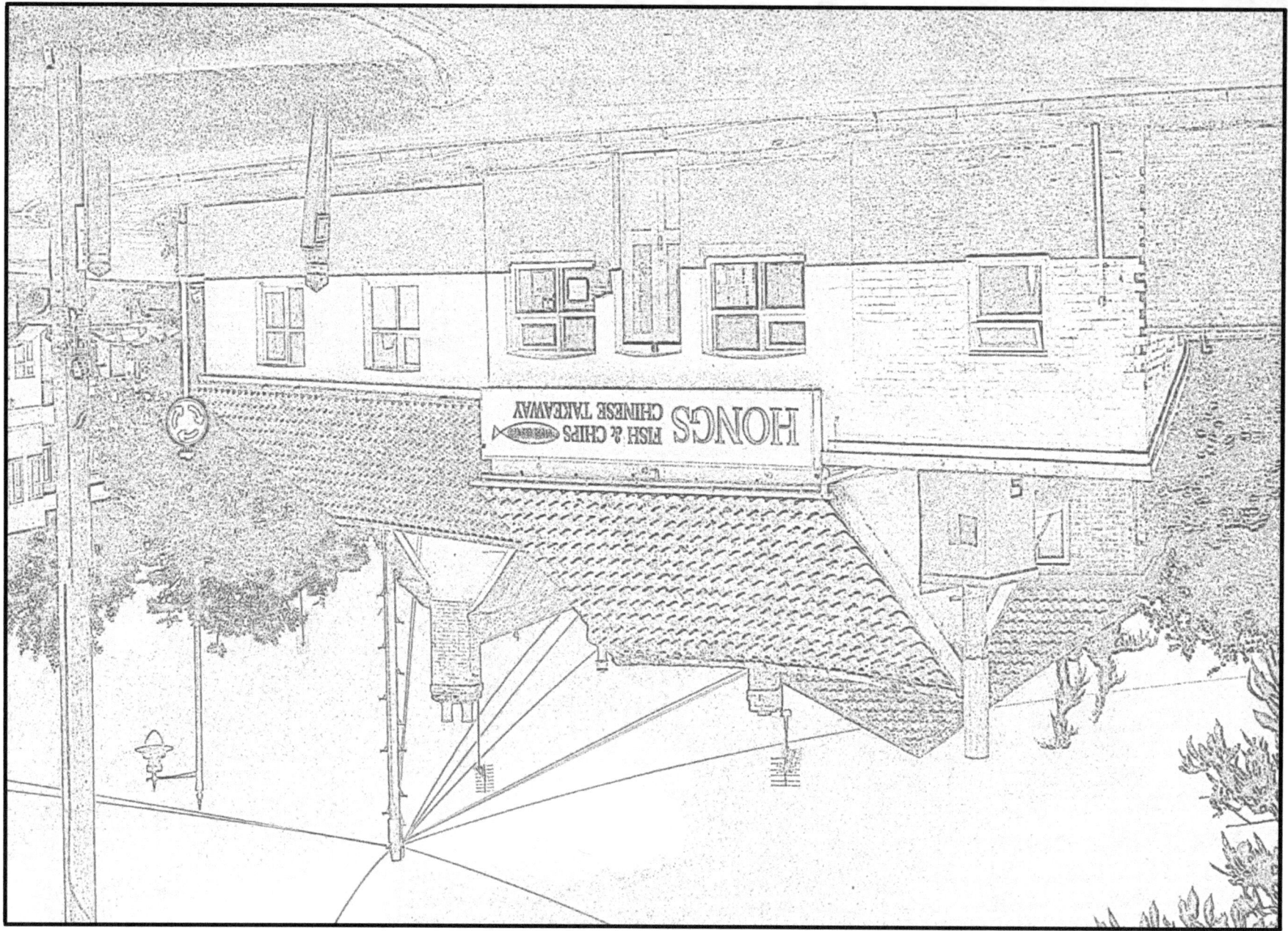

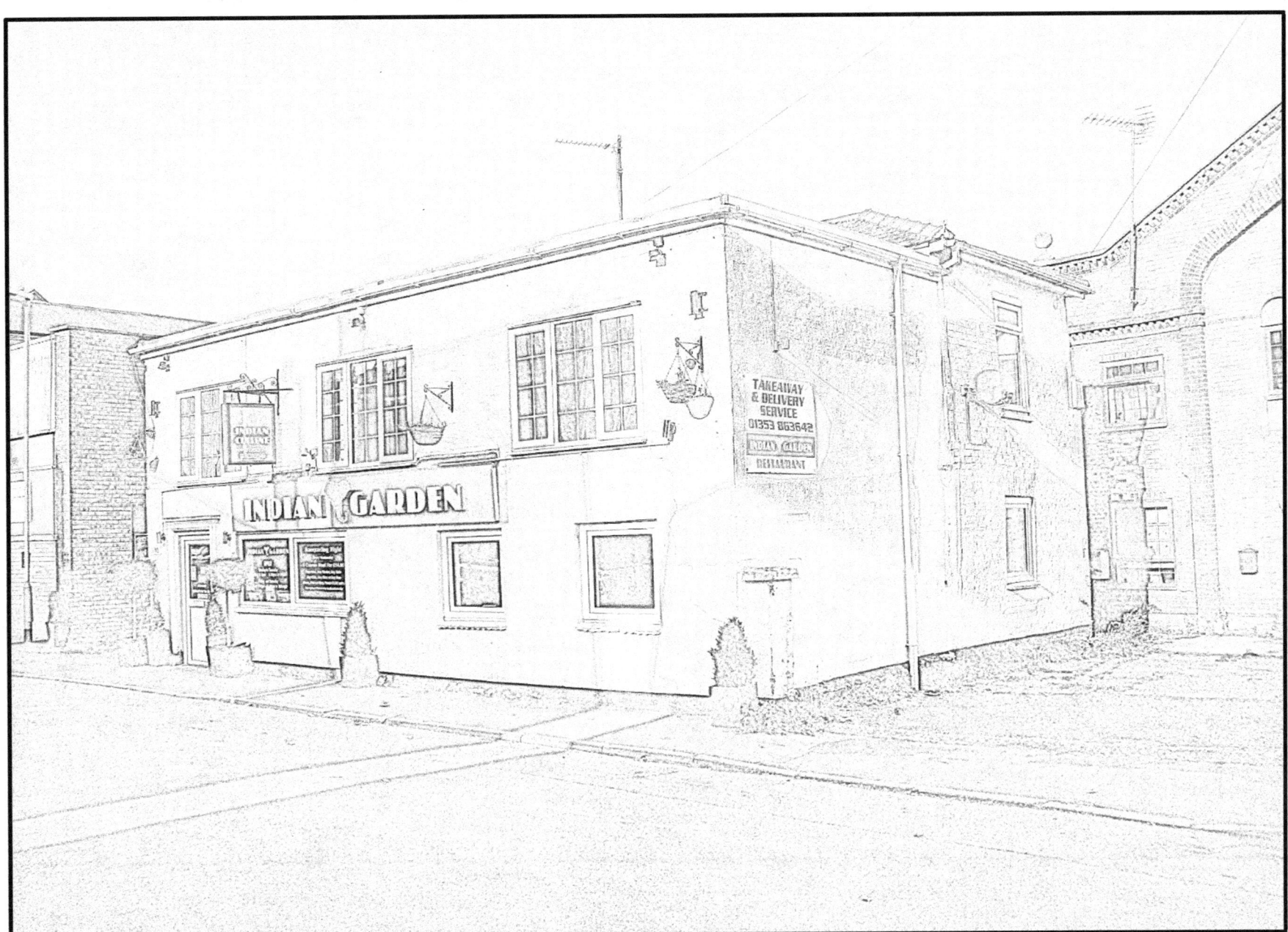

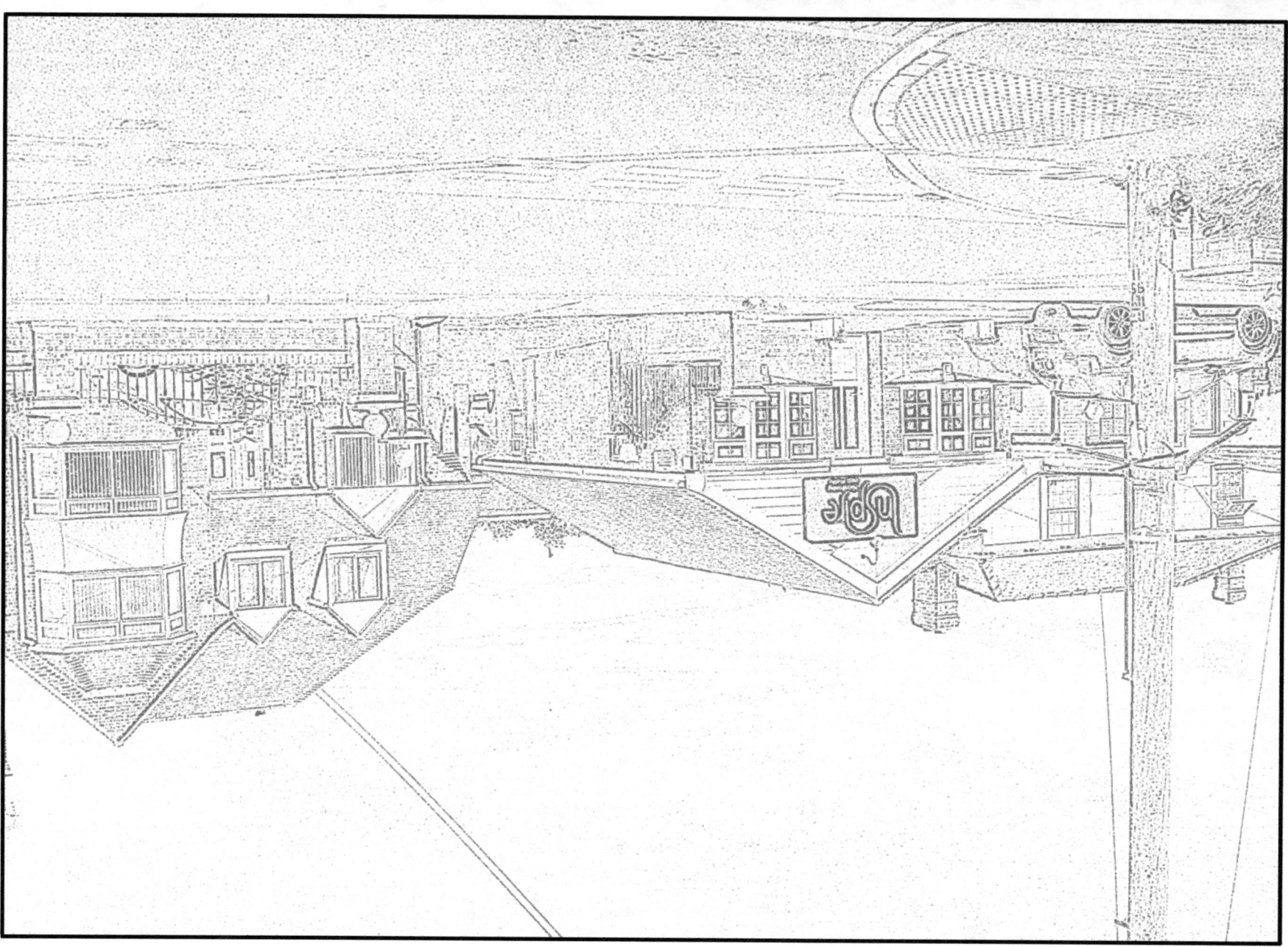

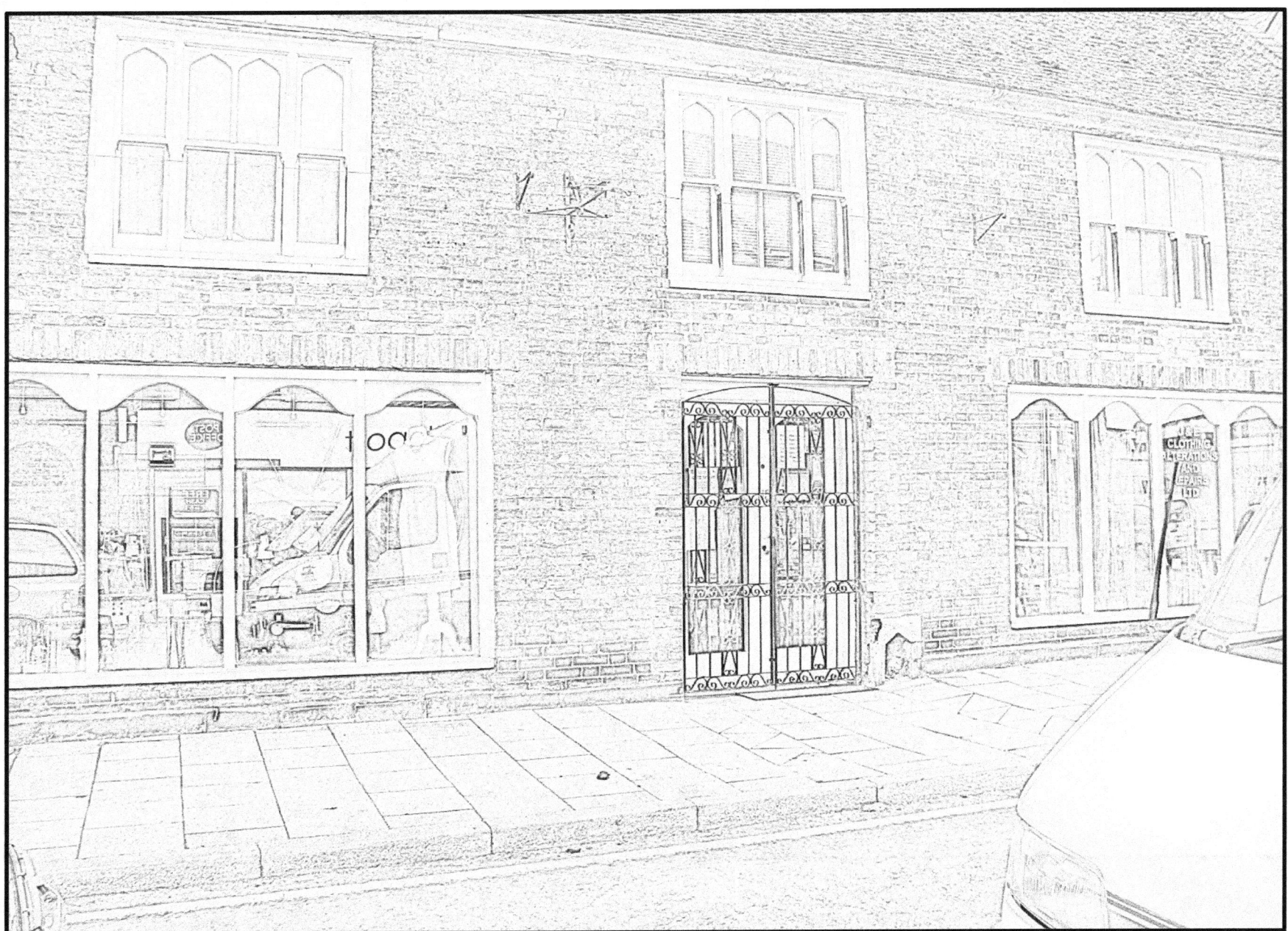

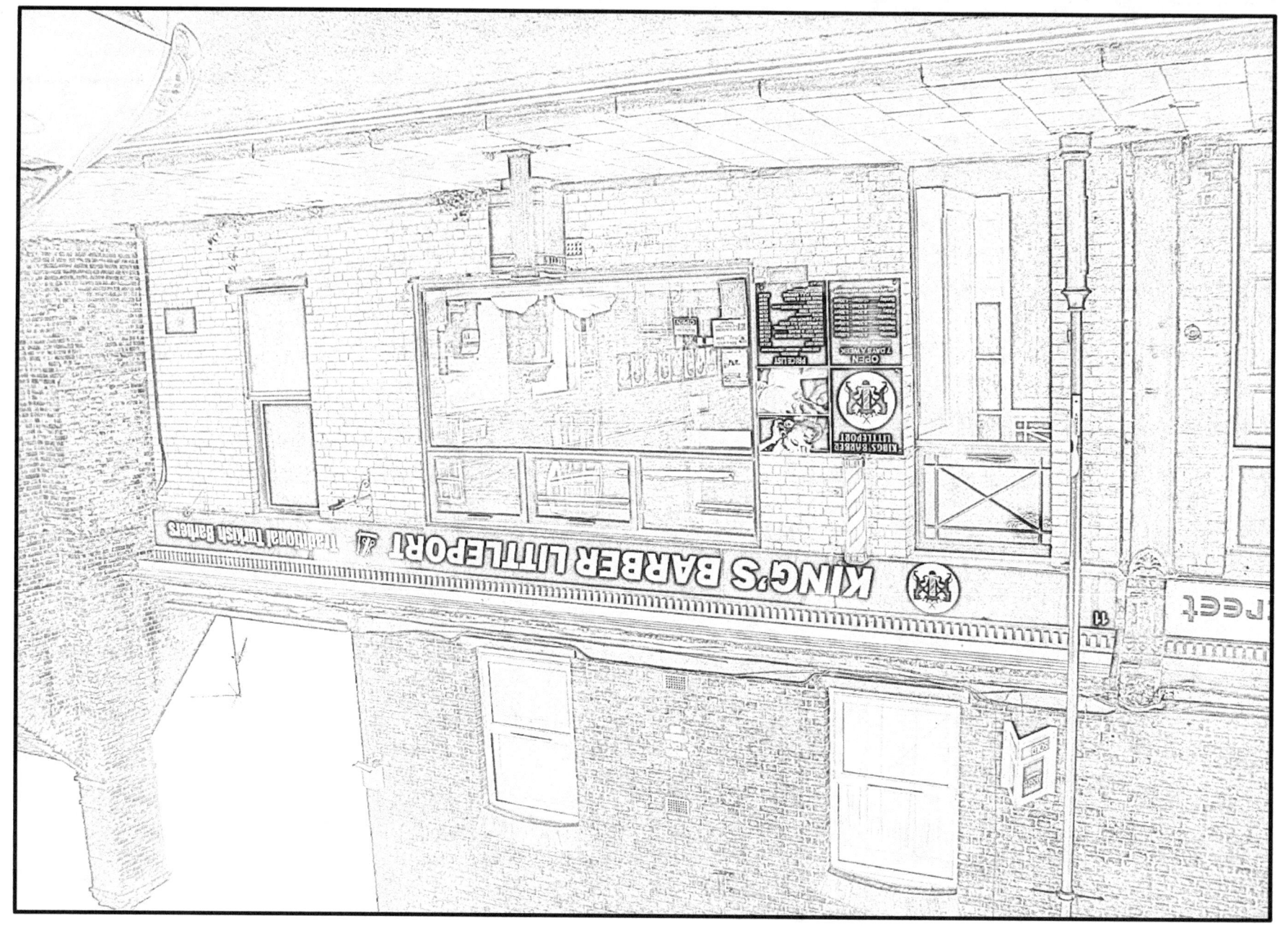

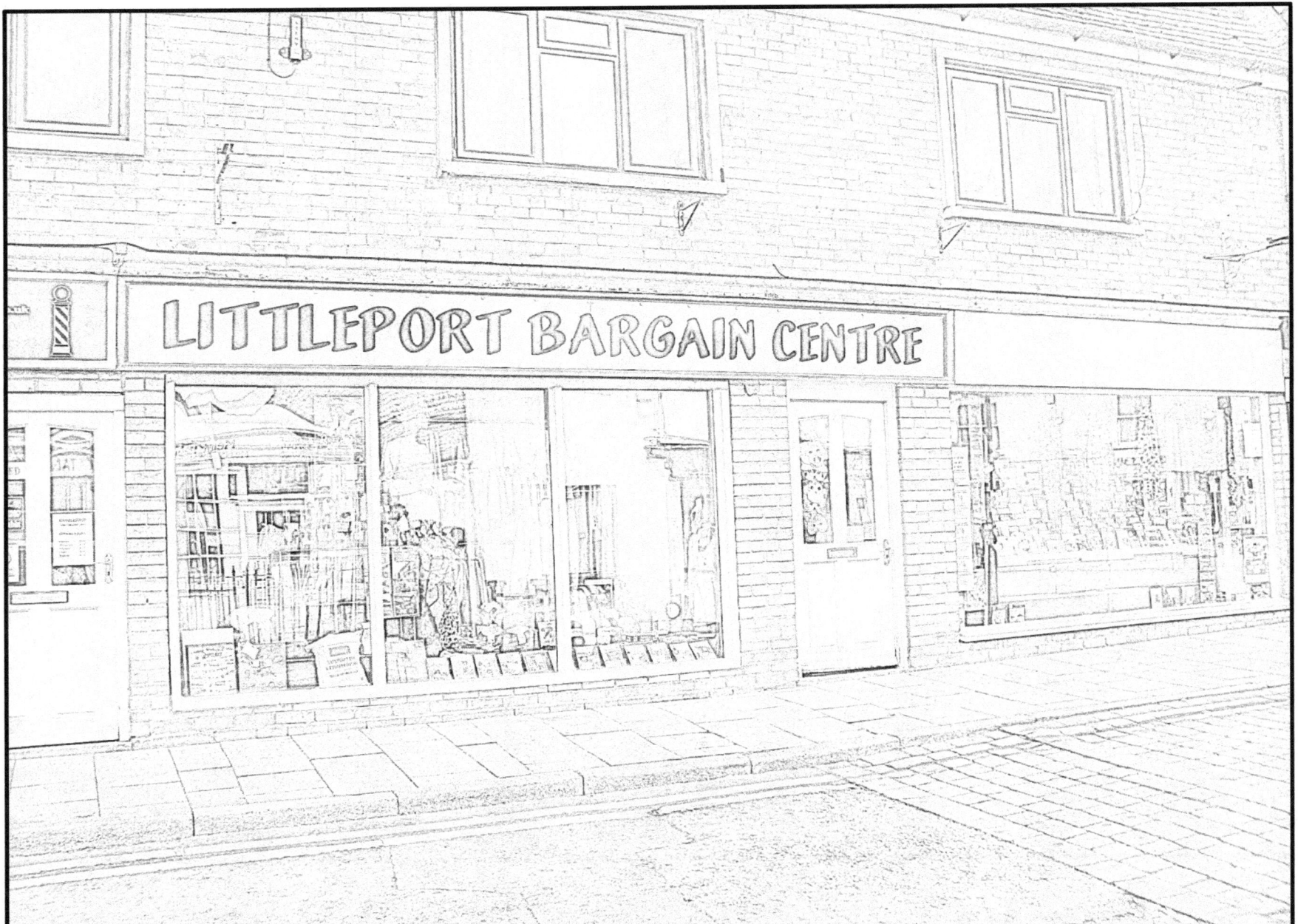

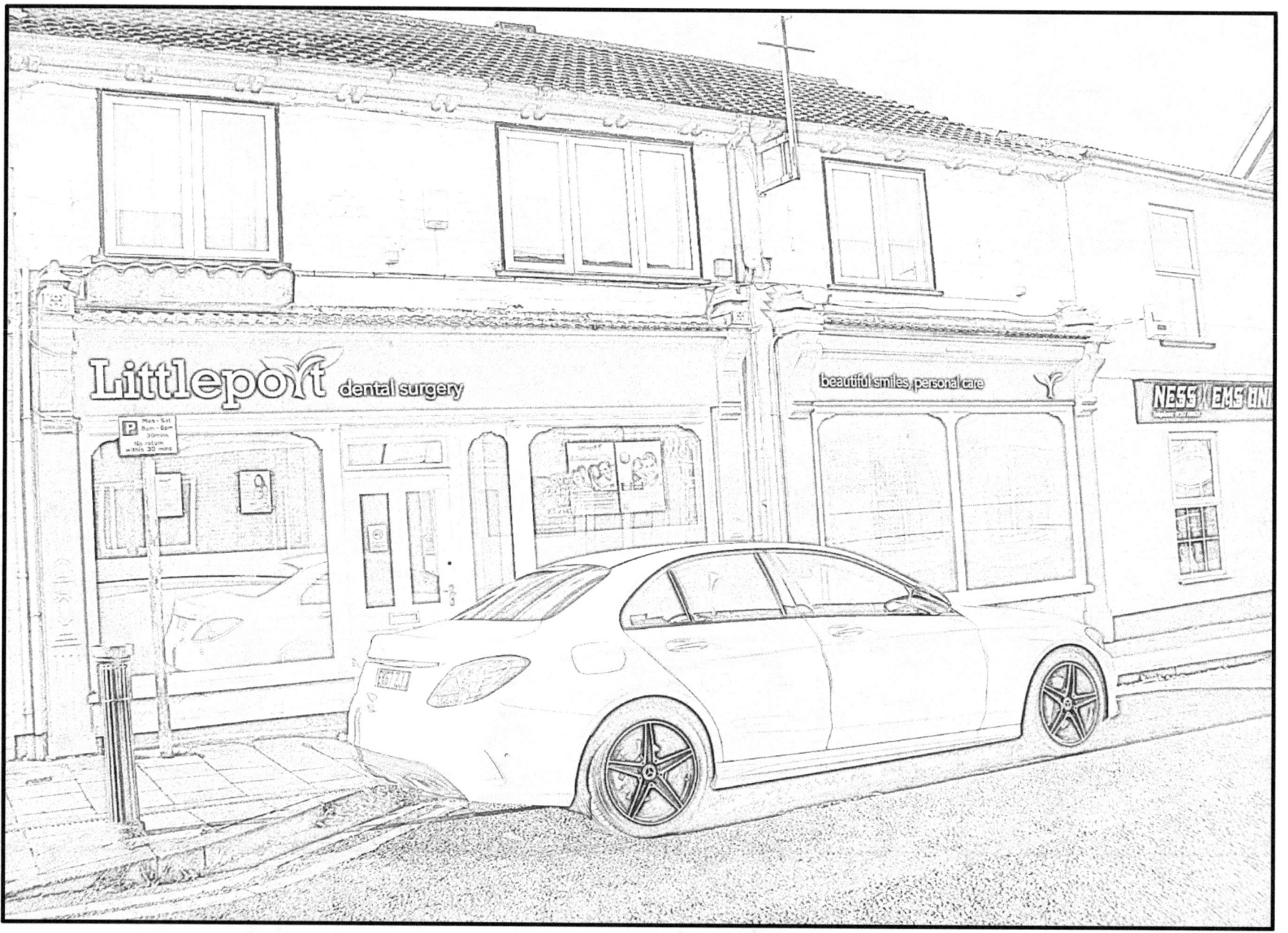

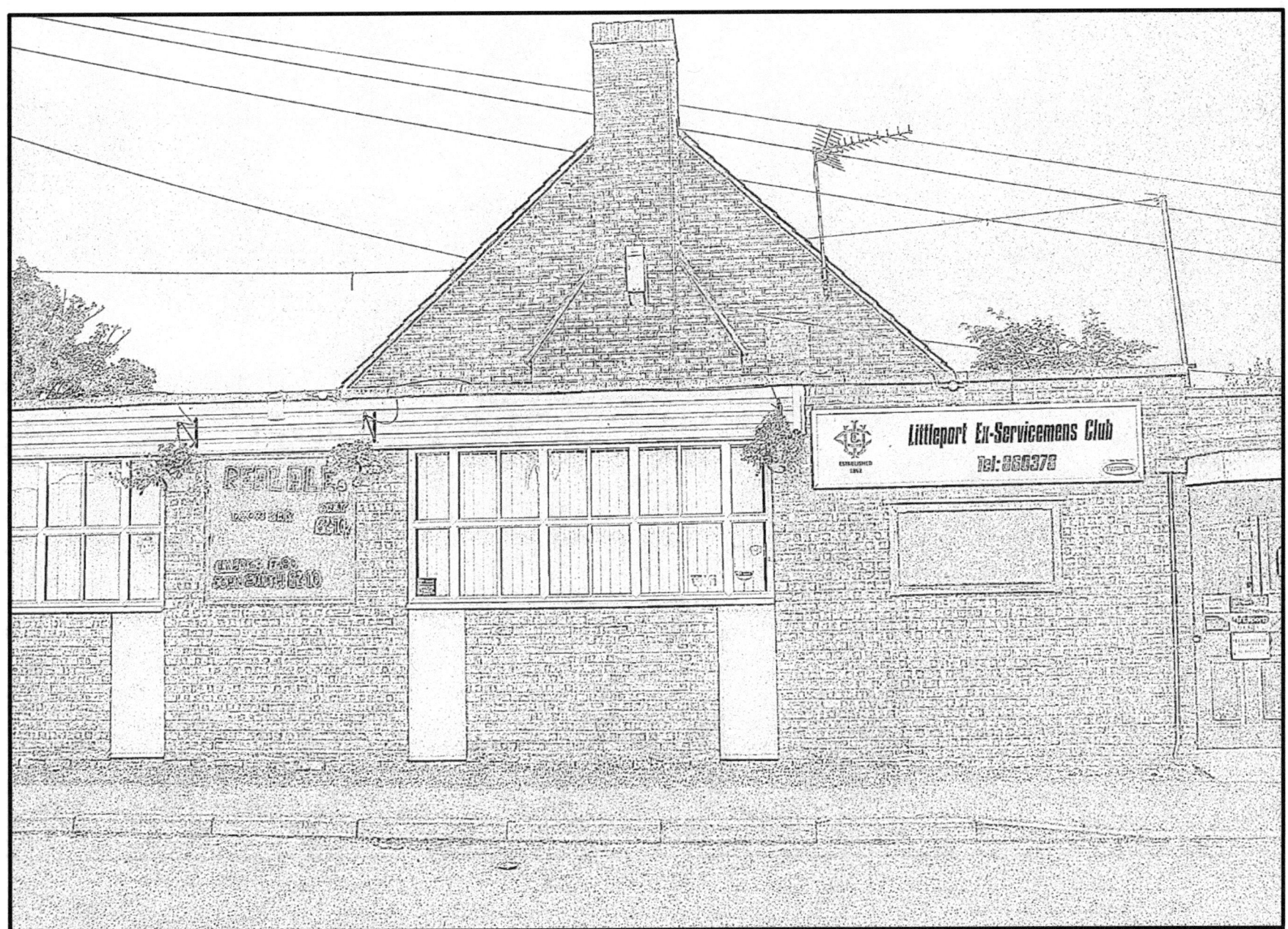

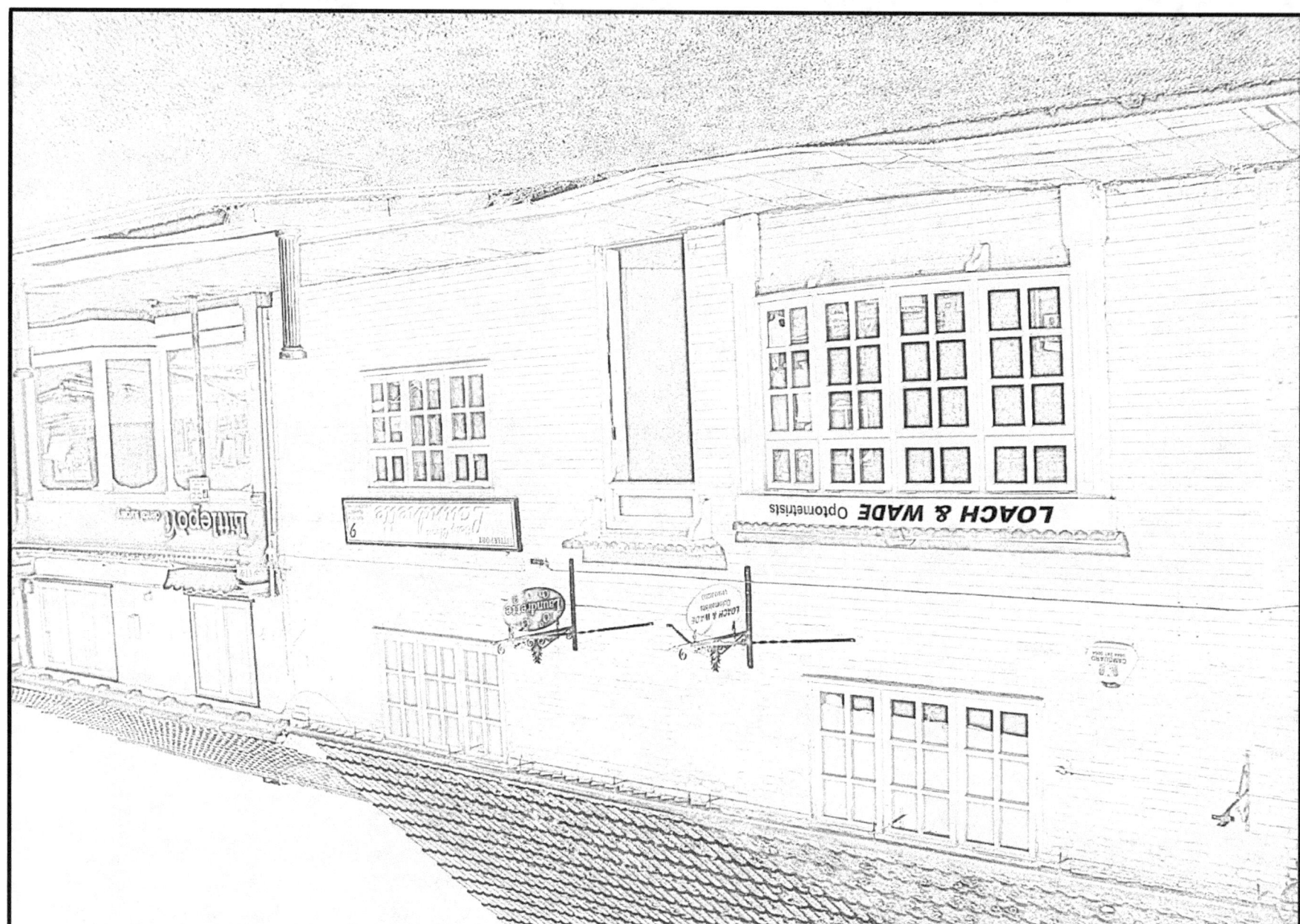

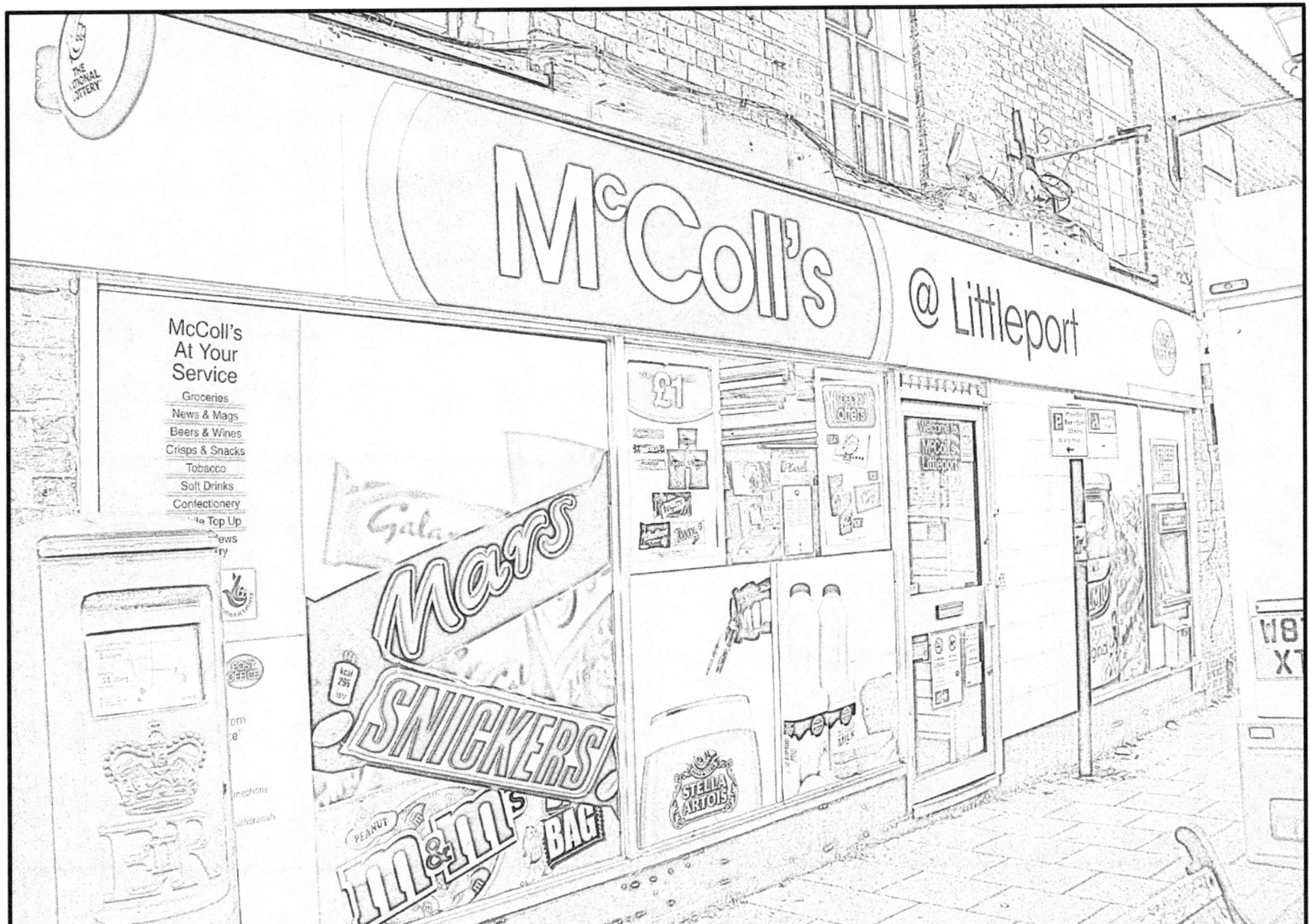

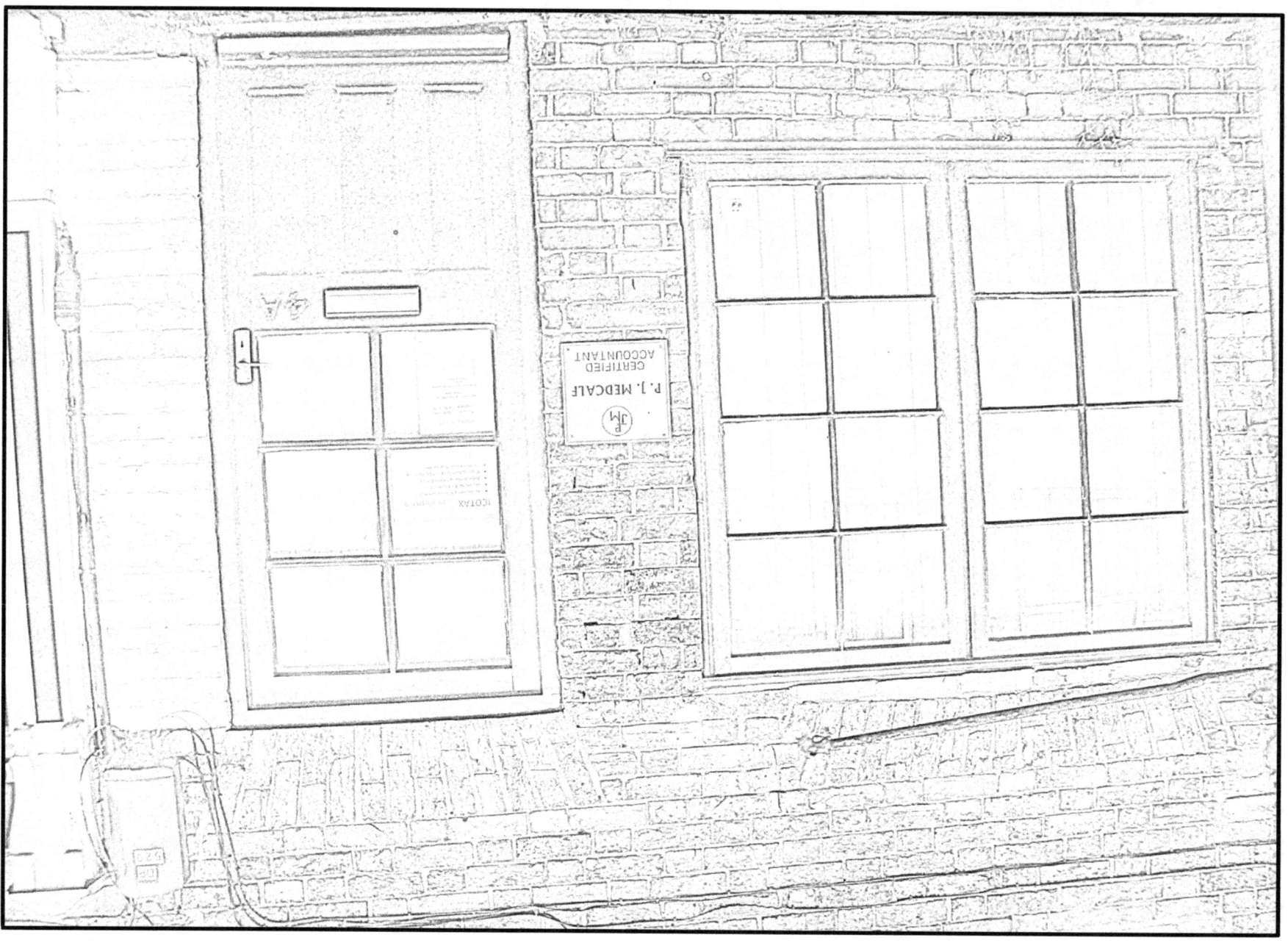

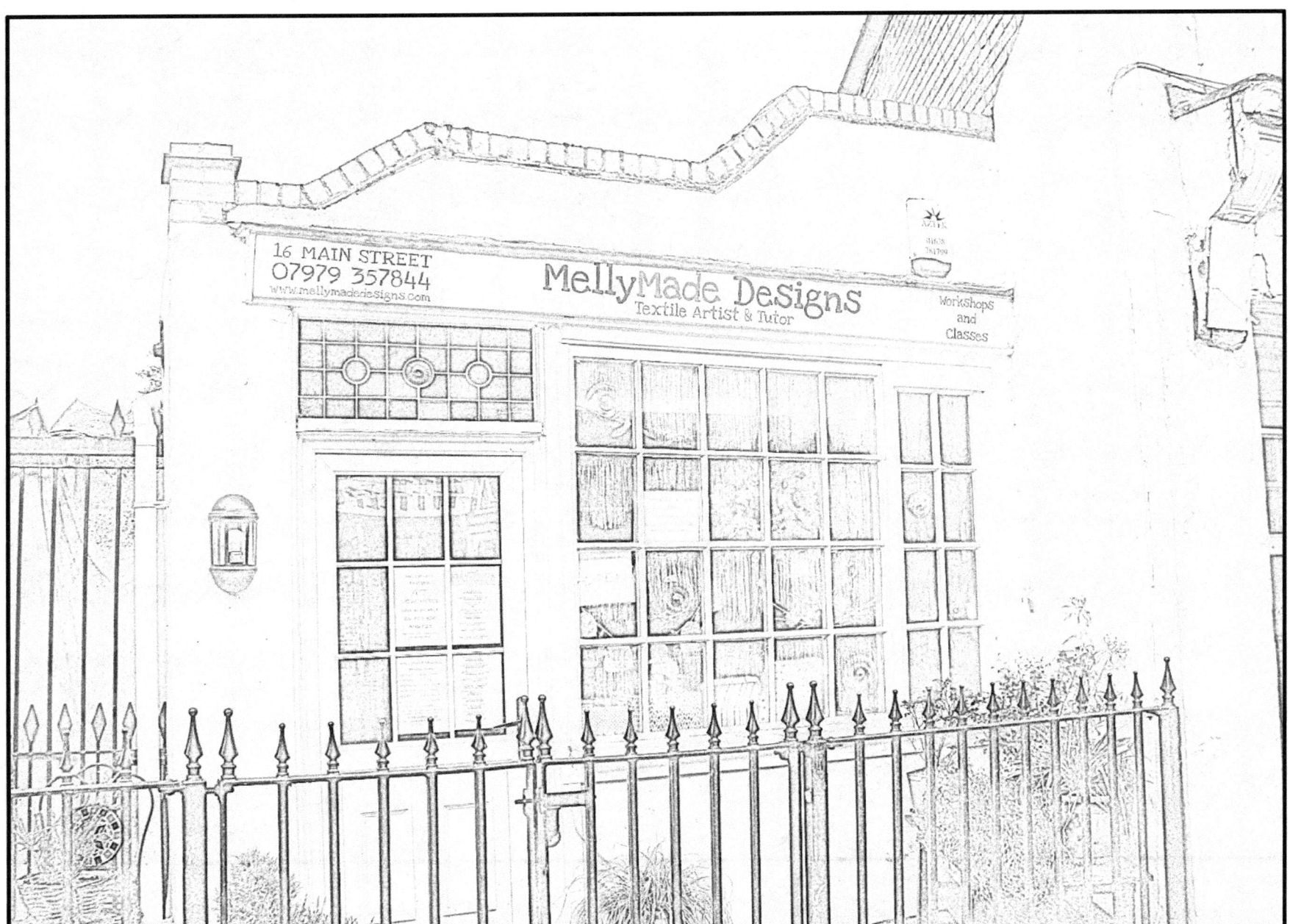

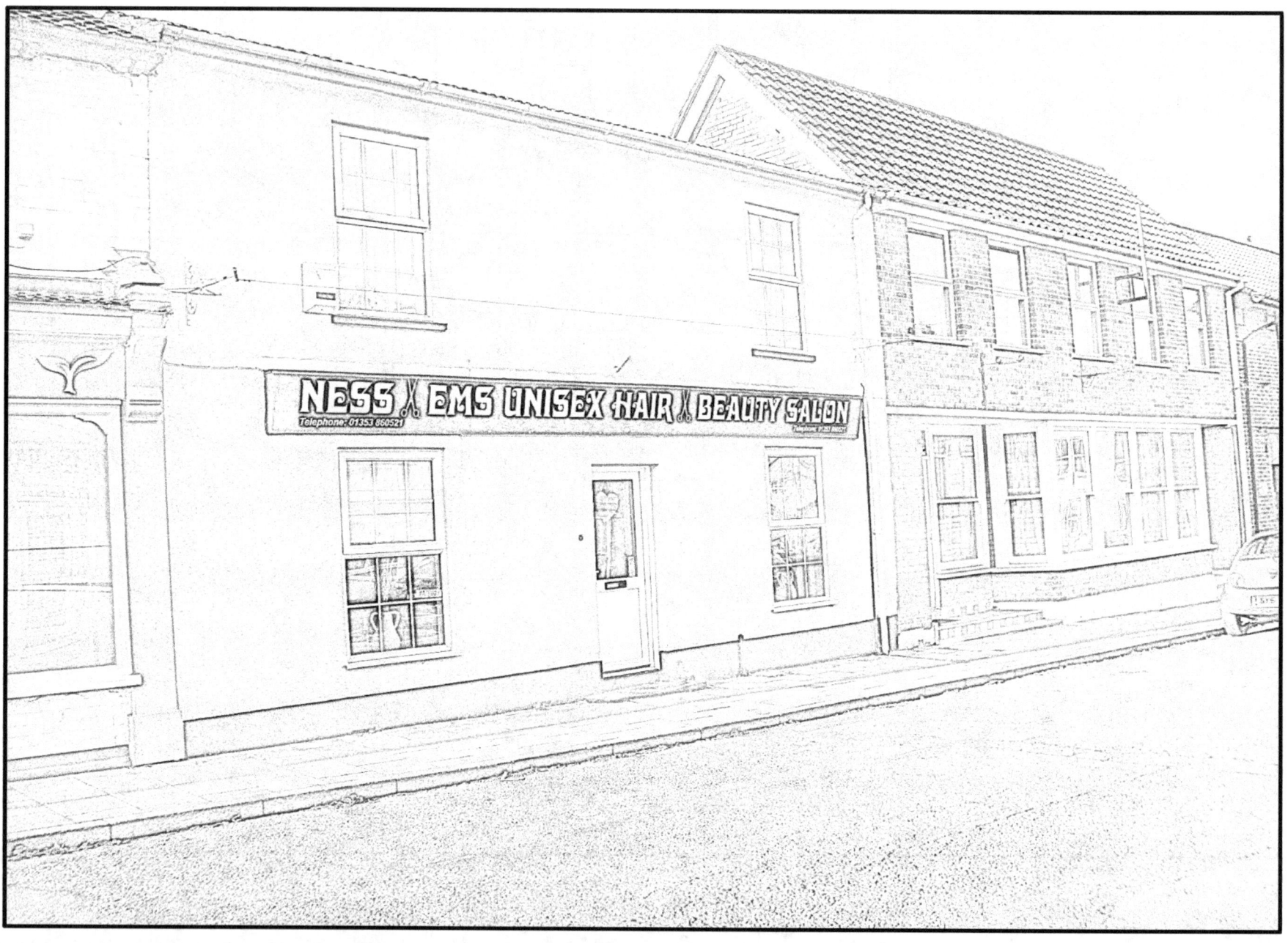

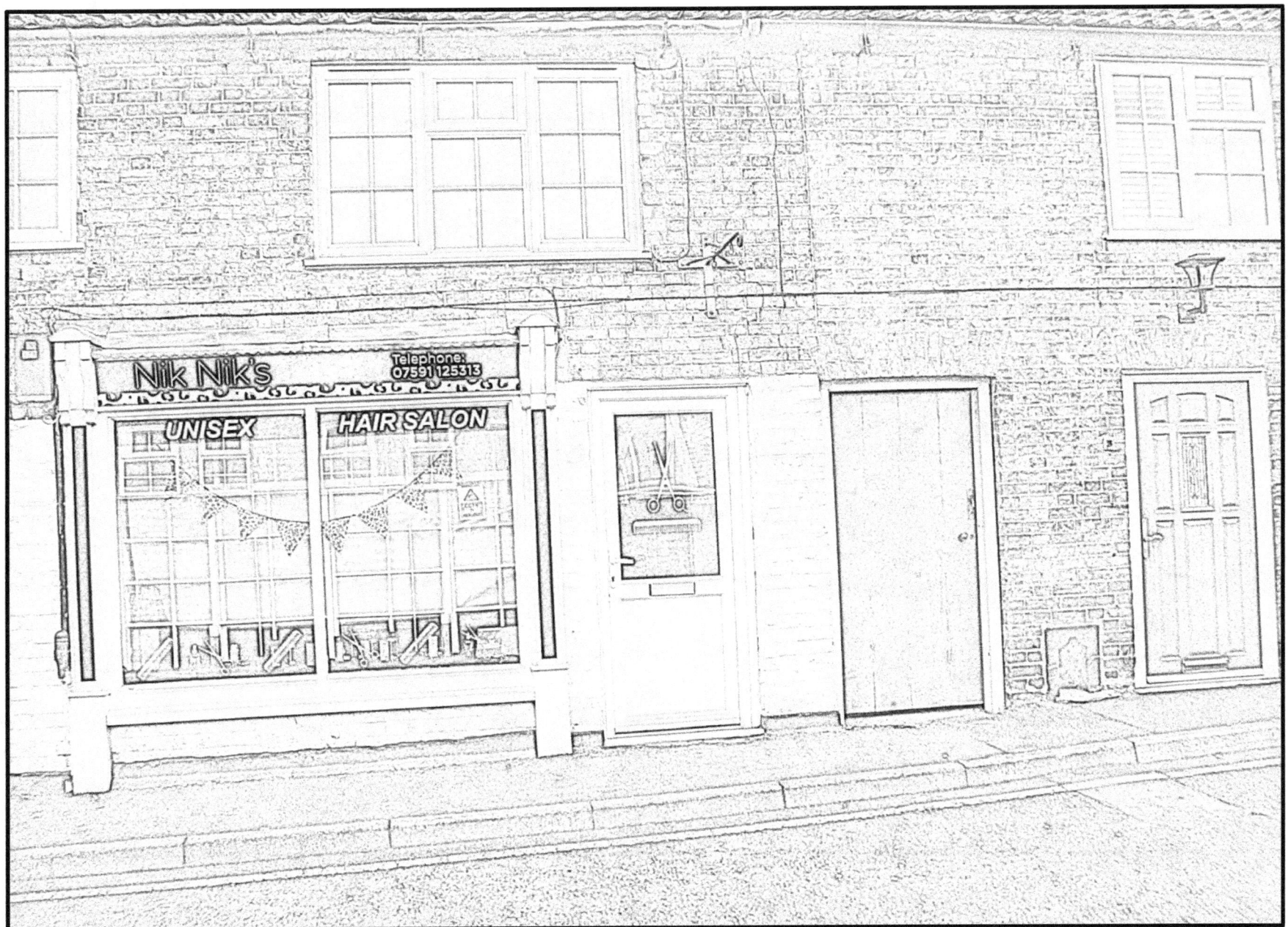

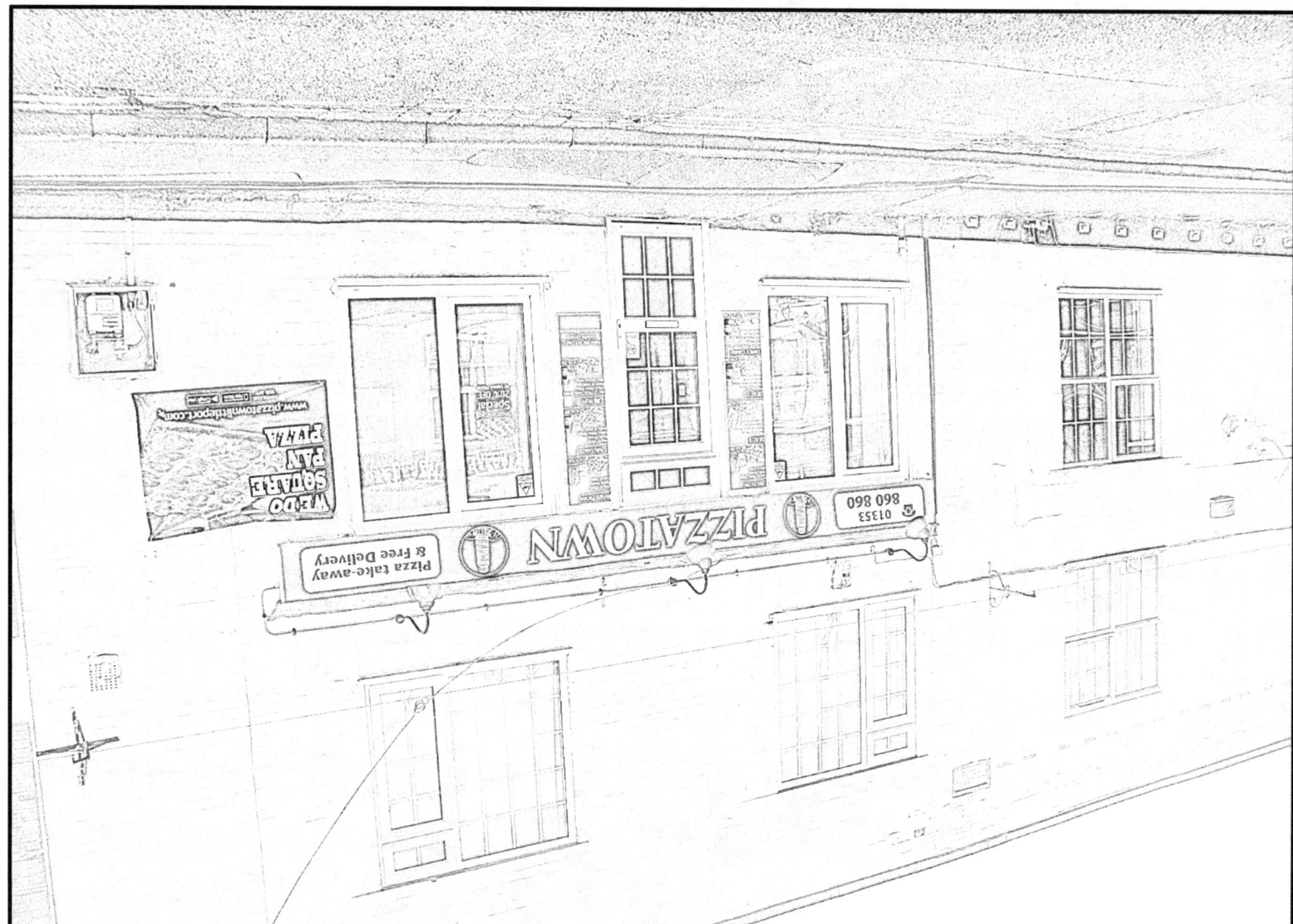

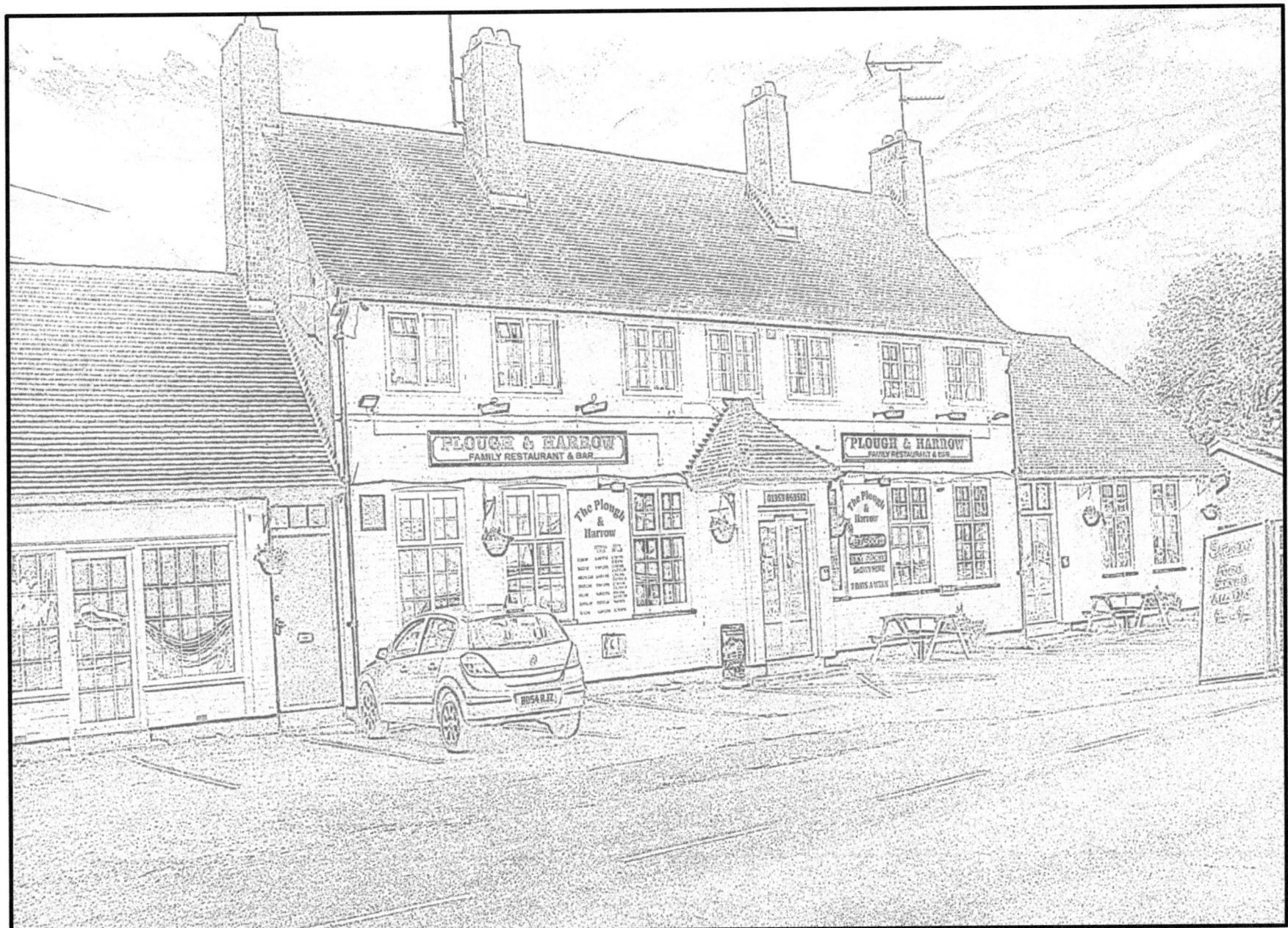

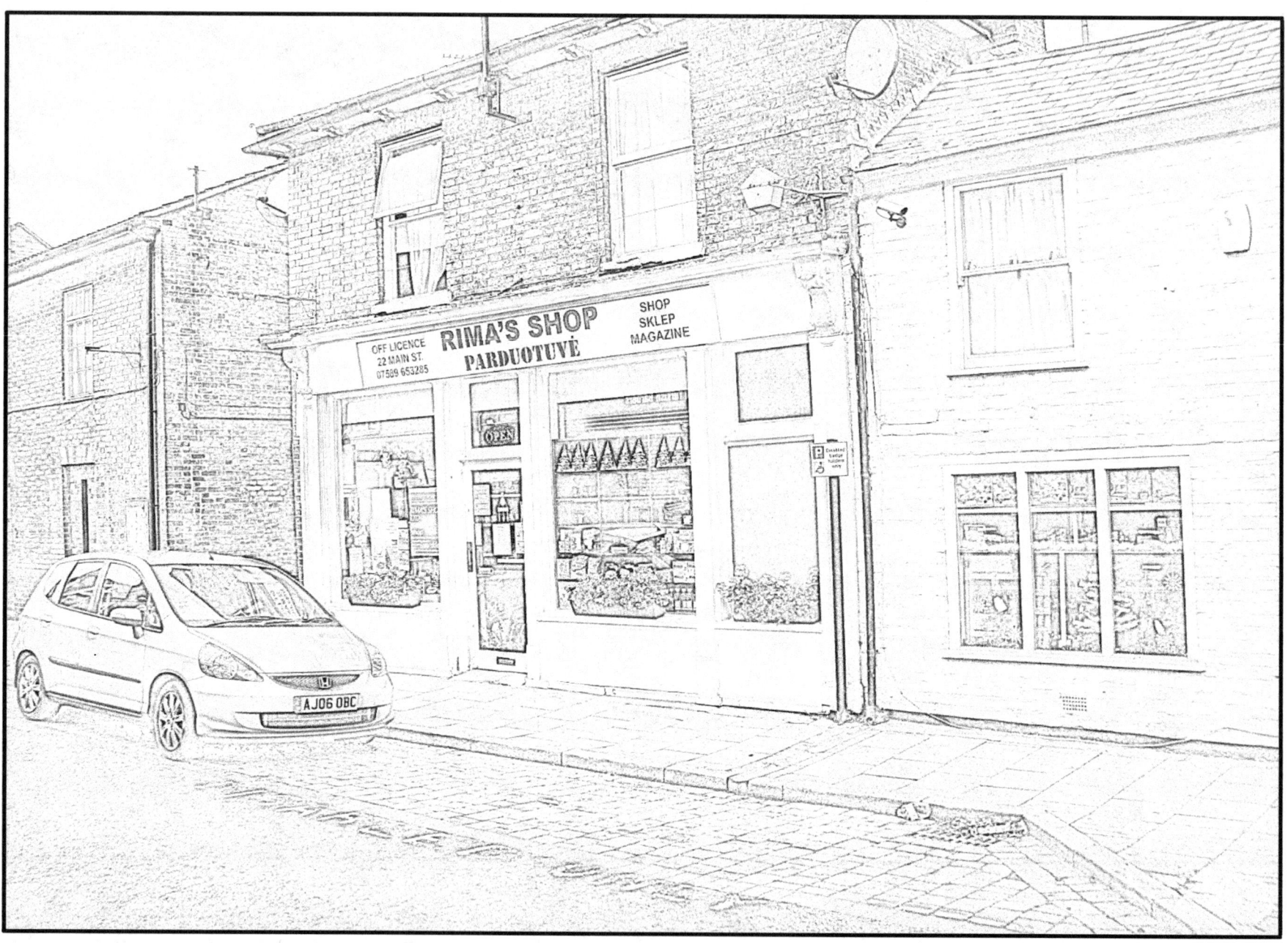

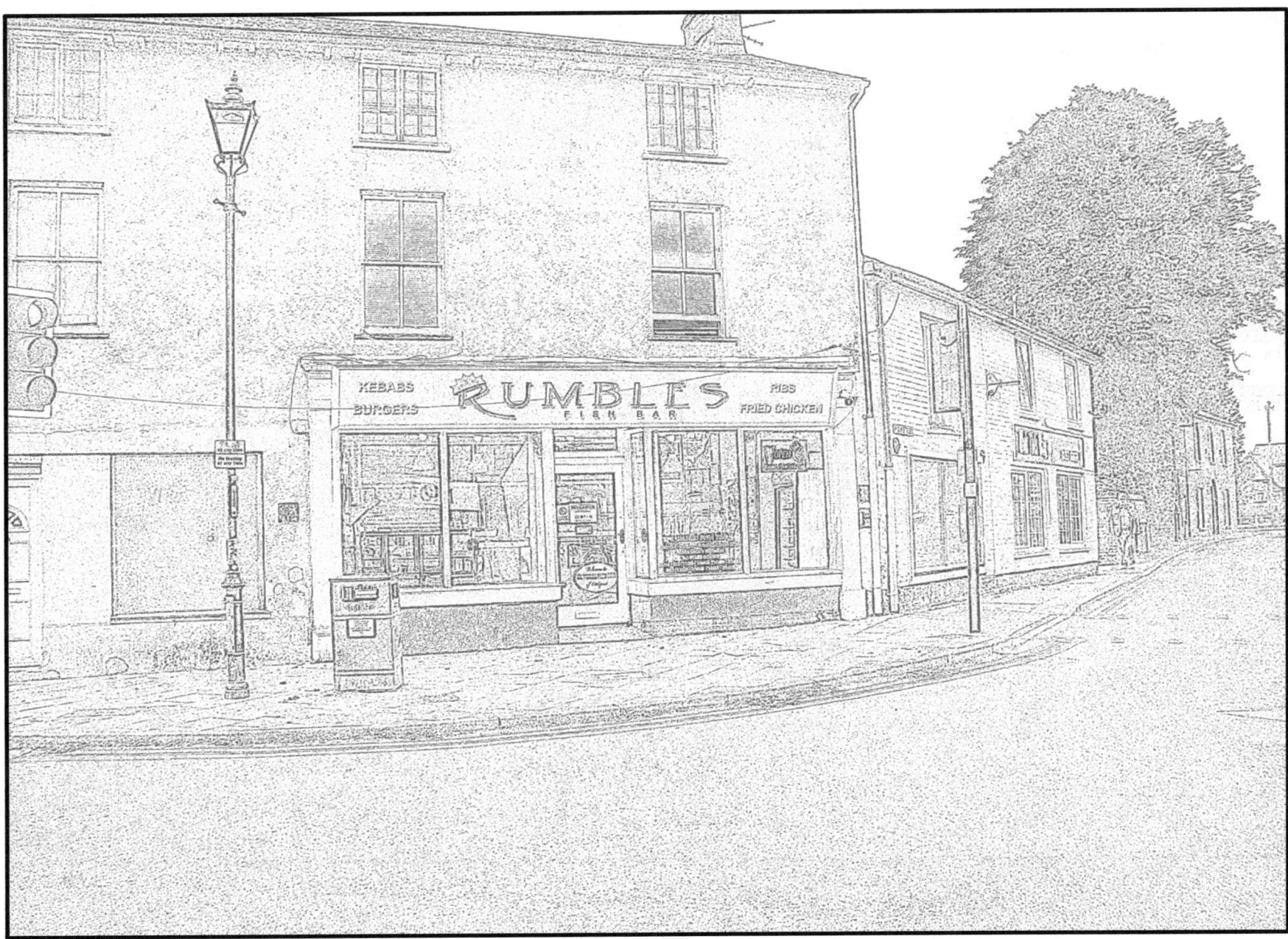

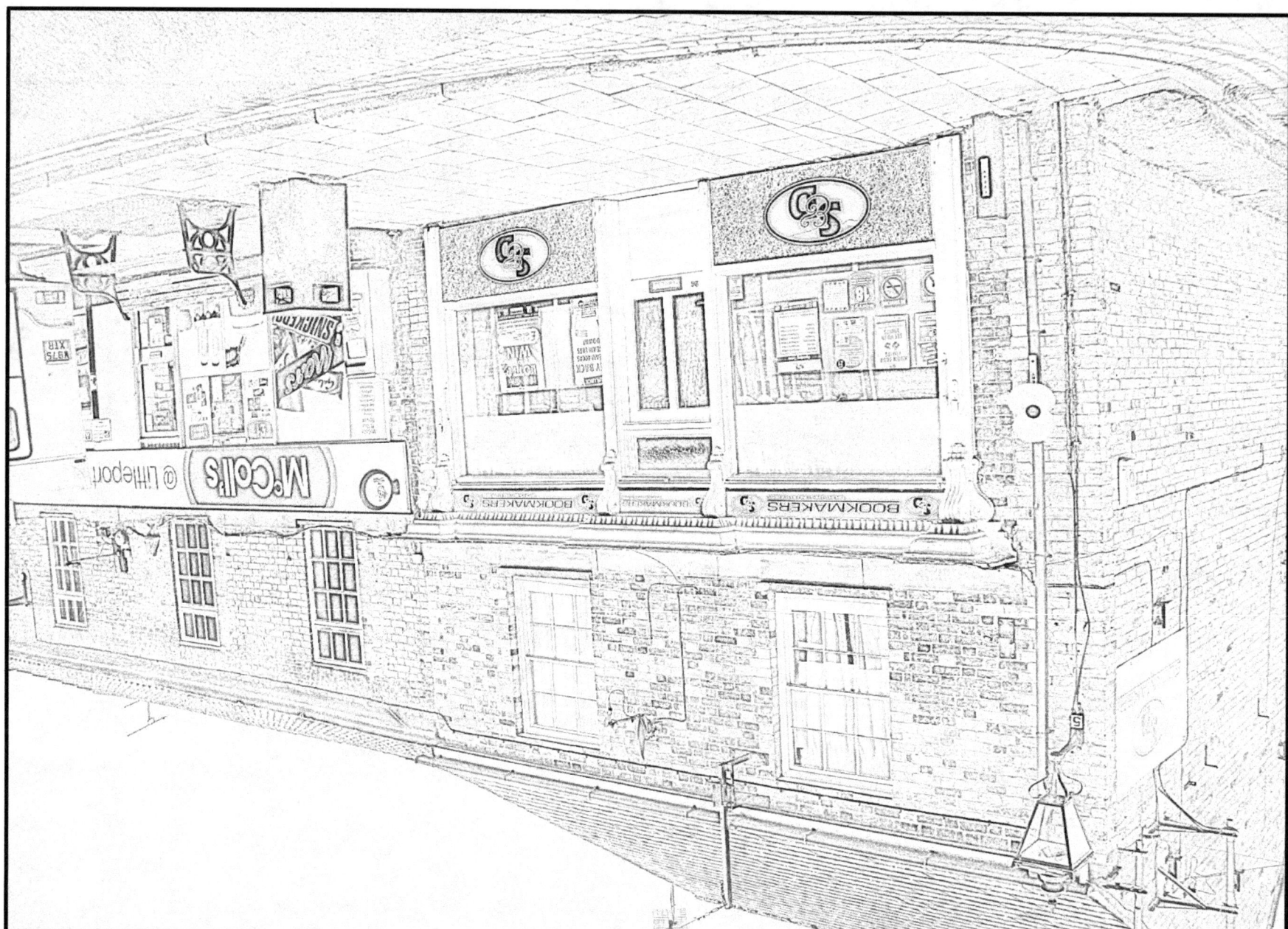

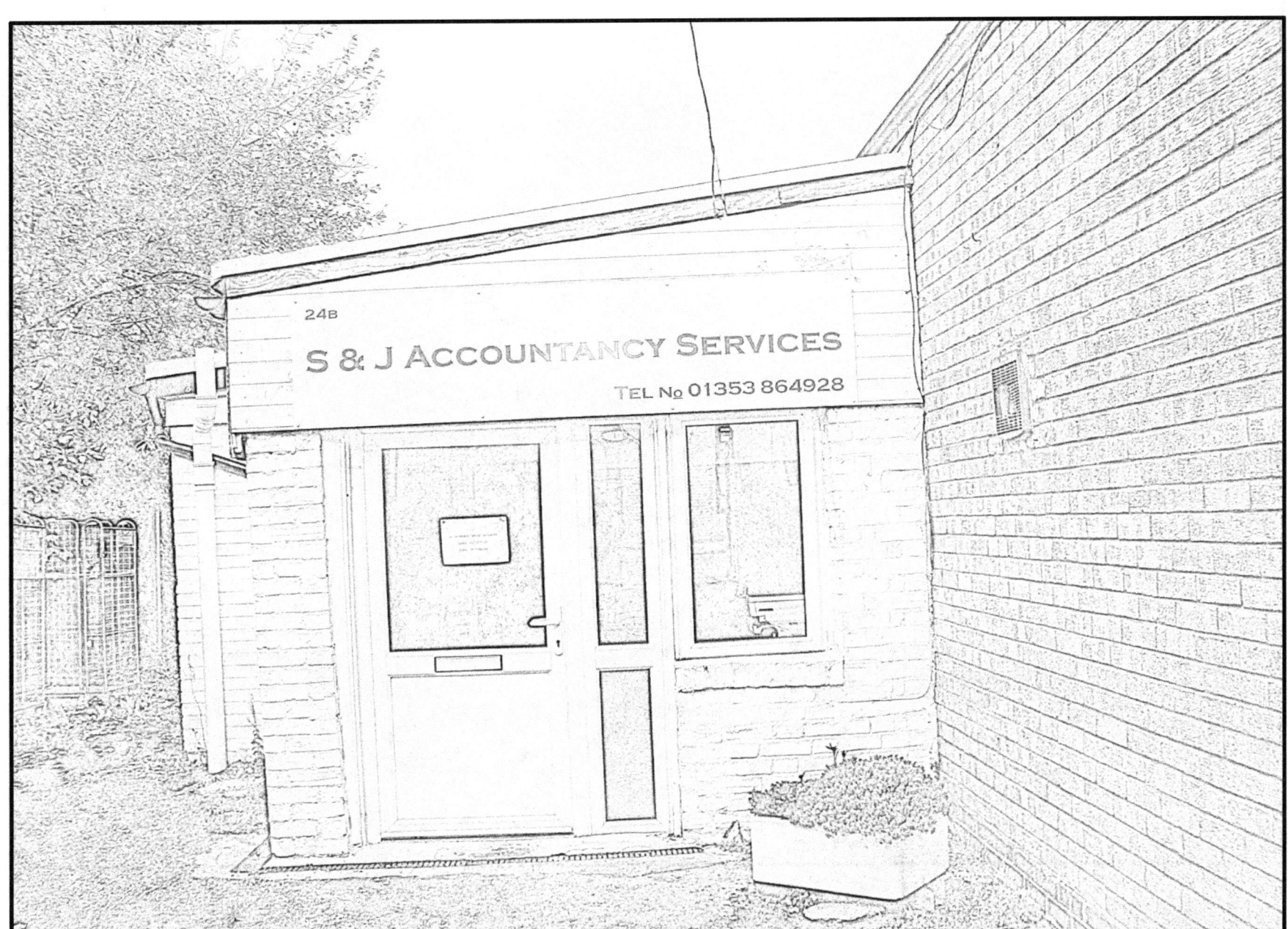

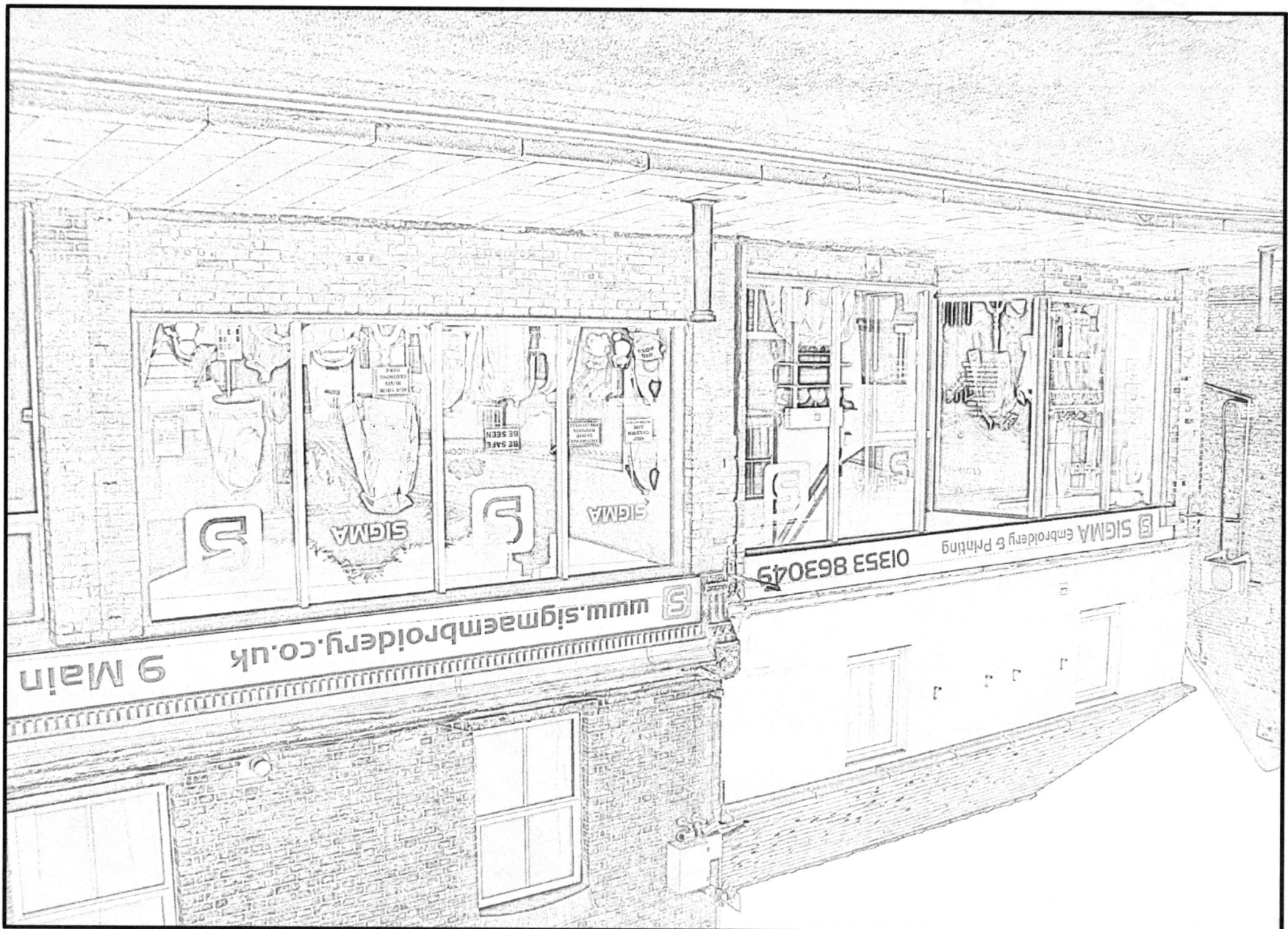

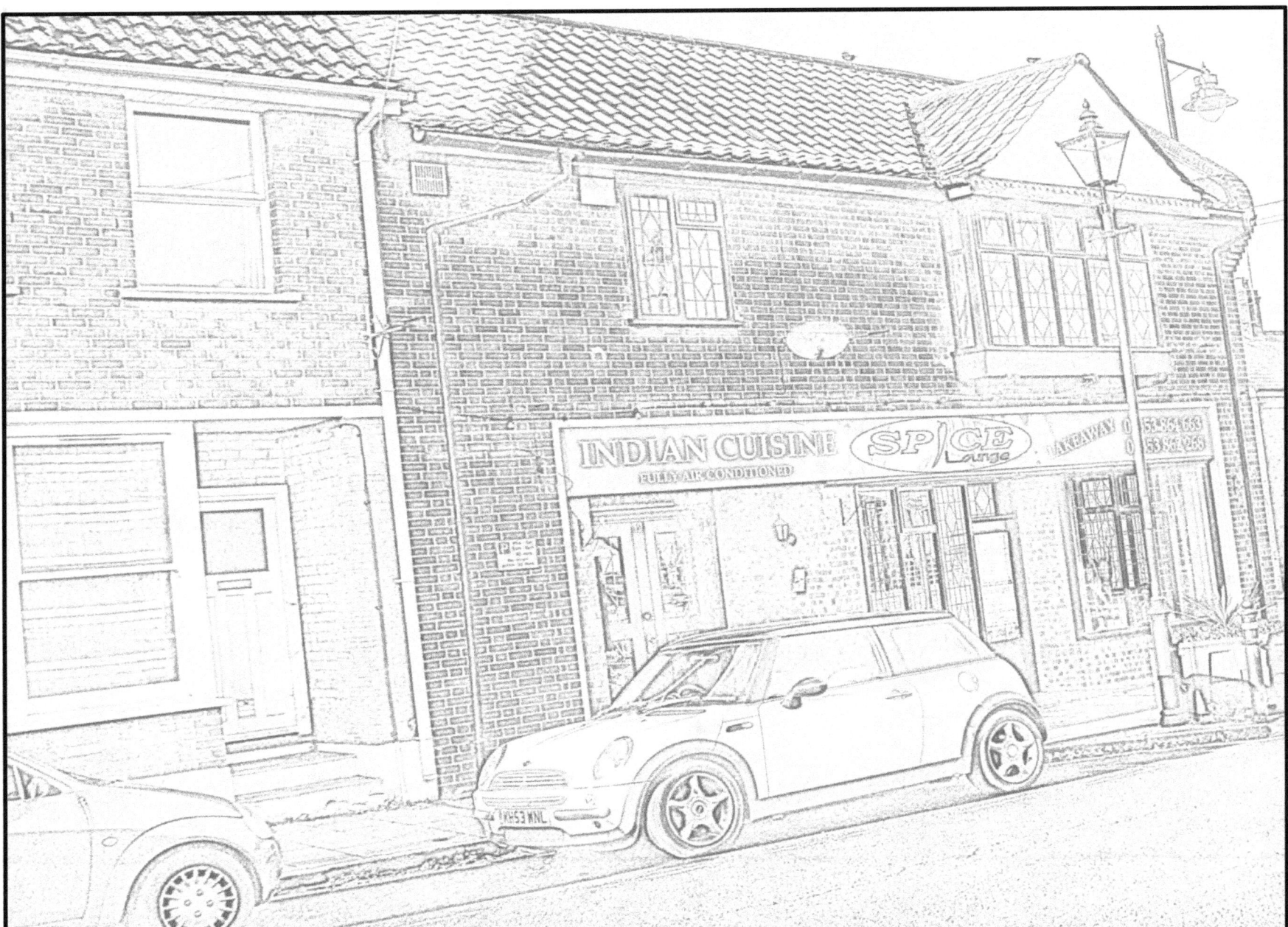

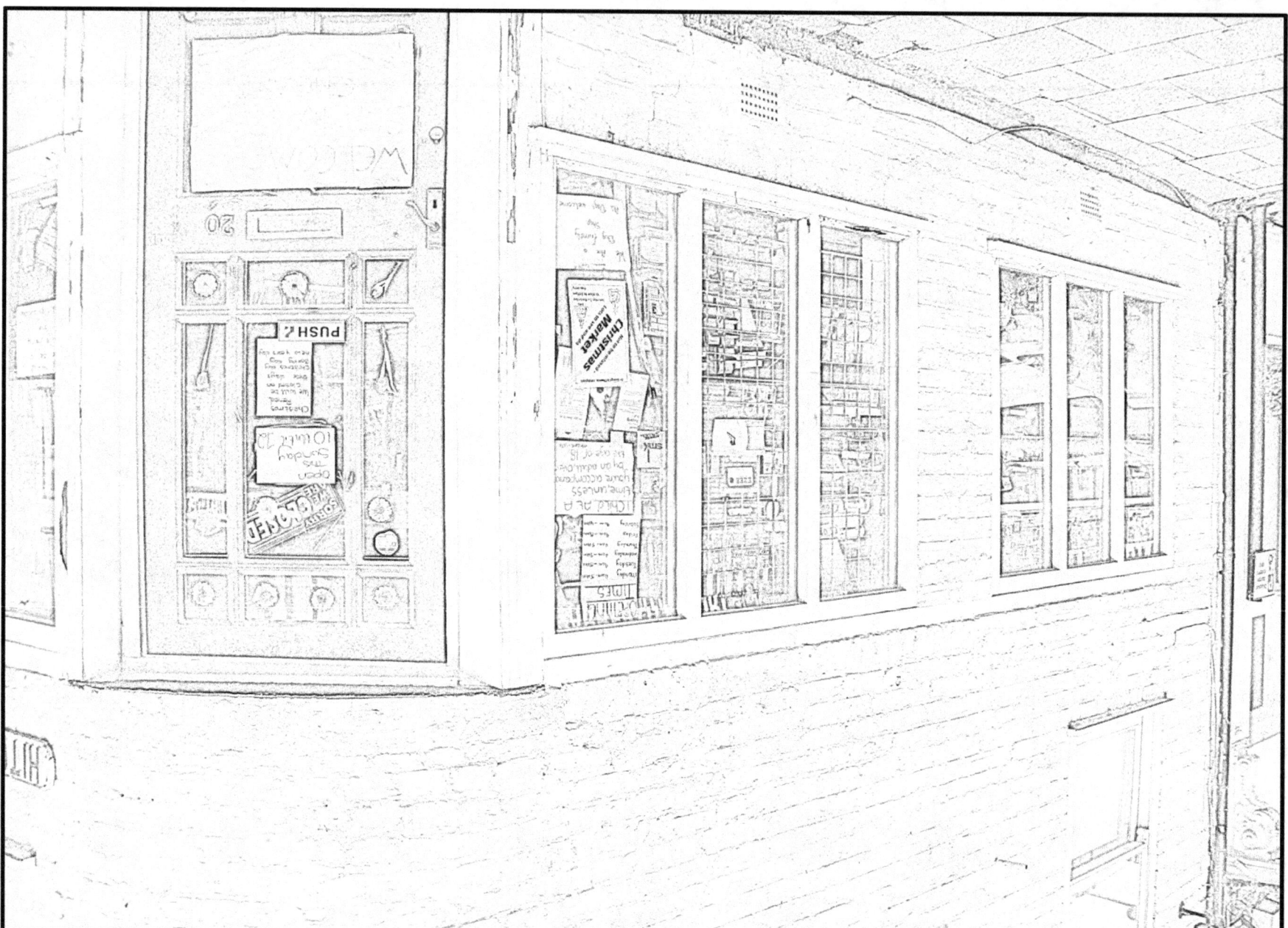

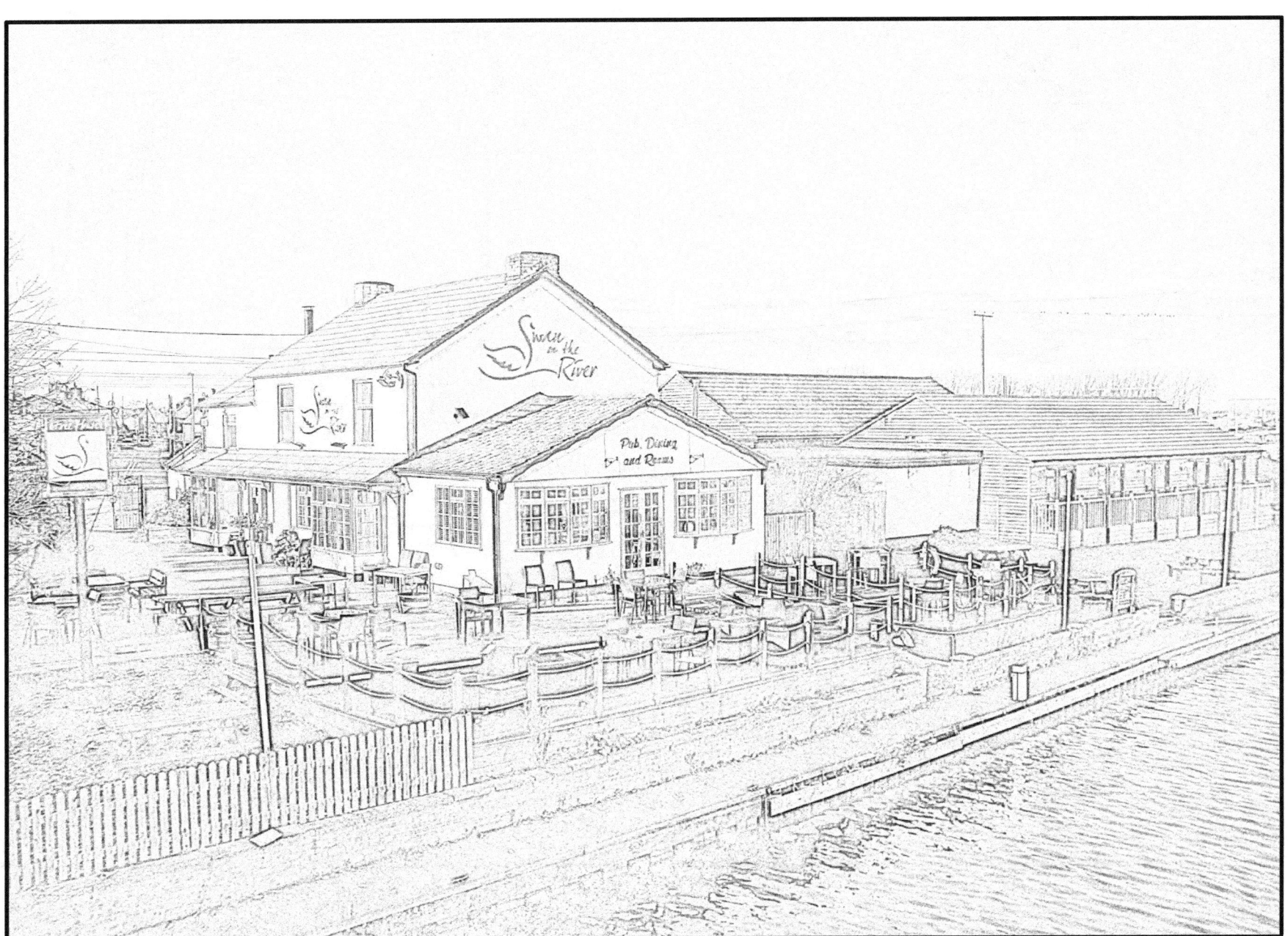

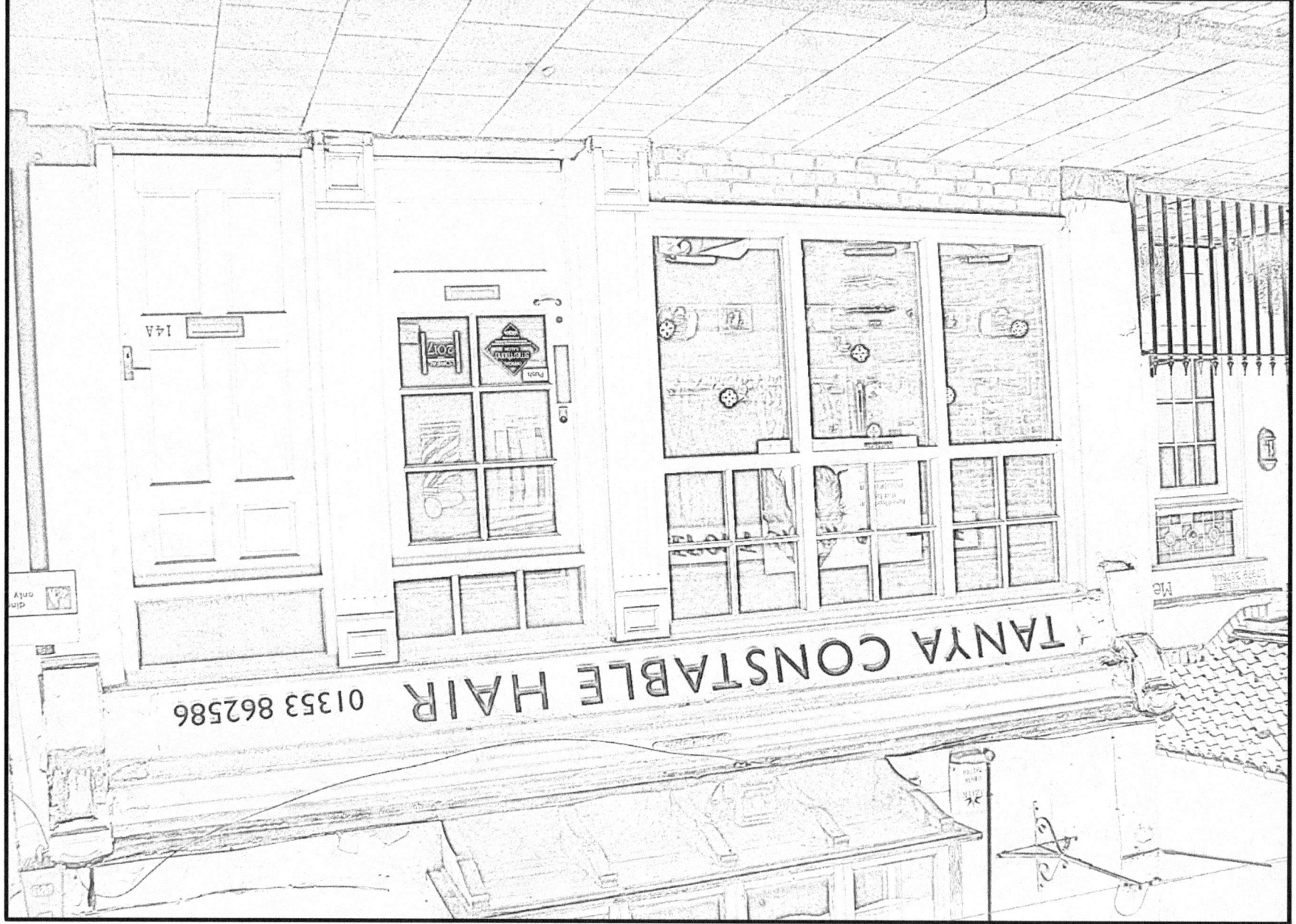

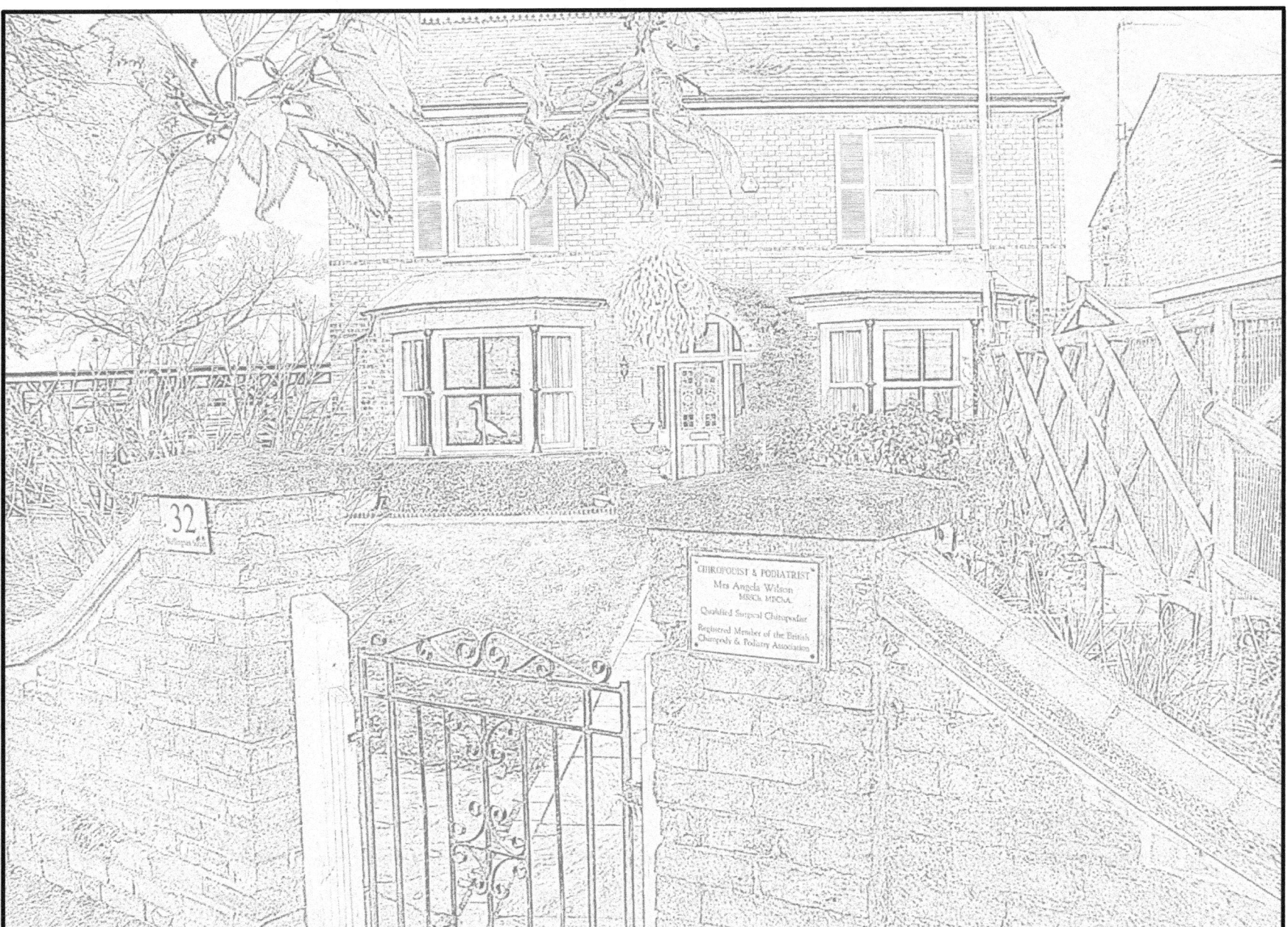

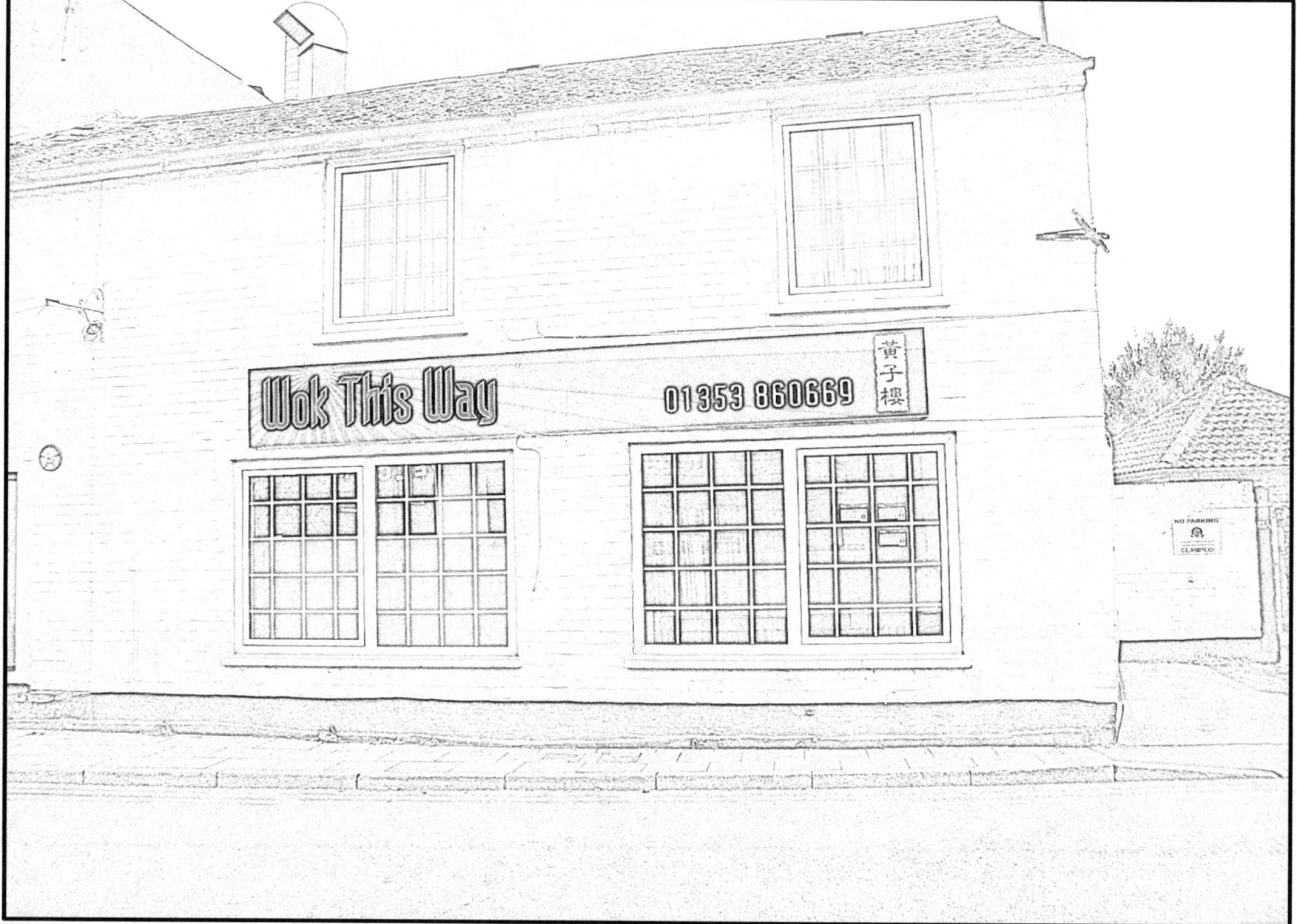

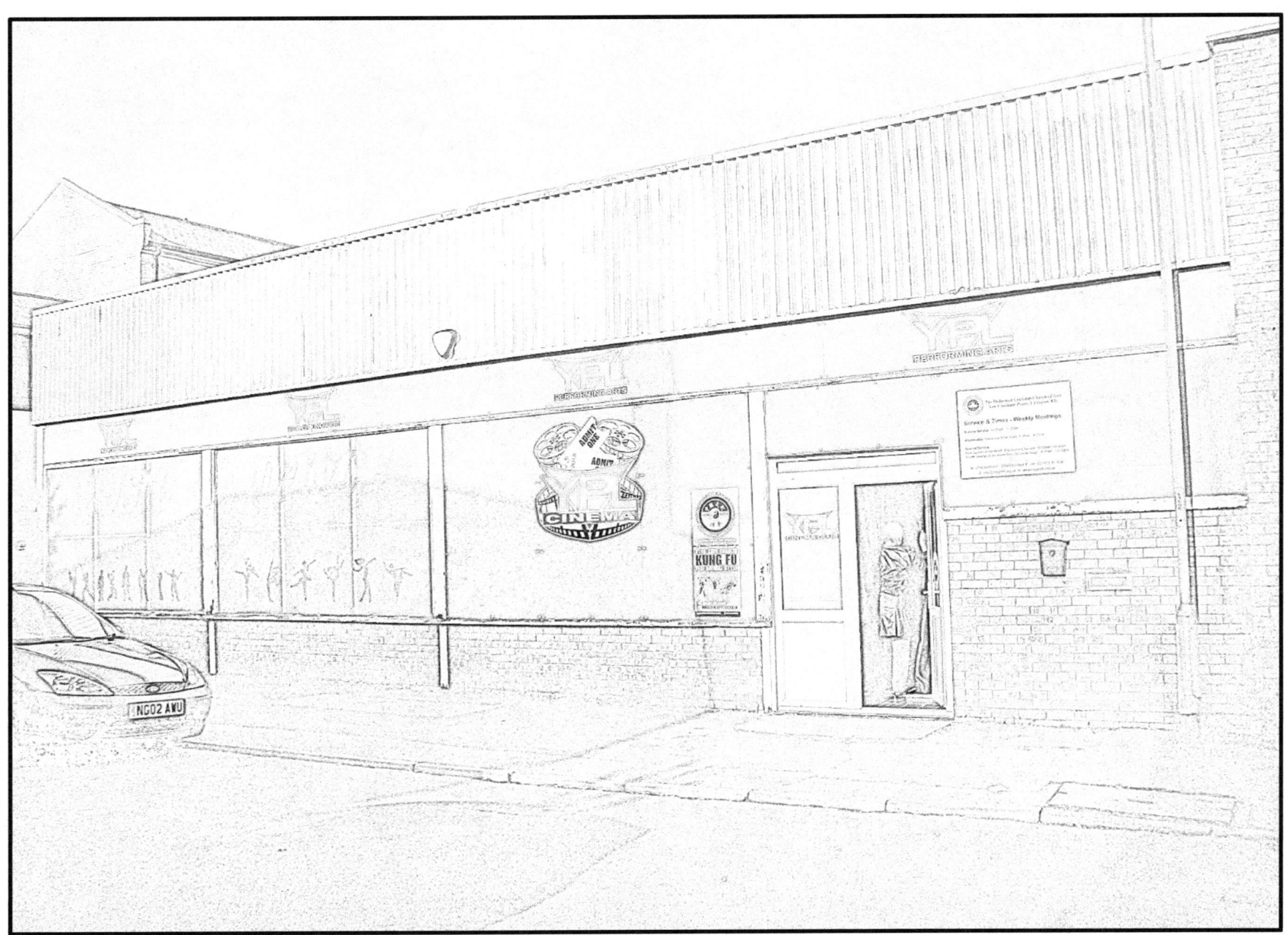

Section 2

- Armourstore   (01353) 860688
- Audley Garage   (01353) 860226
- BP Garage   (01353) 861486
- Branching Out Disability   (01353) 863221
- Criteria Cars   (01353) 863699
- DeLaynie's   (01353) 864414
- Ernest Doe   (01353) 860761
- E-space North   (01353) 865300
- Faraday Road Business Park
- Fenland Arctic Spas and Tubs   (01353) 863115
- Fenland Car Care   (01353) 861444
- Genesis Diagnostics   (01353) 862220
- GTR Motors   (01353) 862166
- It's Wonderful   (01353) 863300
- Jurassic Bark   (01353) 863883
- LG Car Sales   (01353) 862999
- Littleport Timber Buildings   (01353) 861707
- Luke Eyres   (01353) 863125
- M8Trix Precision Engineering   (01353) 860150
- MAM Tiling   (01353) 863916
- FP McCann   (01353) 861416
- Metroseal   (01353) 864880
- Mobi Tech   (01353) 771405
- Performance Conveyor Belting   (01353)864999

- Portley Garage — (01353) 860314
- Port Plumbing — (01353) 860314
- Riverside Caravan and Camping — (01353) 860255
- RPM Motors — (01353) 862894
- Ryder &Amies — (01353) 862286
- Sharman's Garden Centre — (01353) 862298
- Bob Smith — (01353) 861161
- Sumo Power — (01945) 479125
- Techneat Engineers Ltd — (01353) 862044
- Thurlow Nunn Standen — (01353) 863038
- The Woodmakers — 07943013050
- Victoria Tyres — (01353) 860057
- Woodfen Lodge — (01353) 862495
- Woodlands Farm Units
- YPL Auction — (01353) 864611

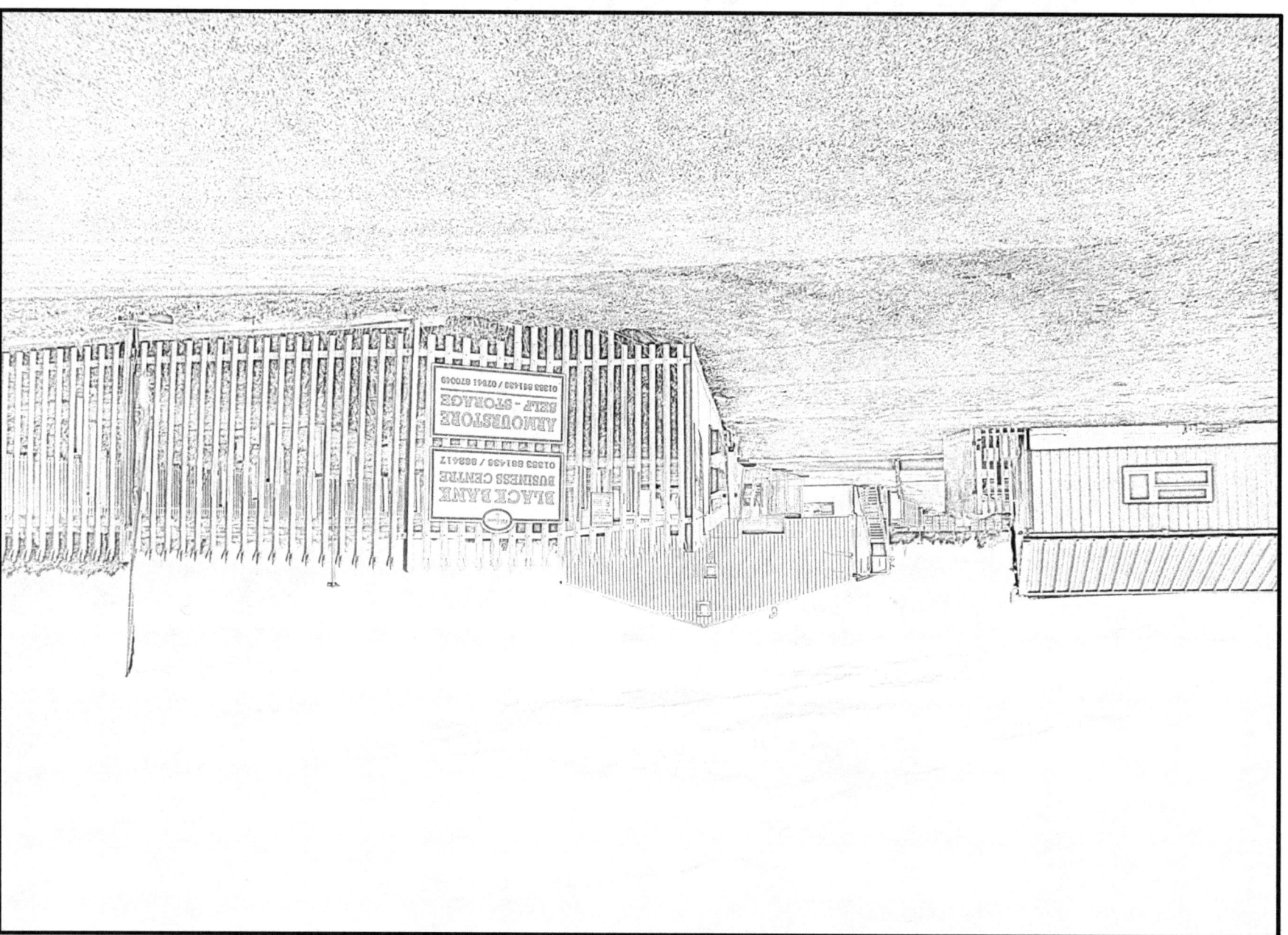

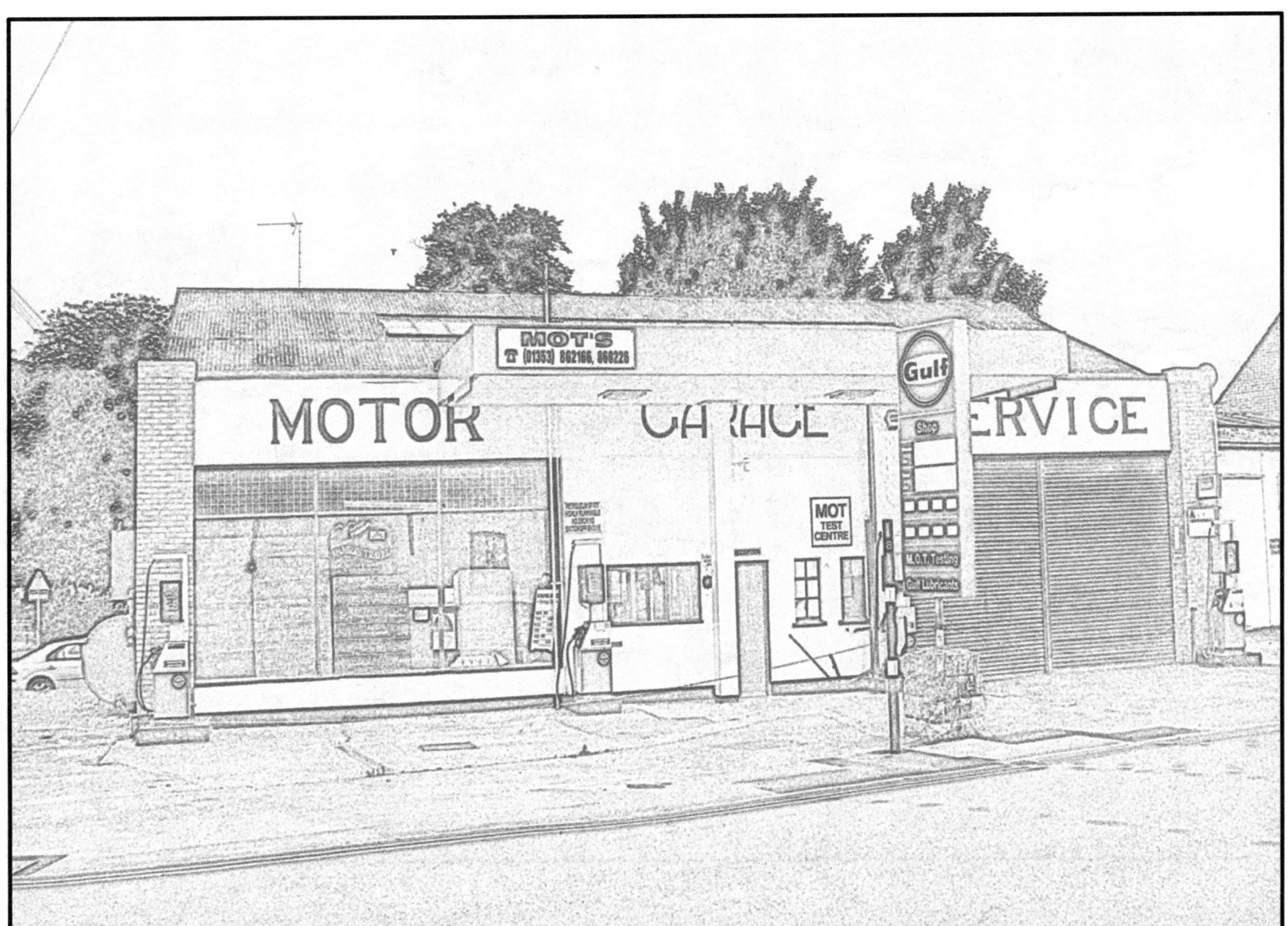

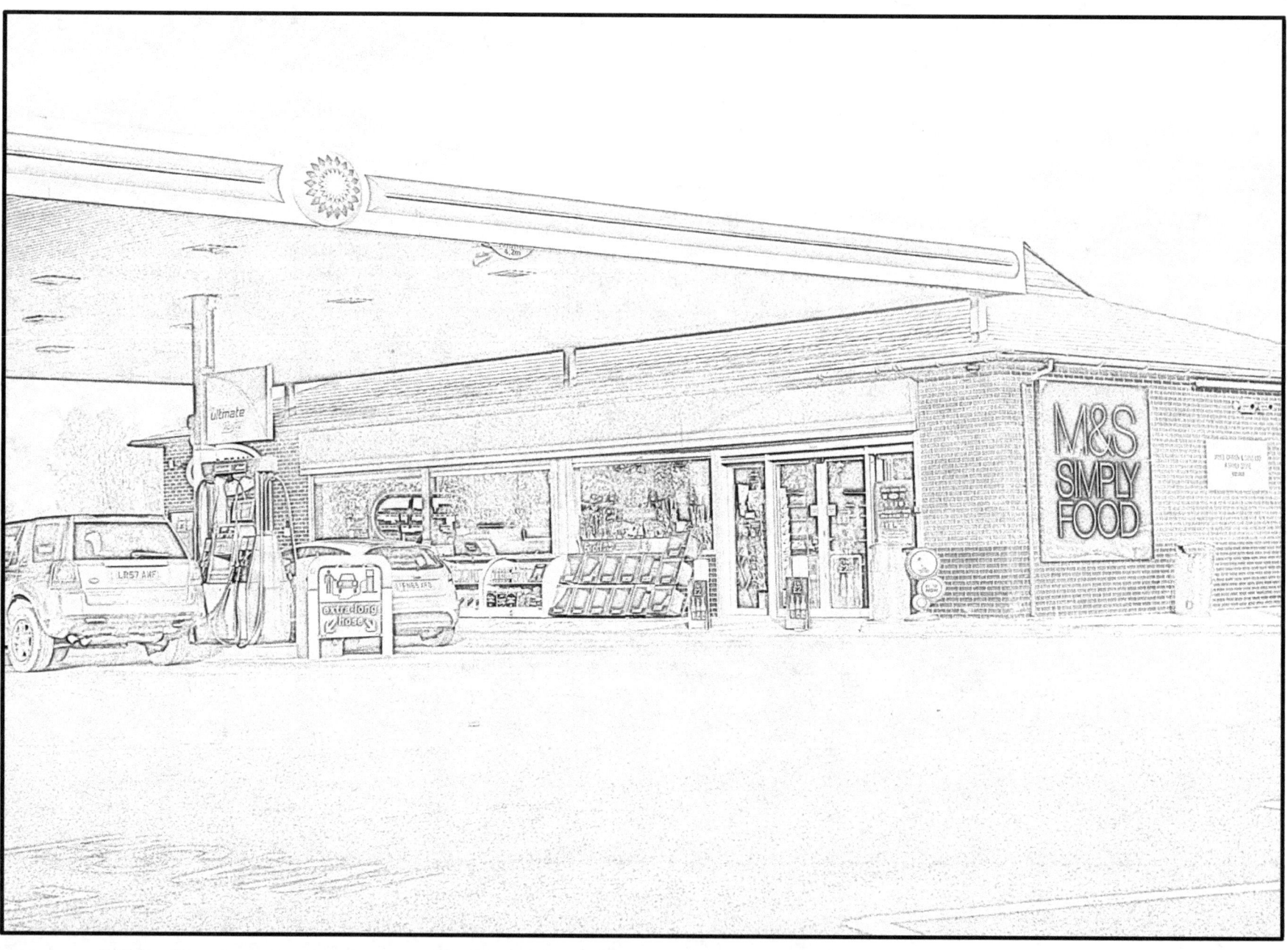

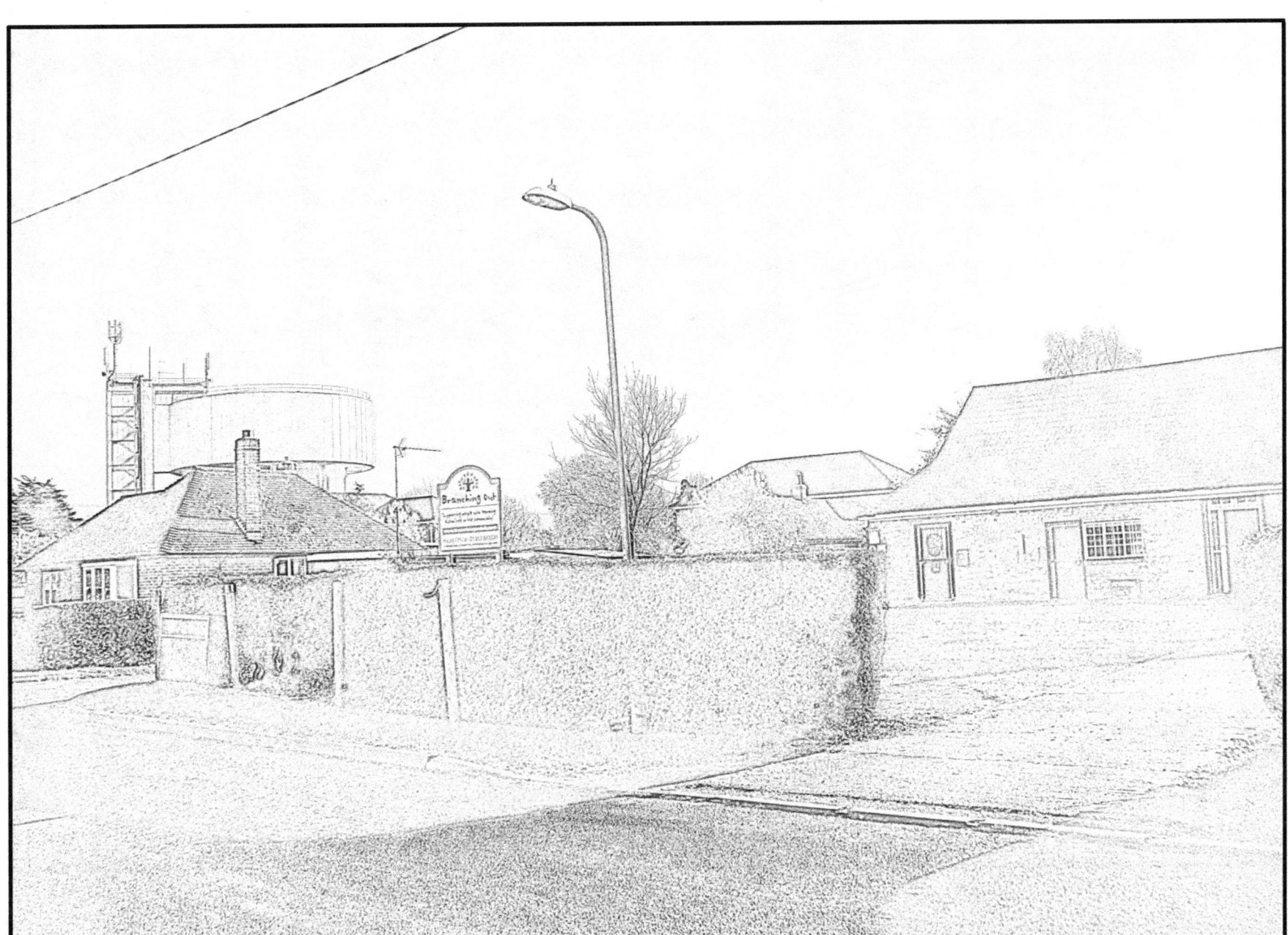

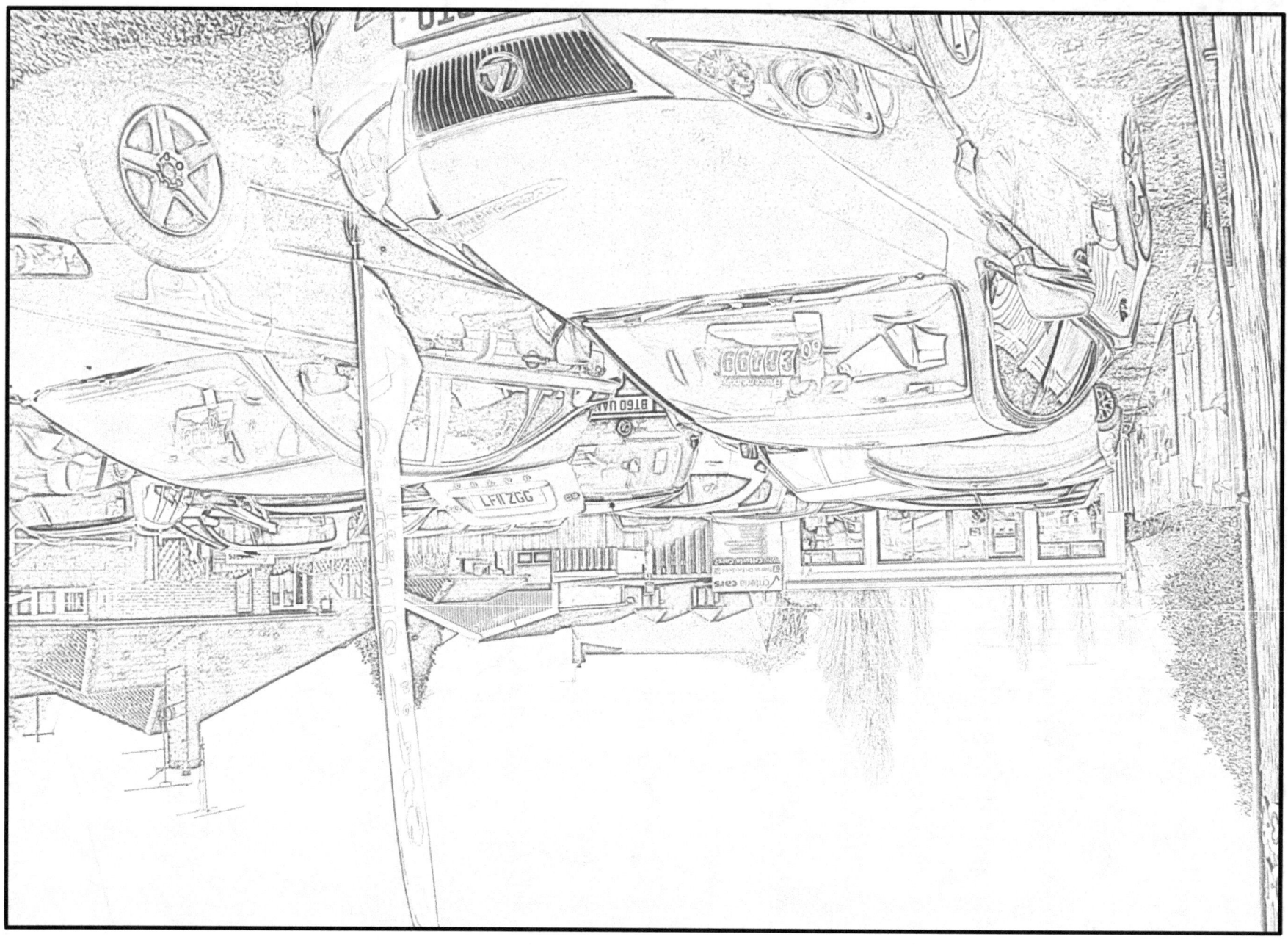

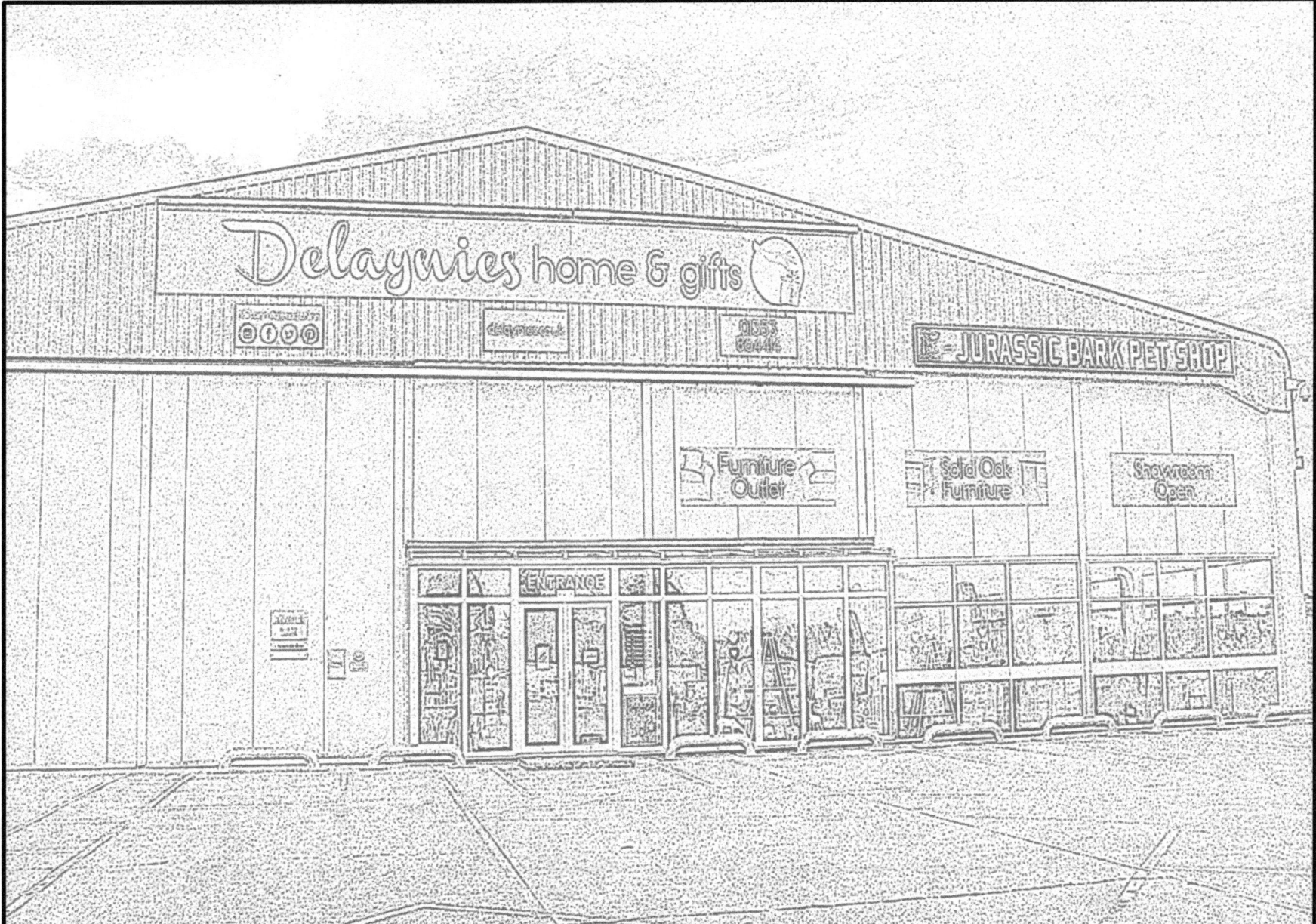

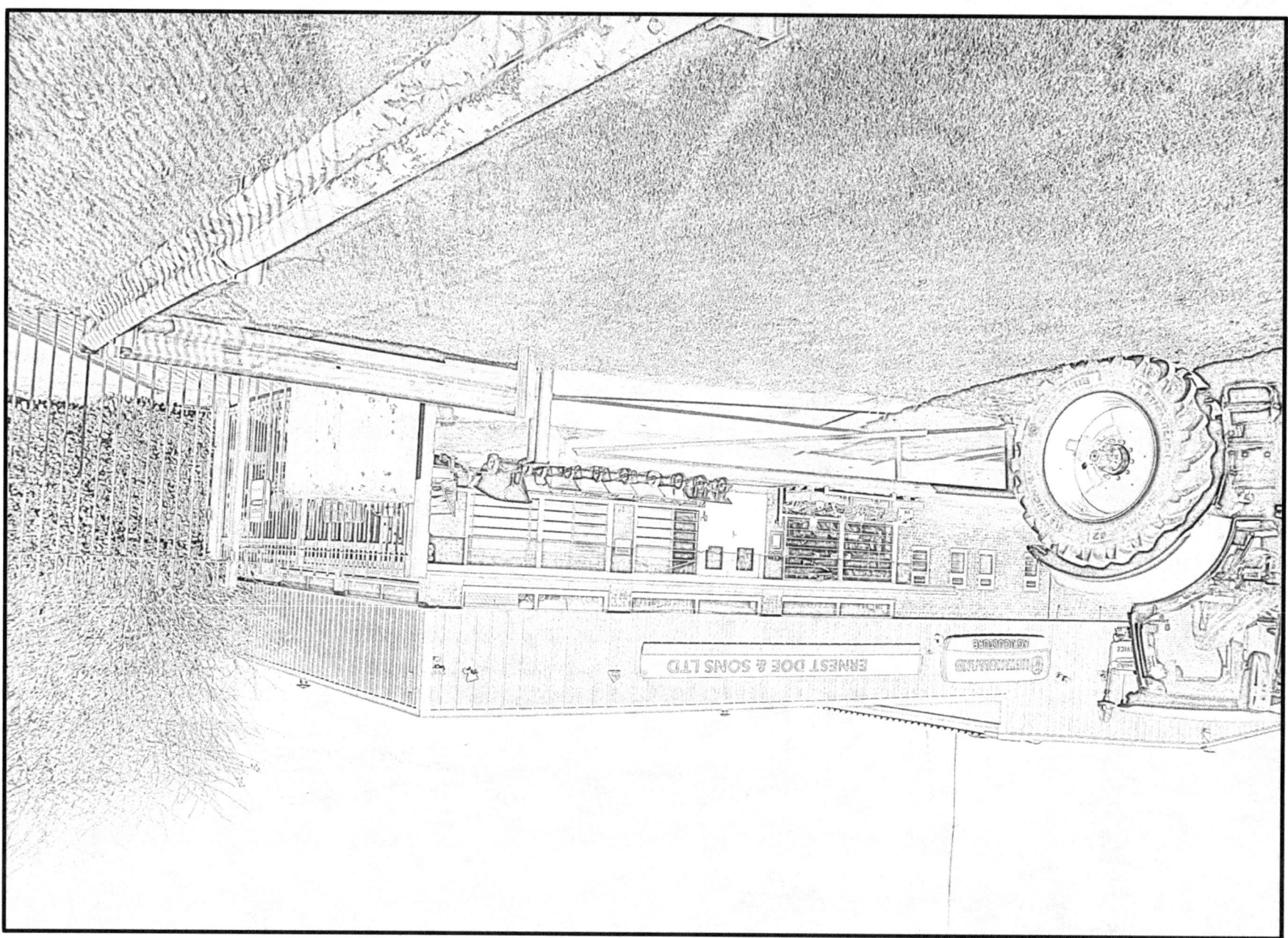

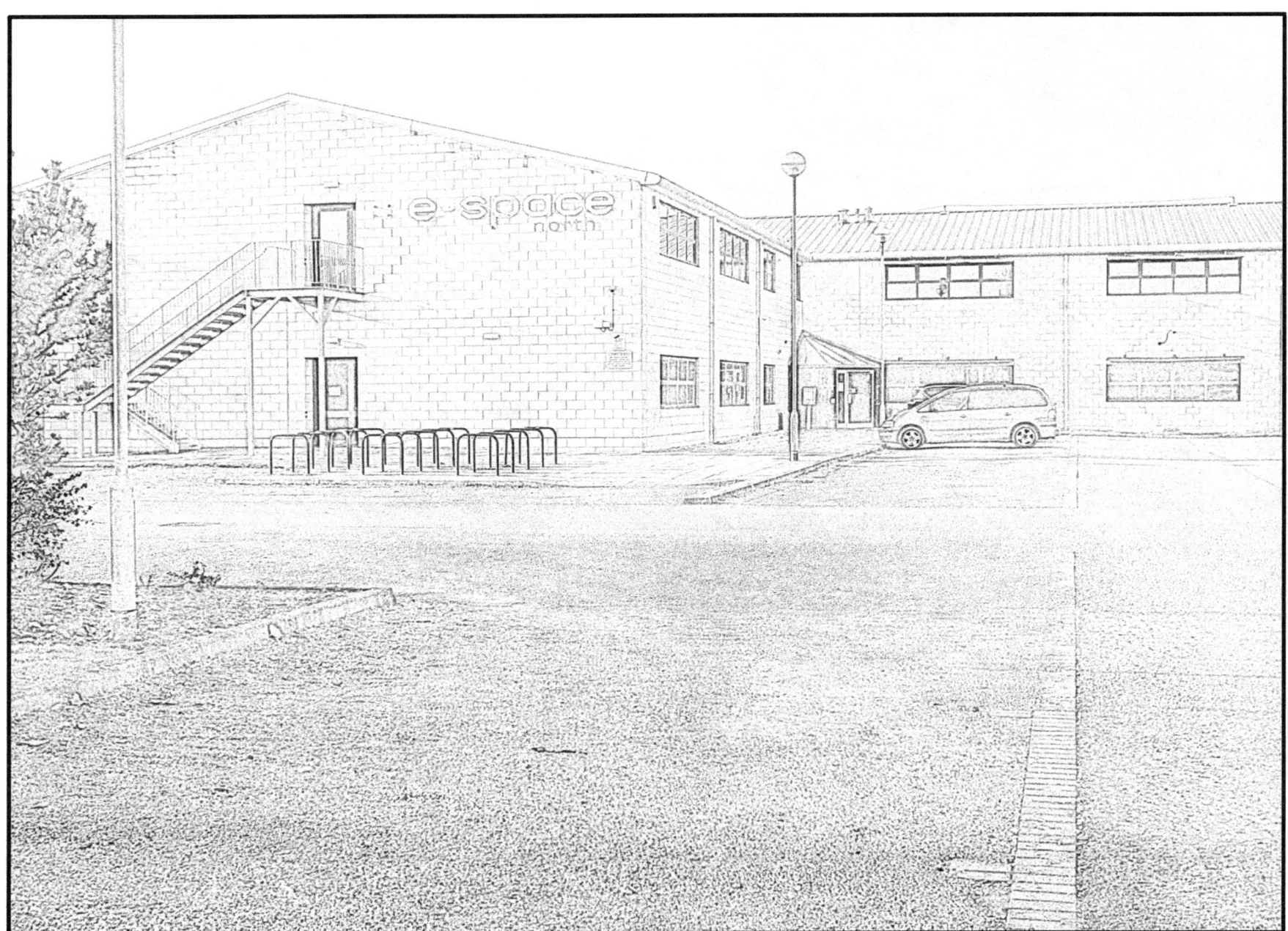

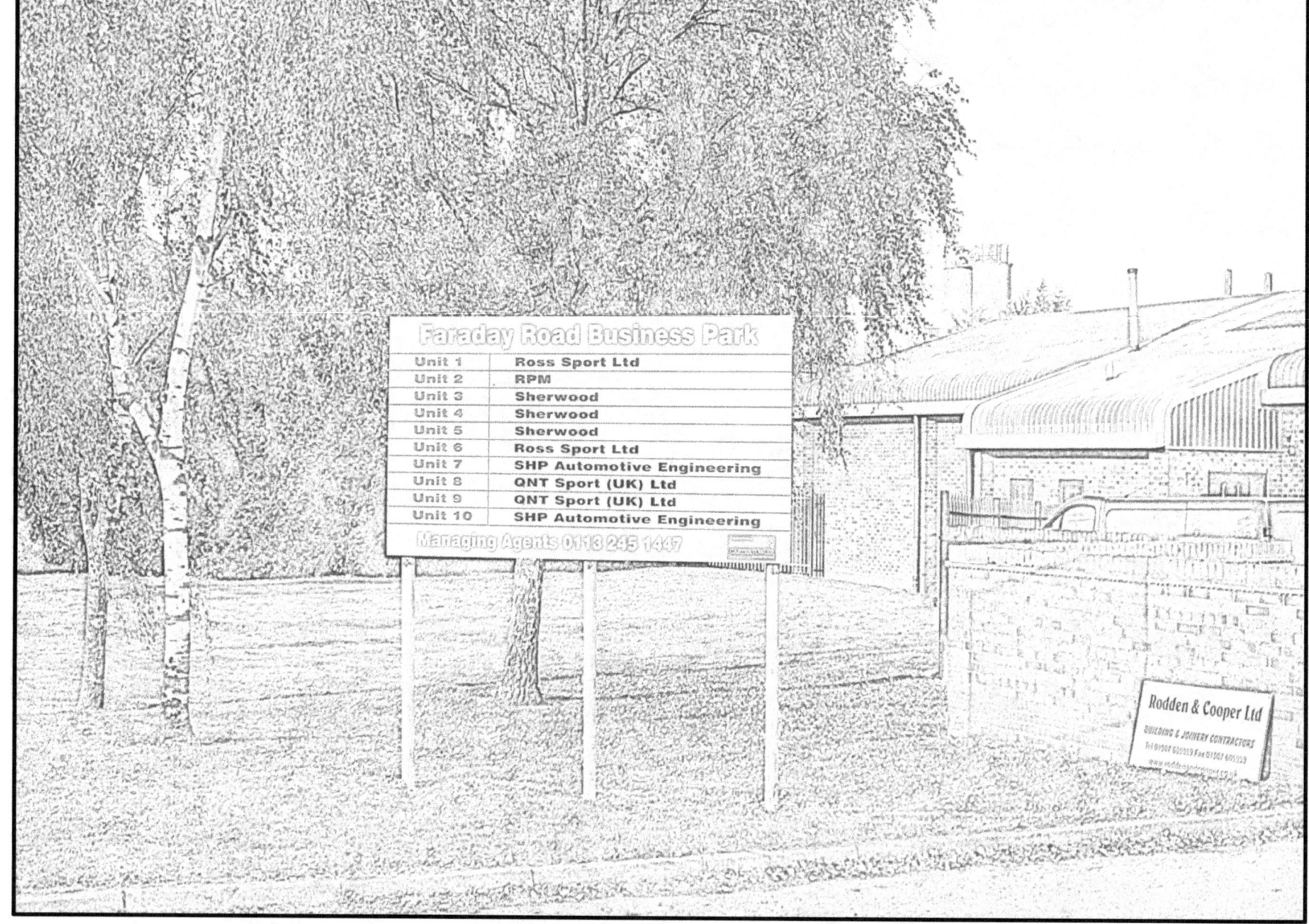

Faraday Road Business Park

Unit 1	Ross Sport Ltd
Unit 2	RPM
Unit 3	Sherwood
Unit 4	Sherwood
Unit 5	Sherwood
Unit 6	Ross Sport Ltd
Unit 7	SHP Automotive Engineering
Unit 8	QNT Sport (UK) Ltd
Unit 9	QNT Sport (UK) Ltd
Unit 10	SHP Automotive Engineering

Managing Agents 0113 245 1447

Rodden & Cooper Ltd
BUILDING & JOINERY CONTRACTORS

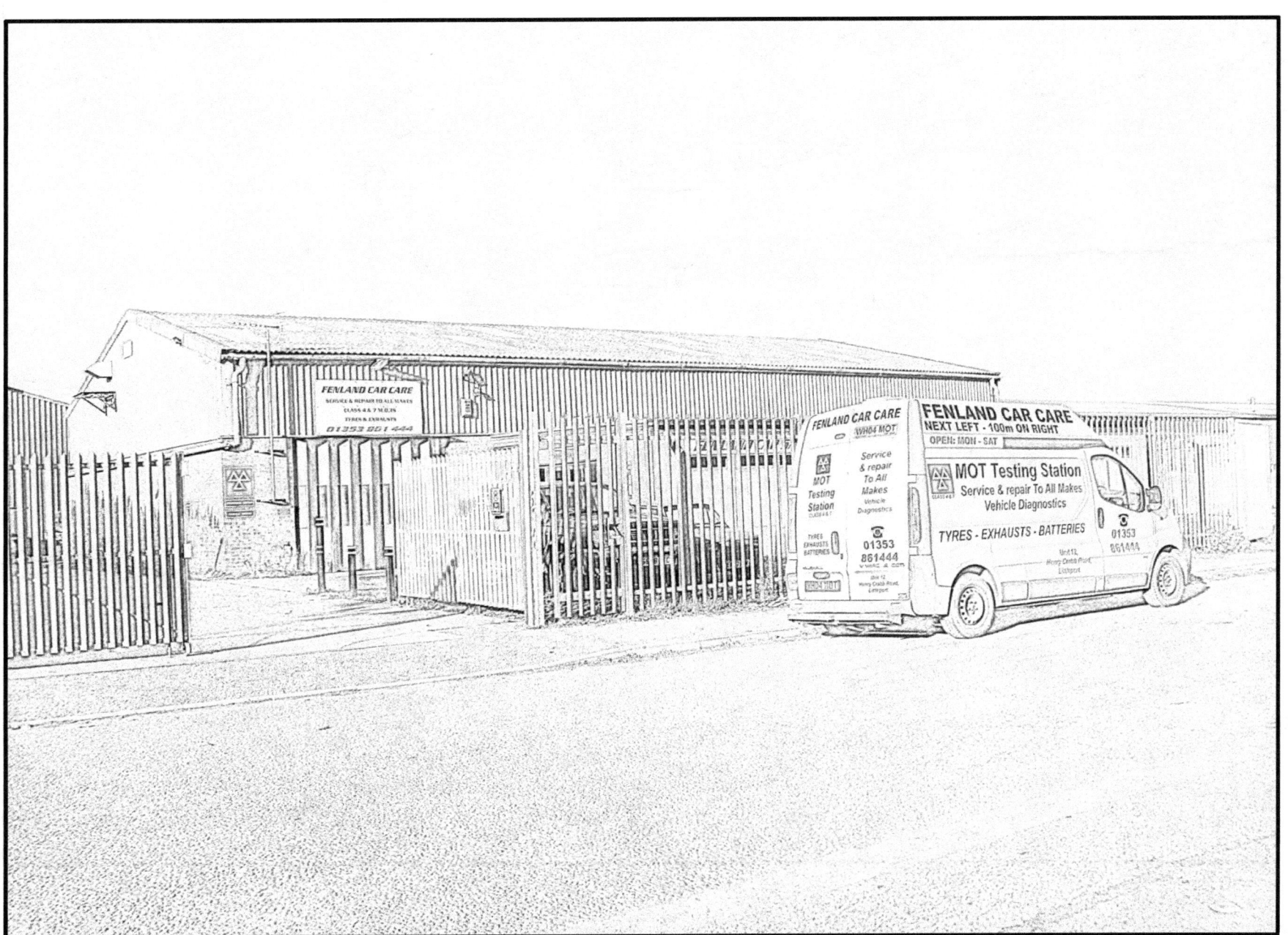

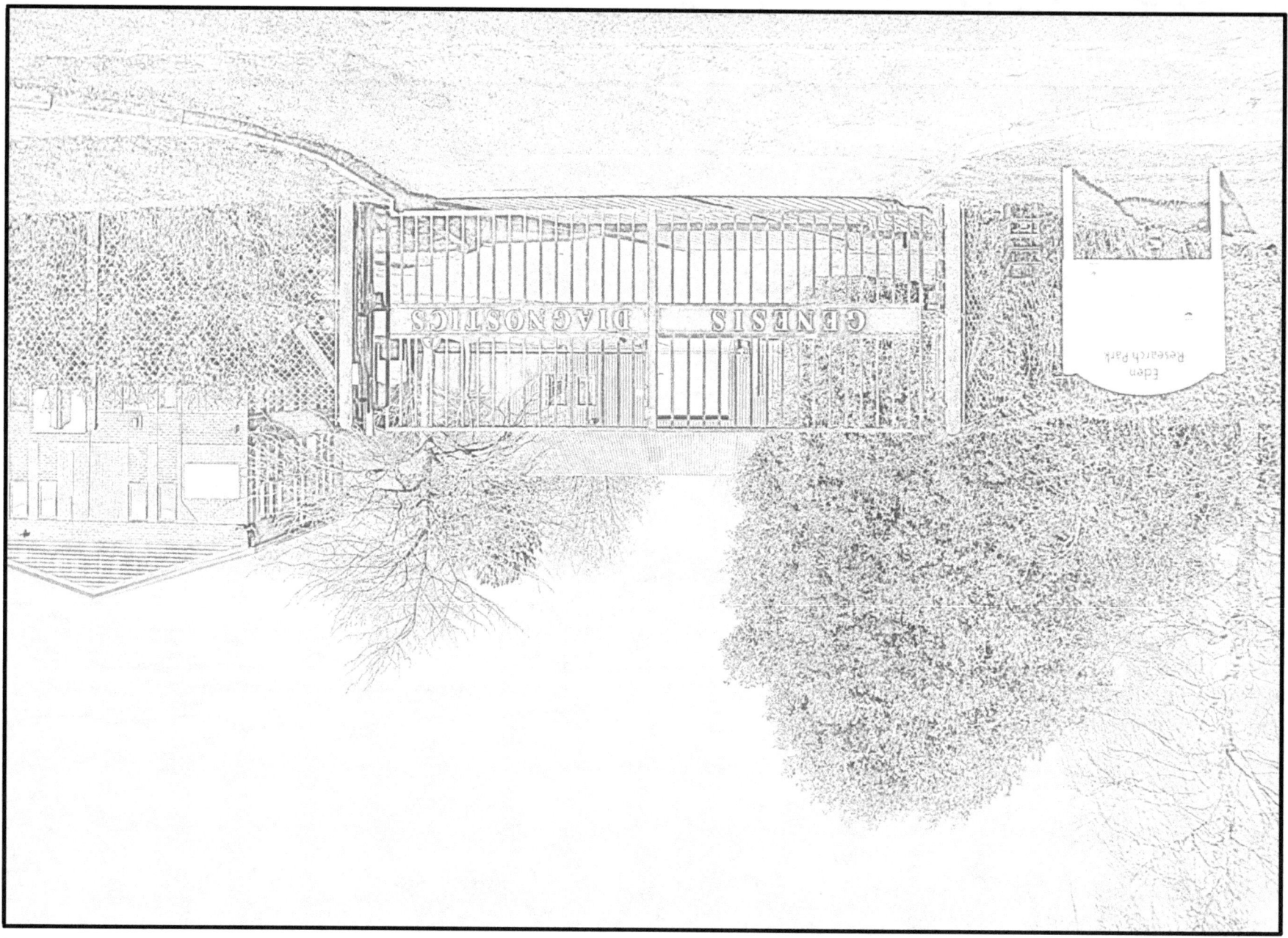

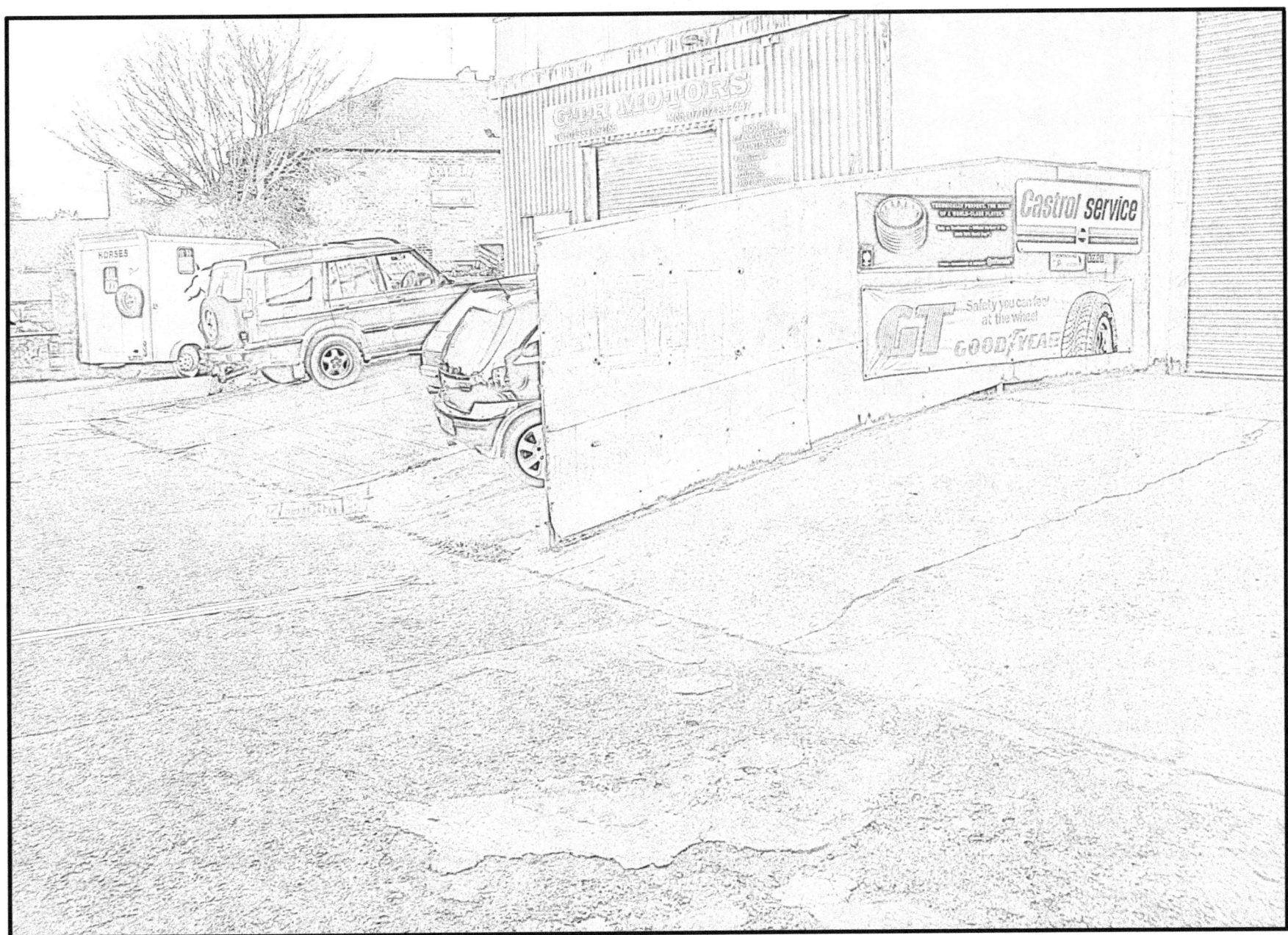

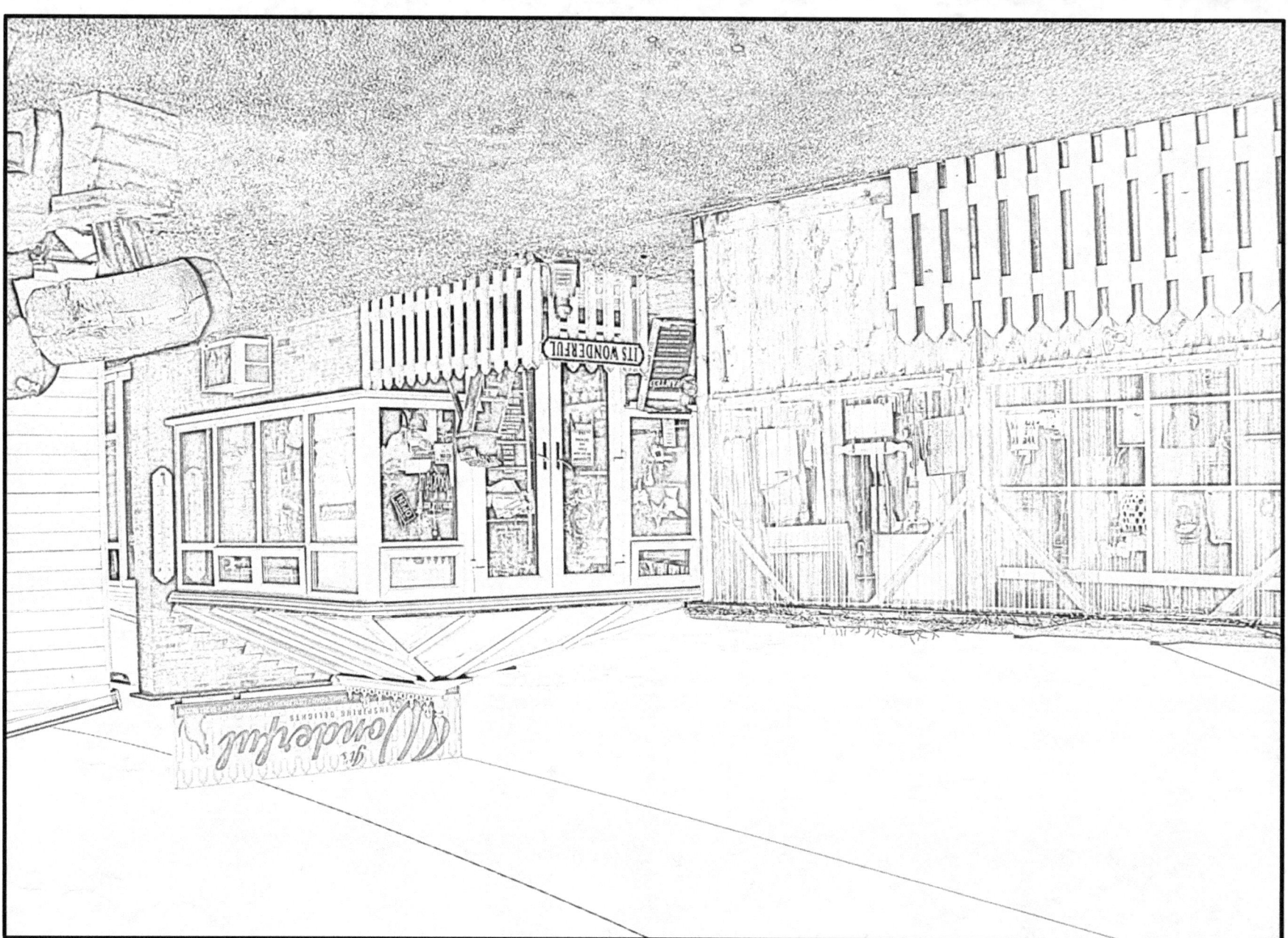

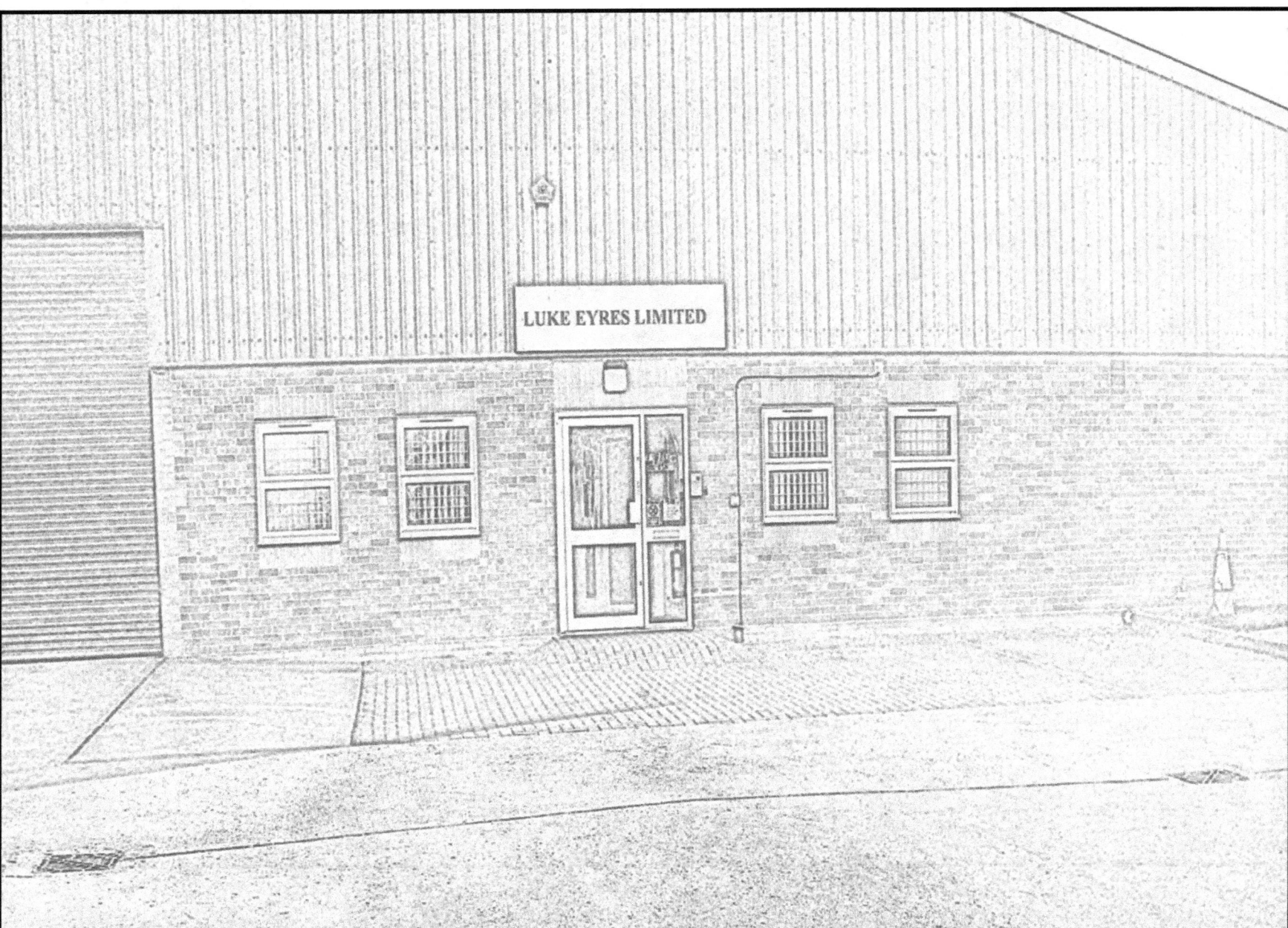

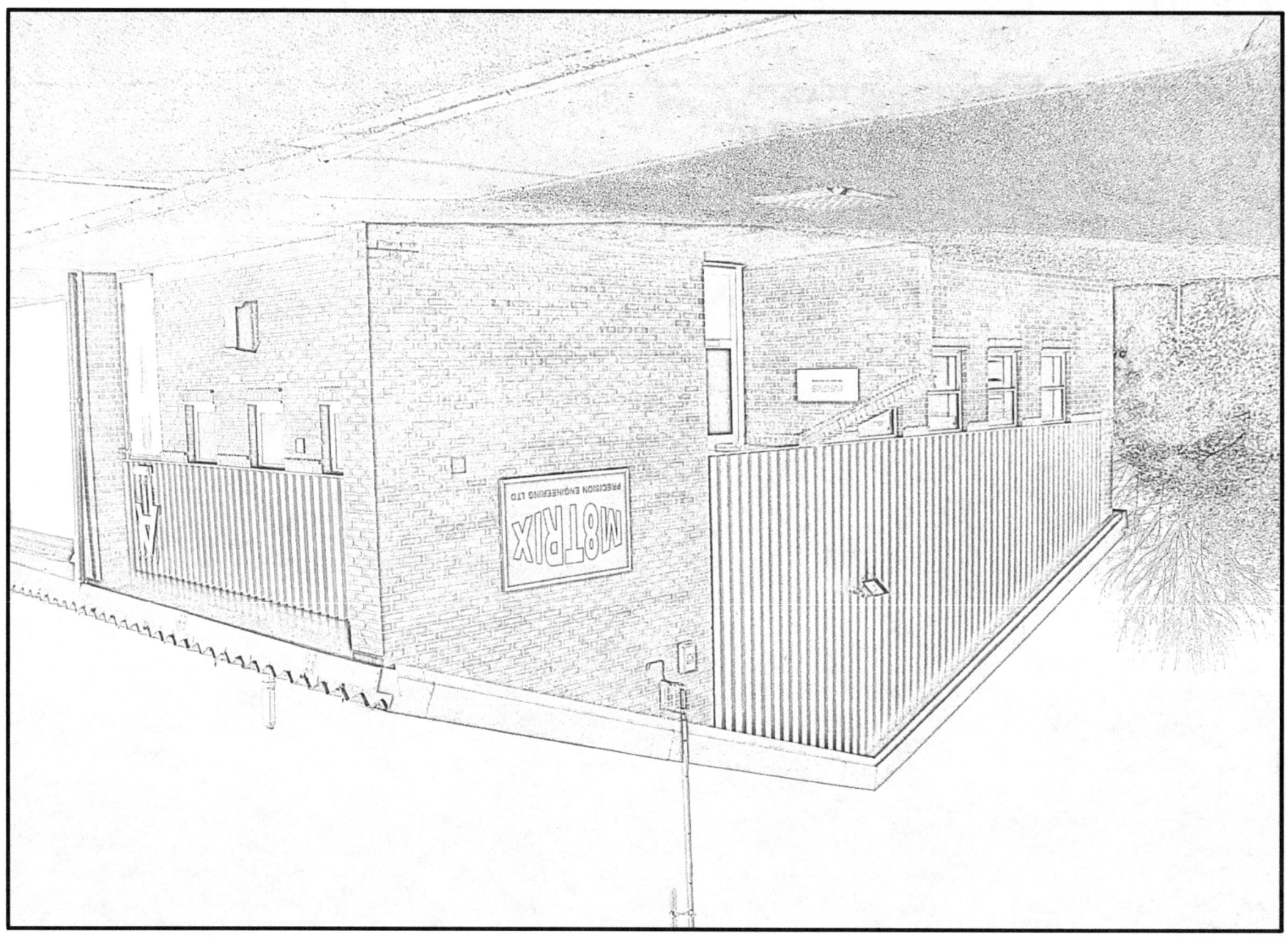

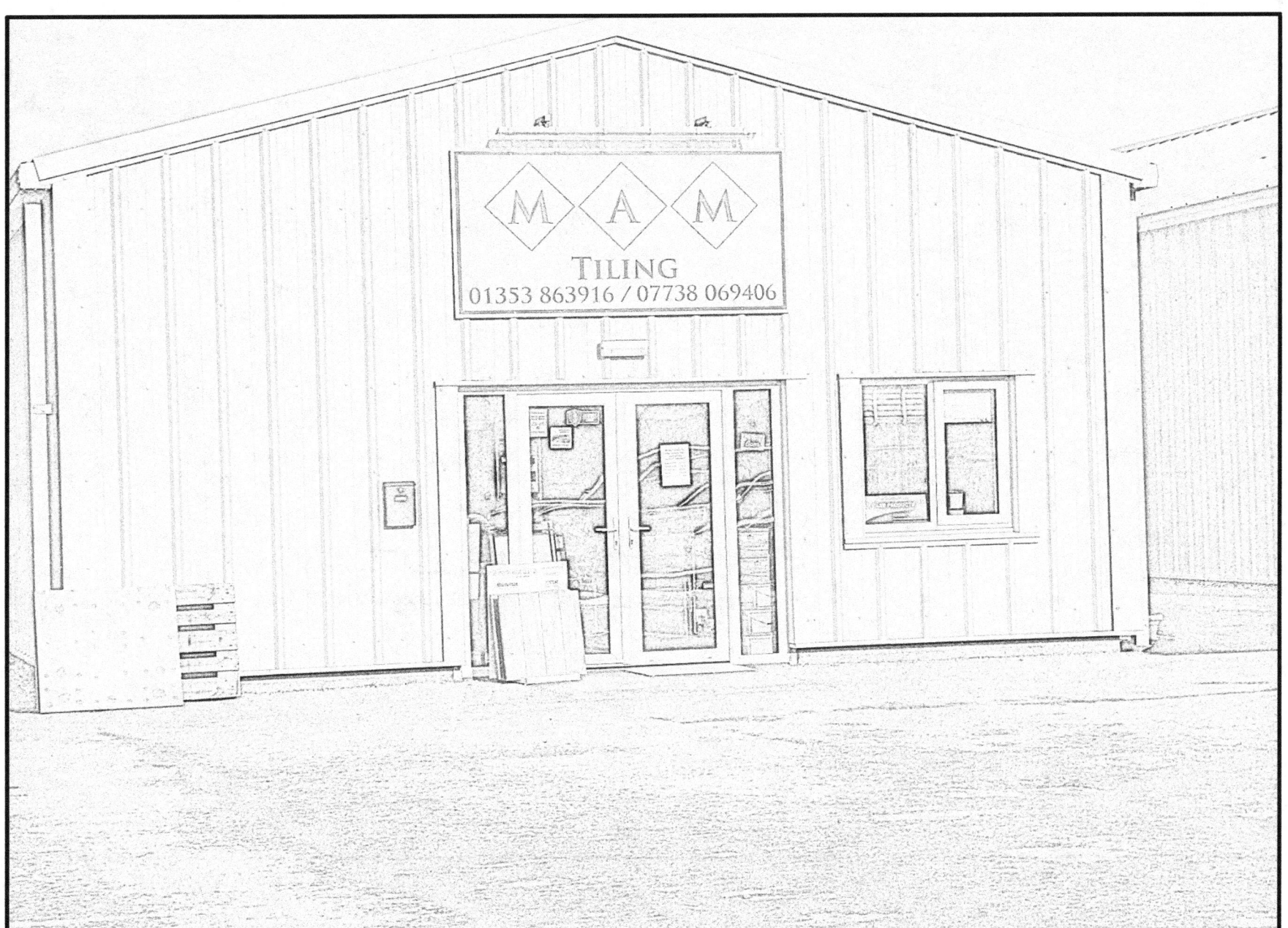

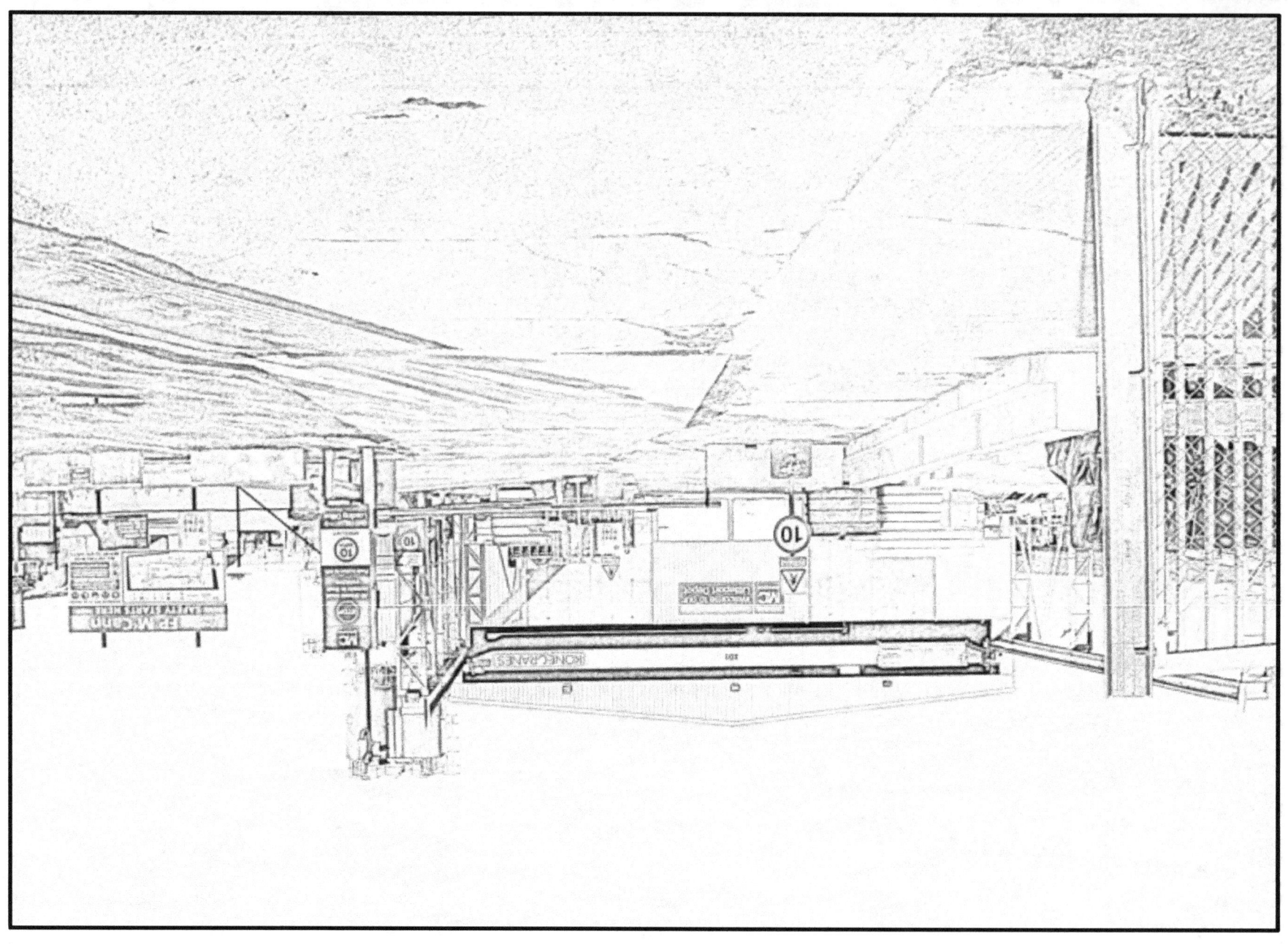

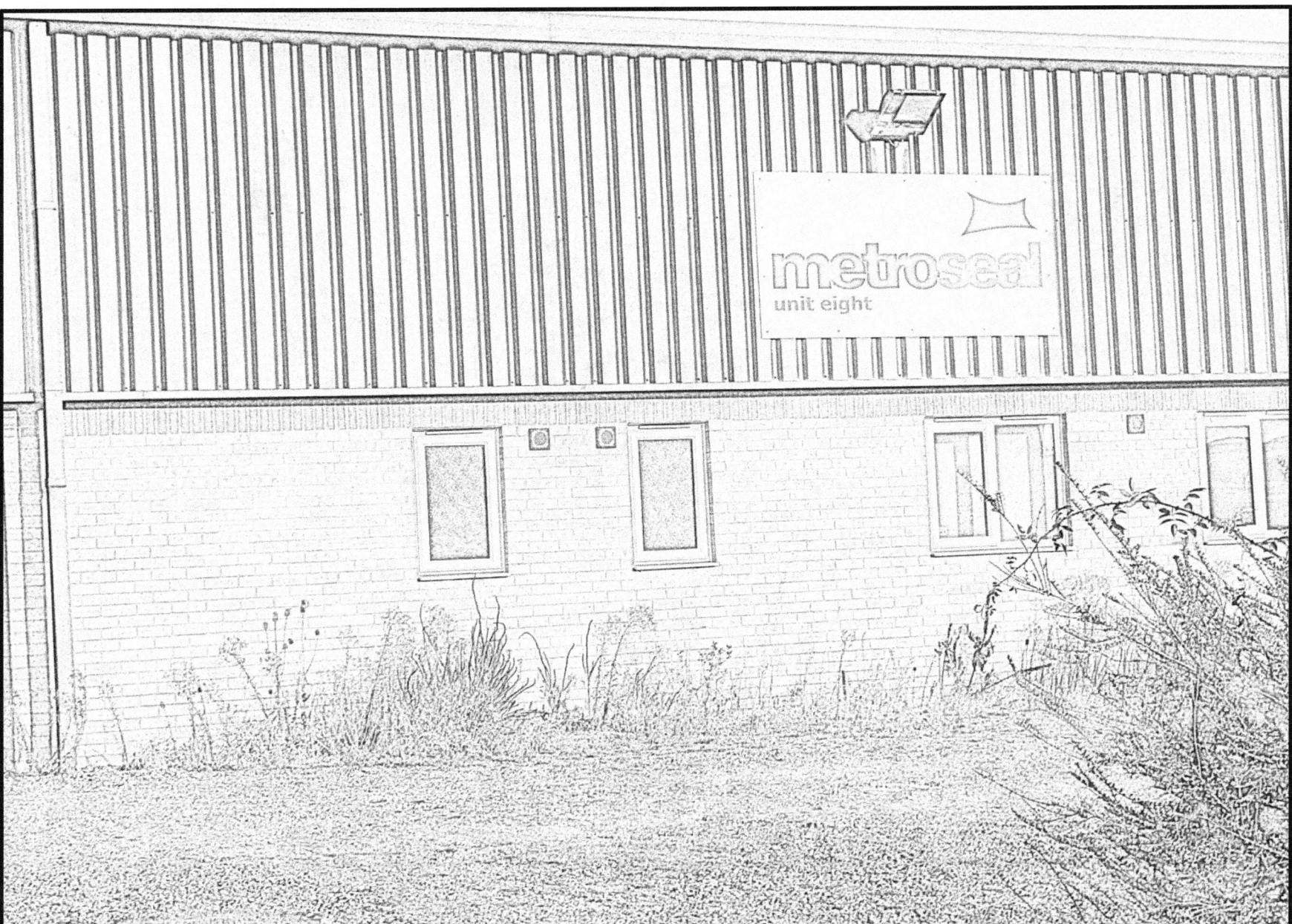

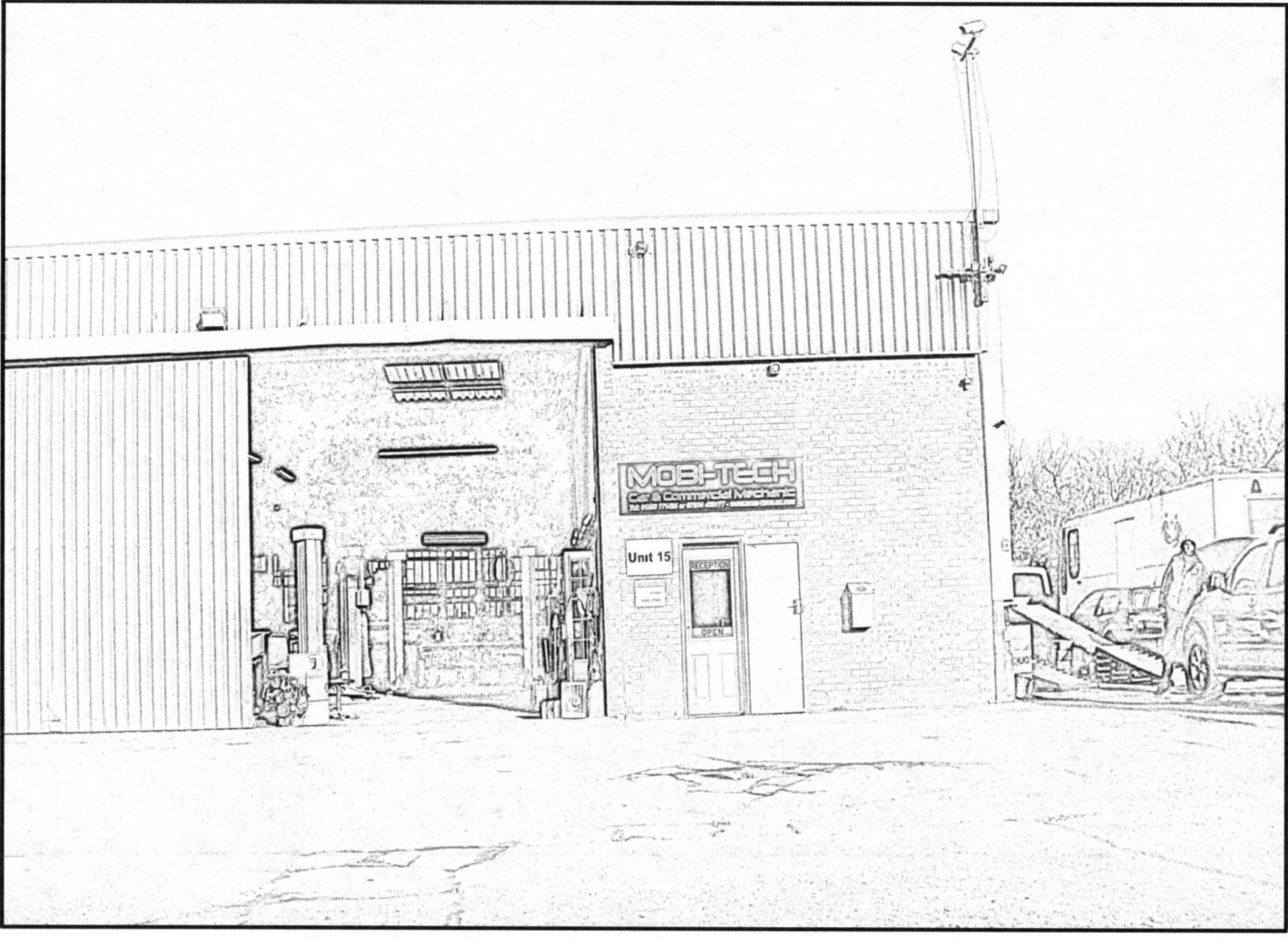

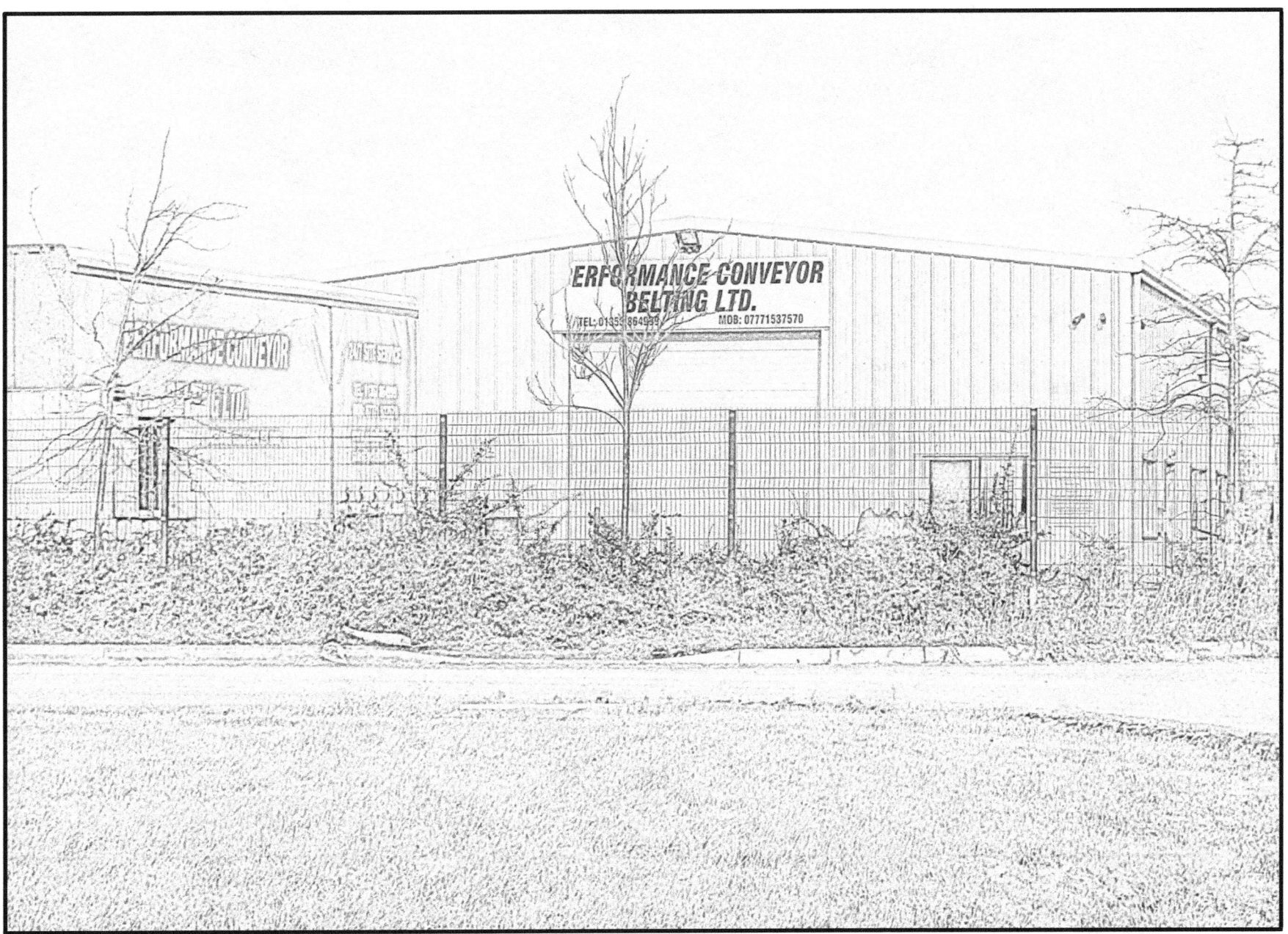

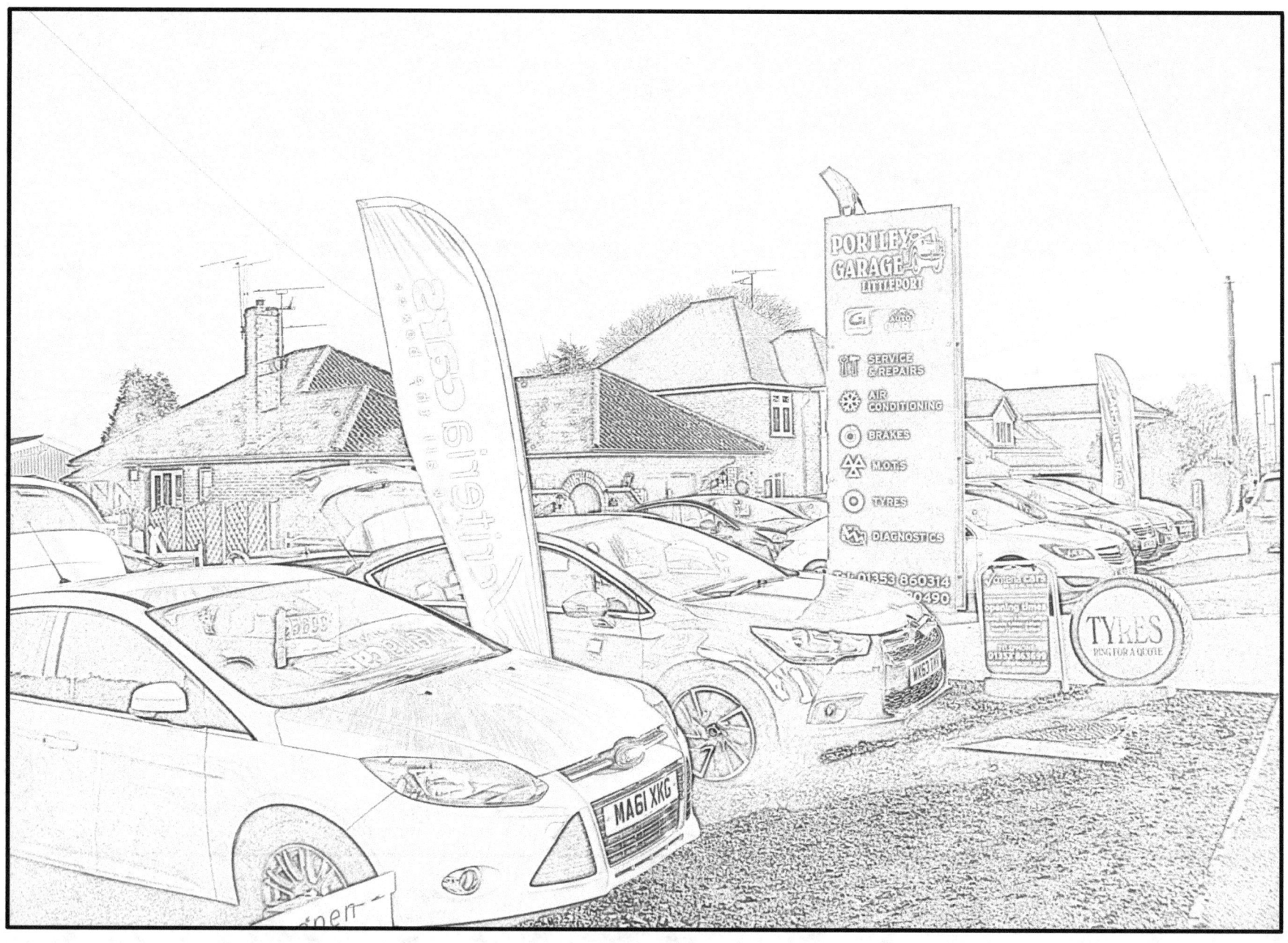

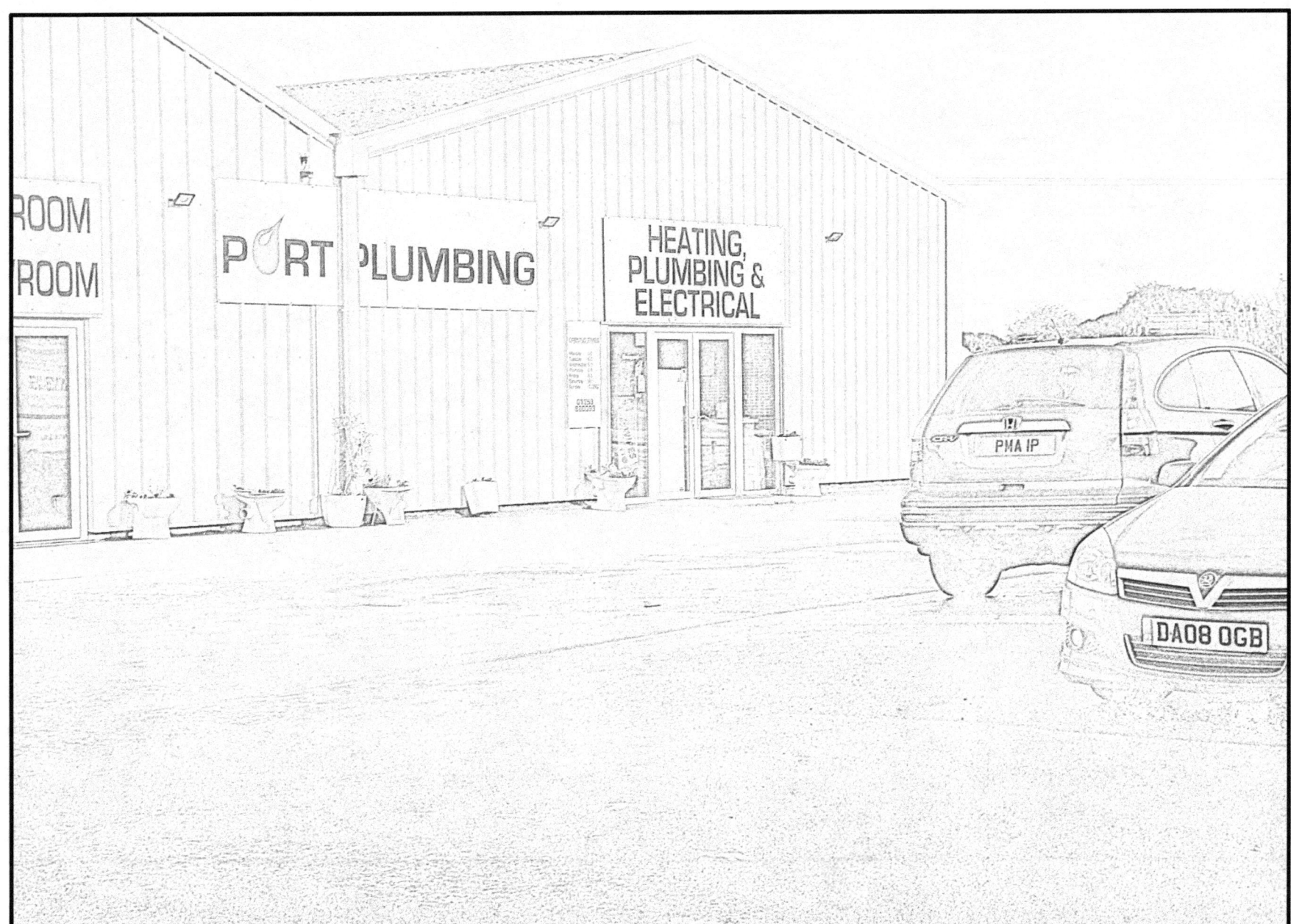

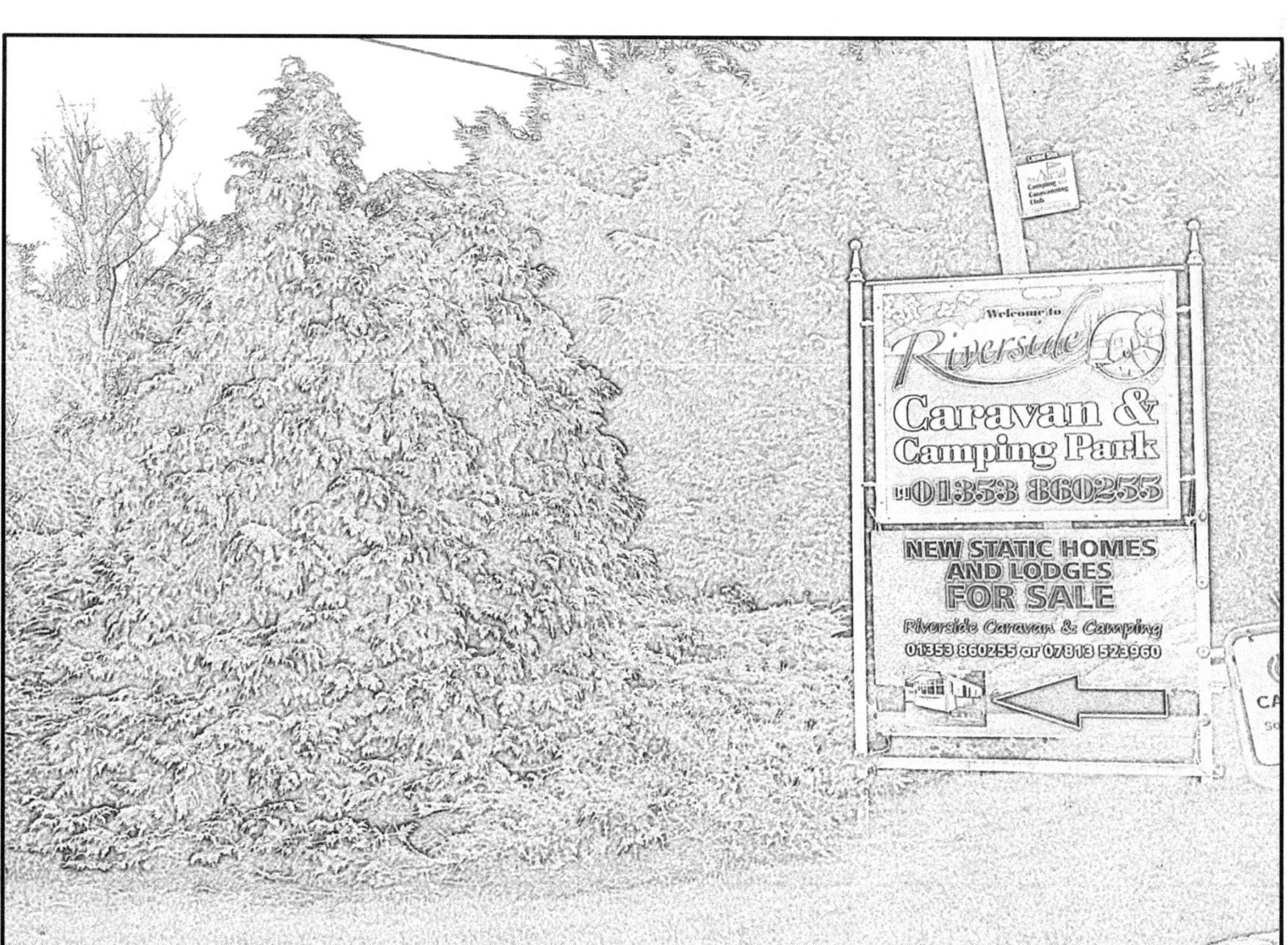

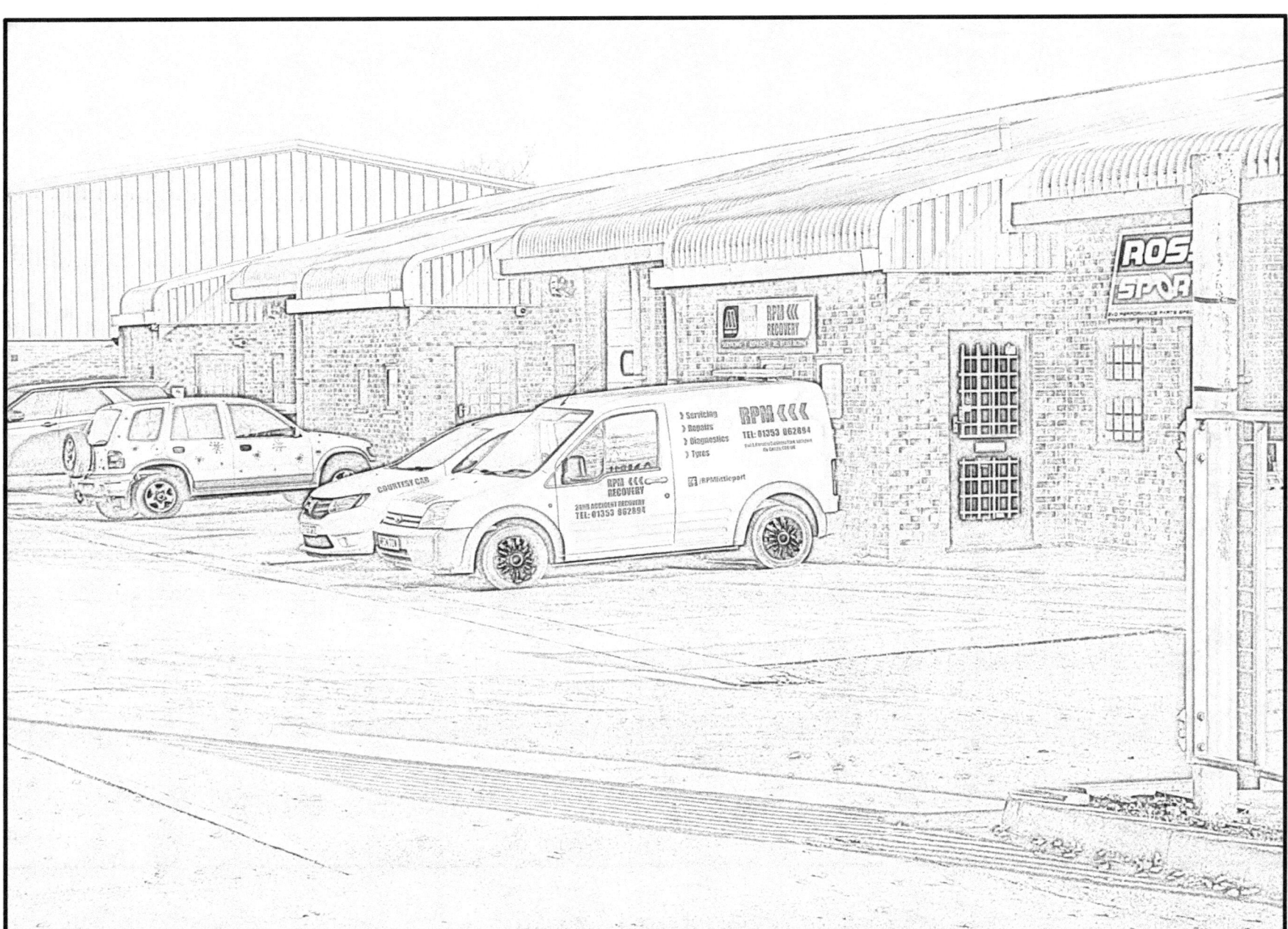

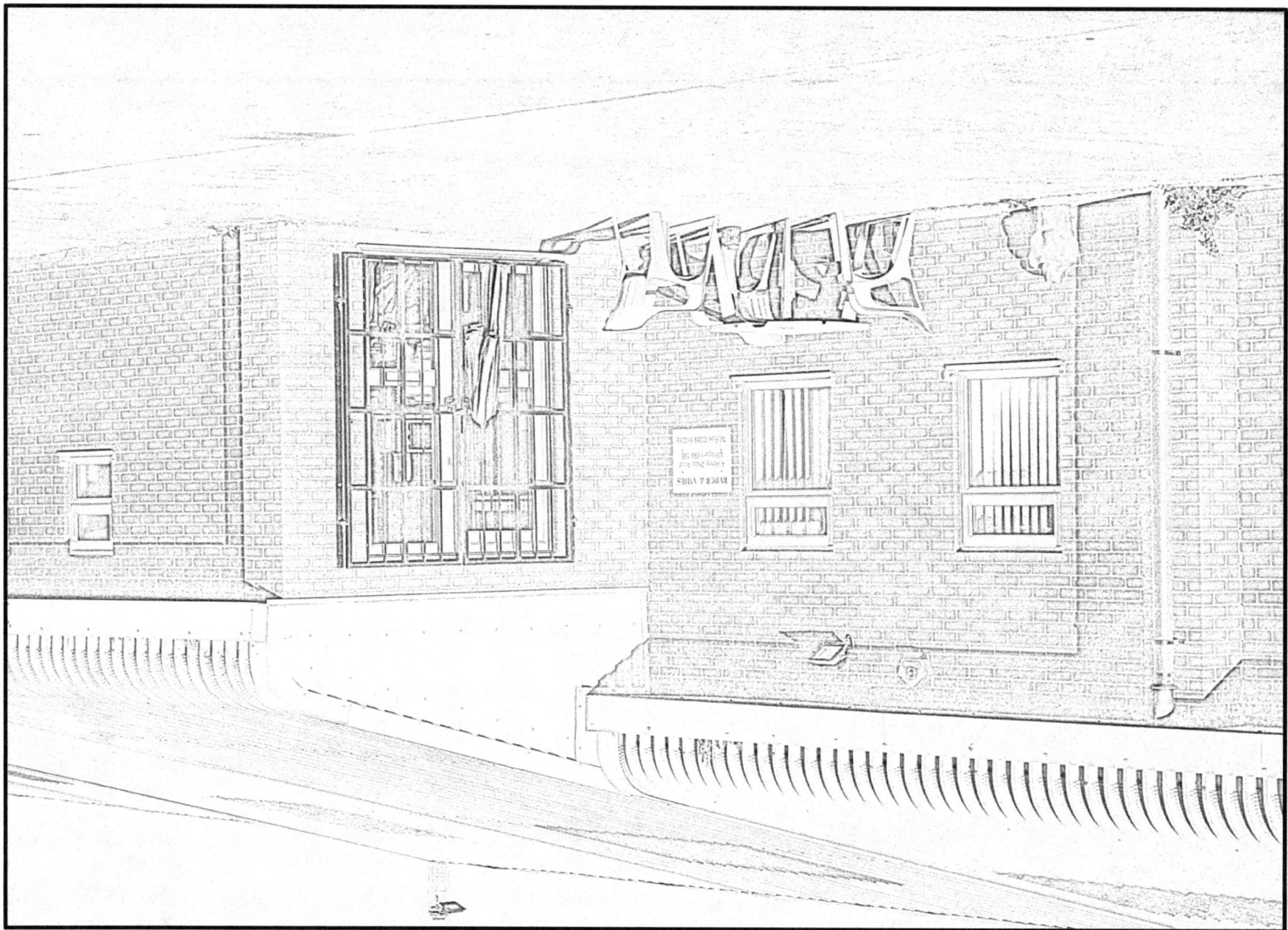

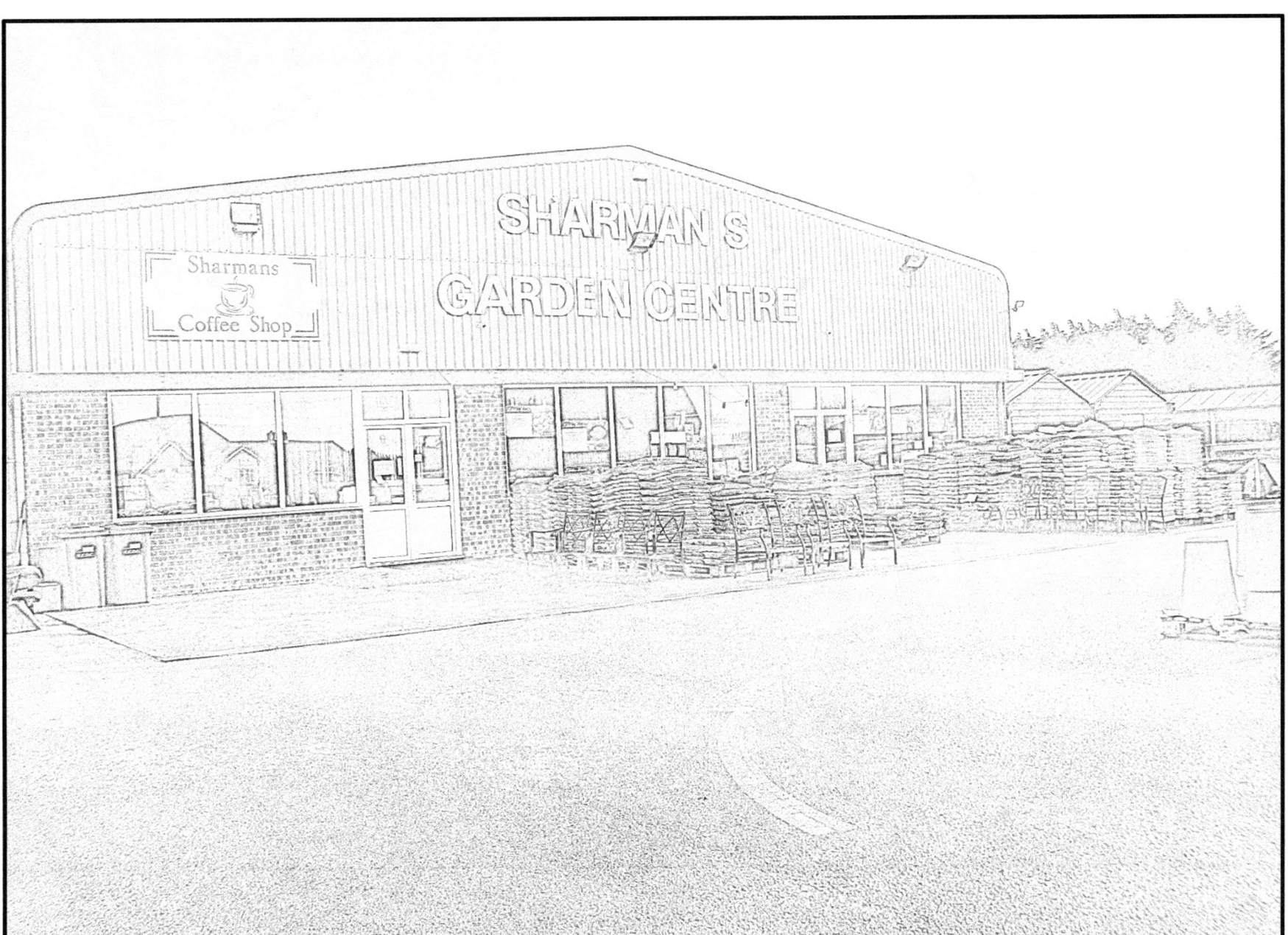

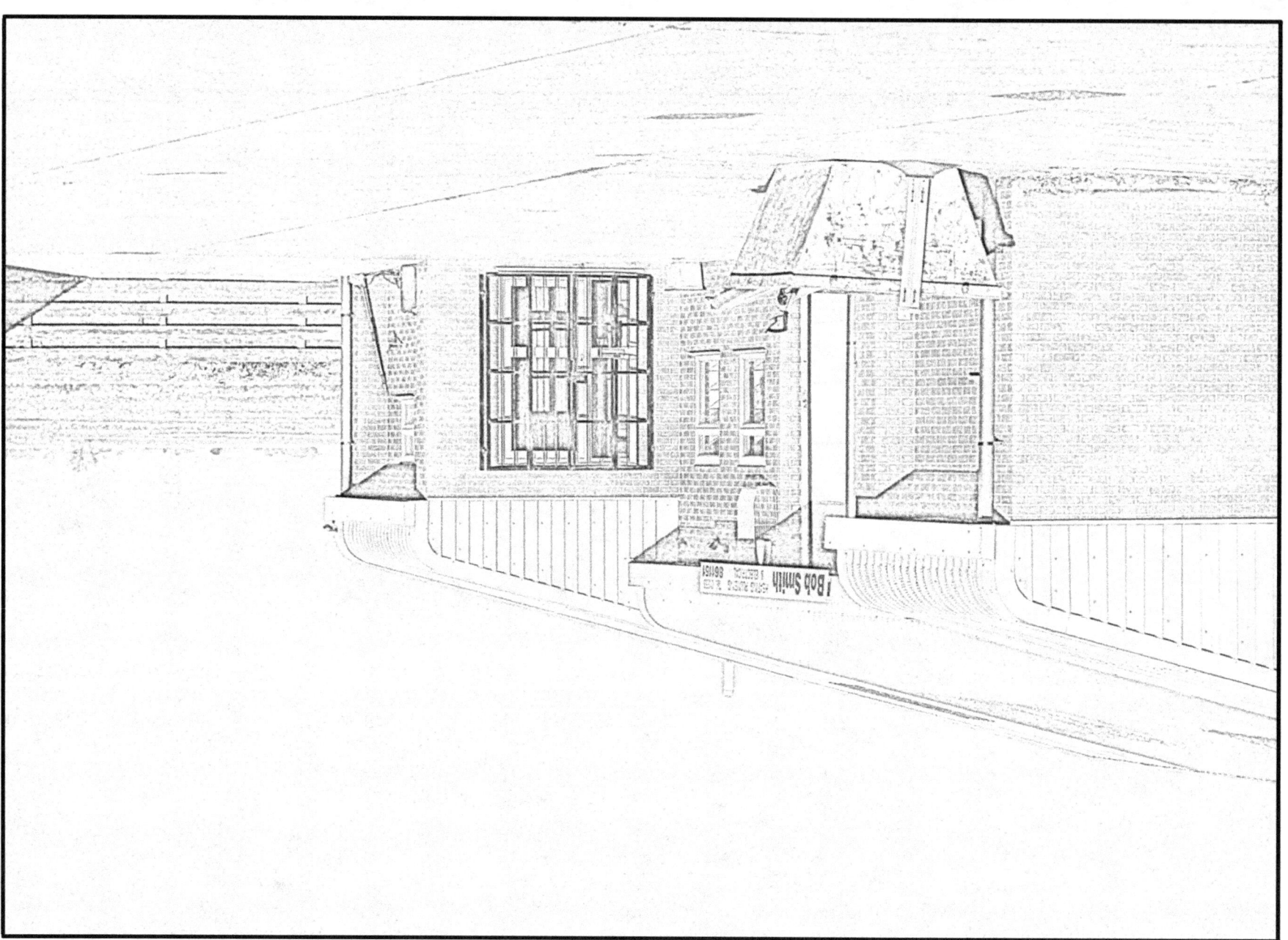

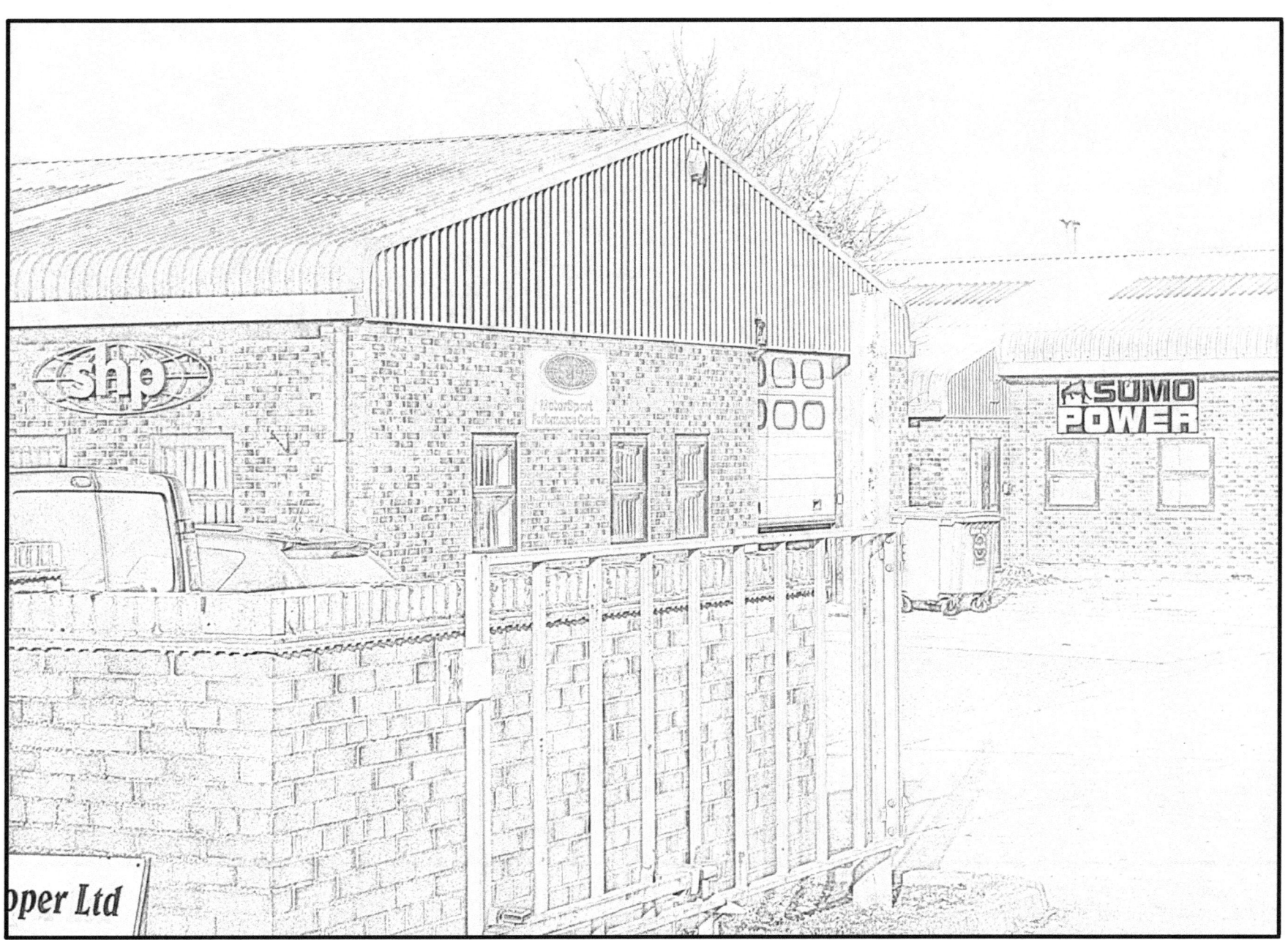

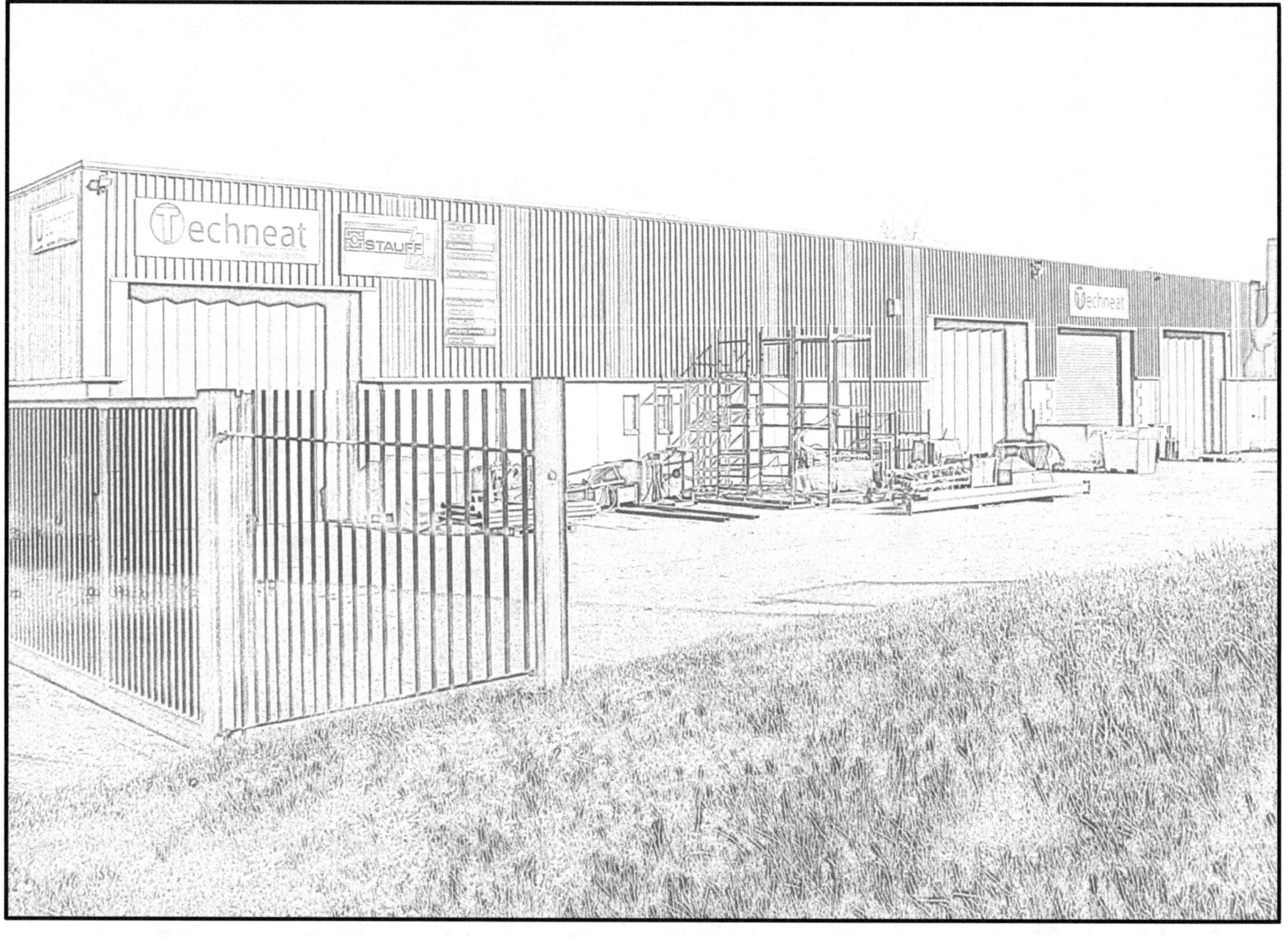

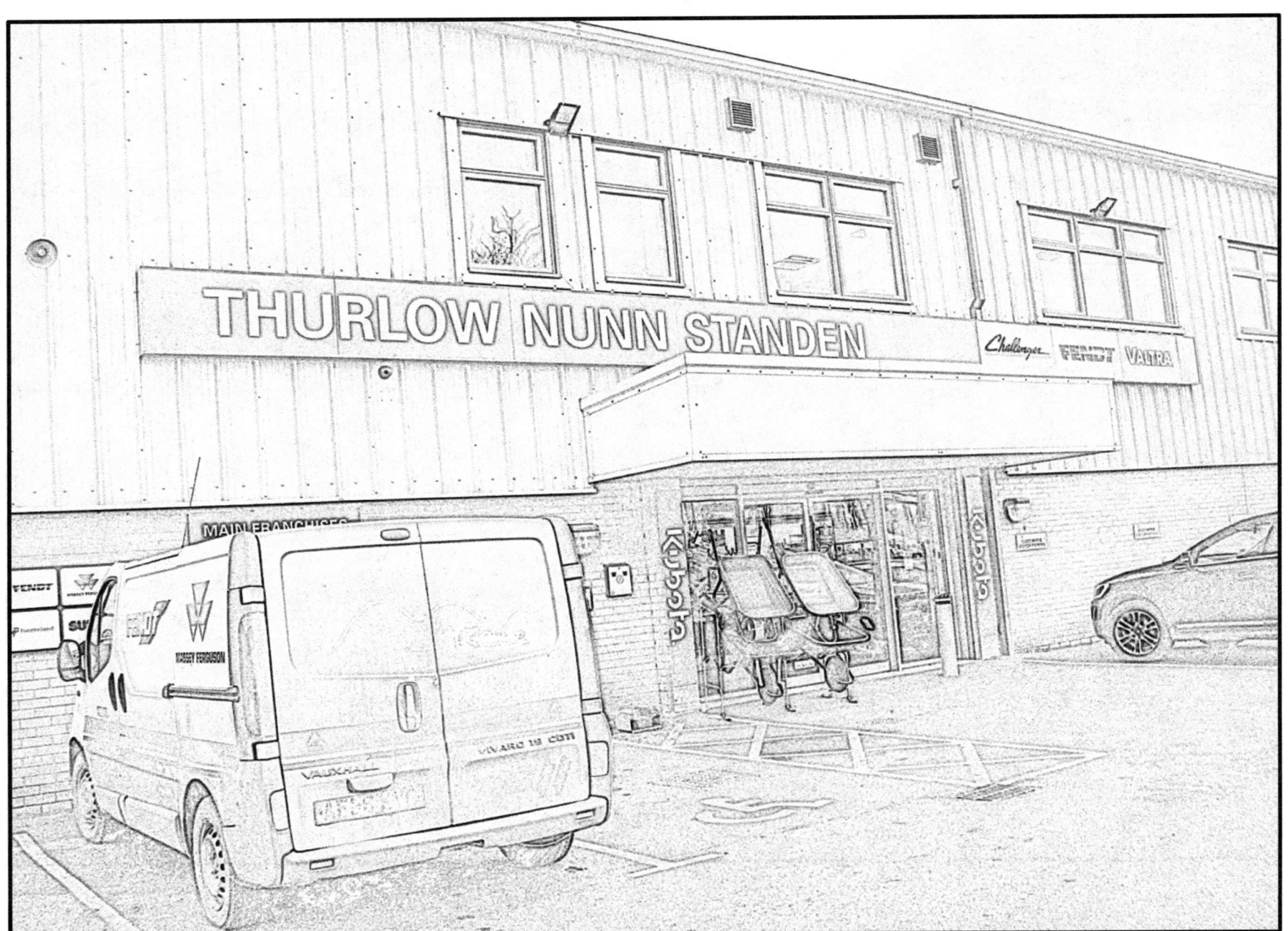

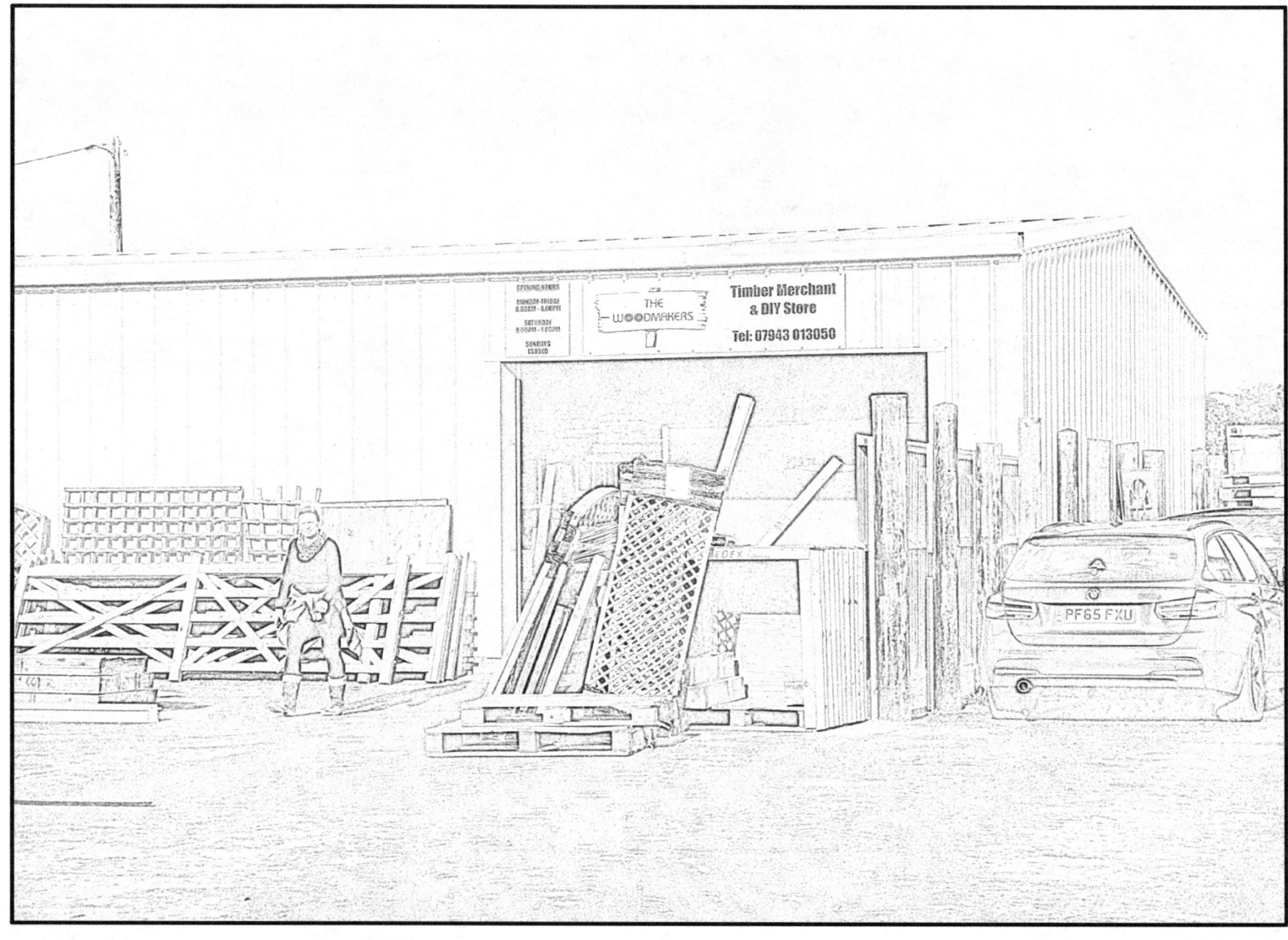

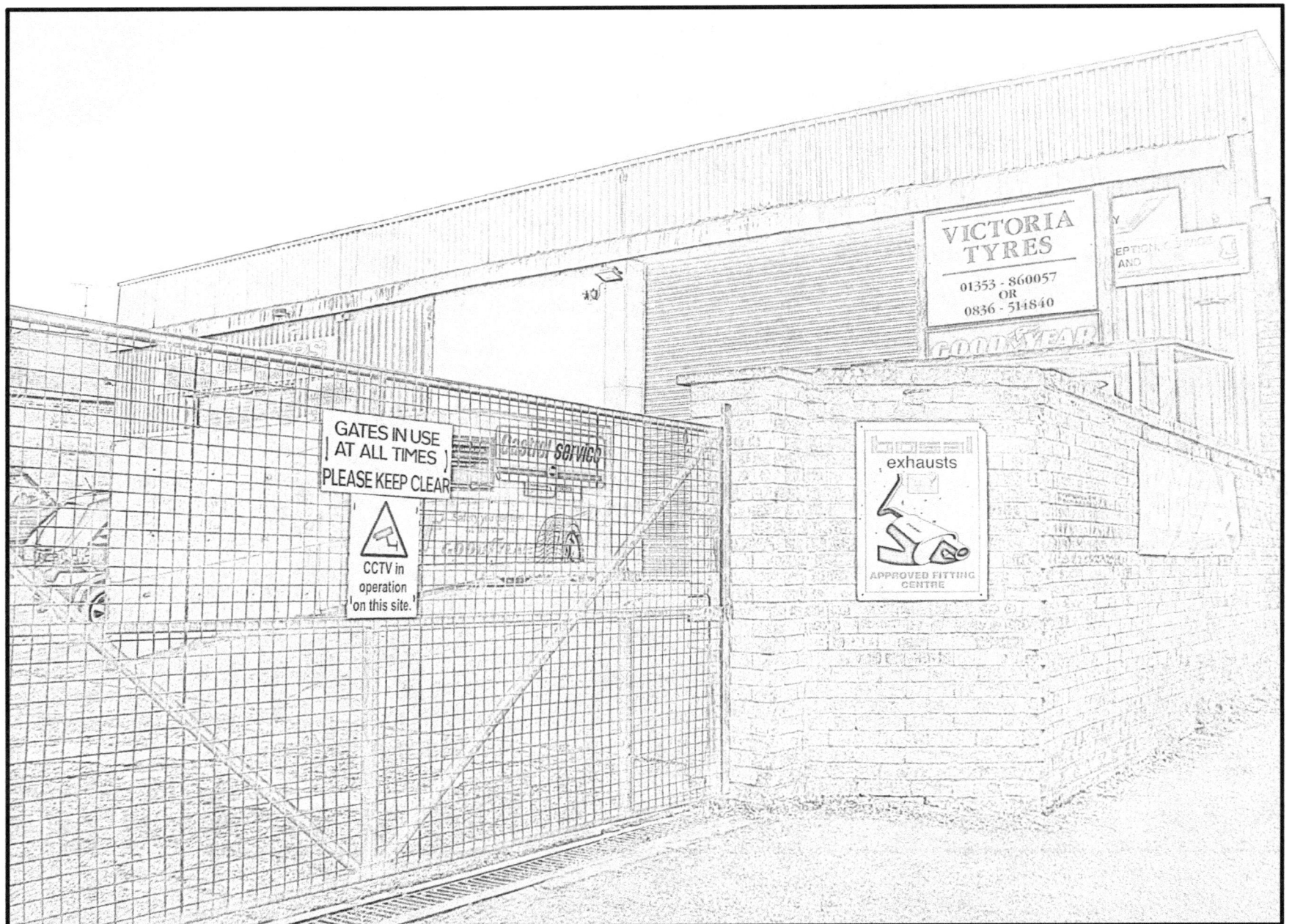

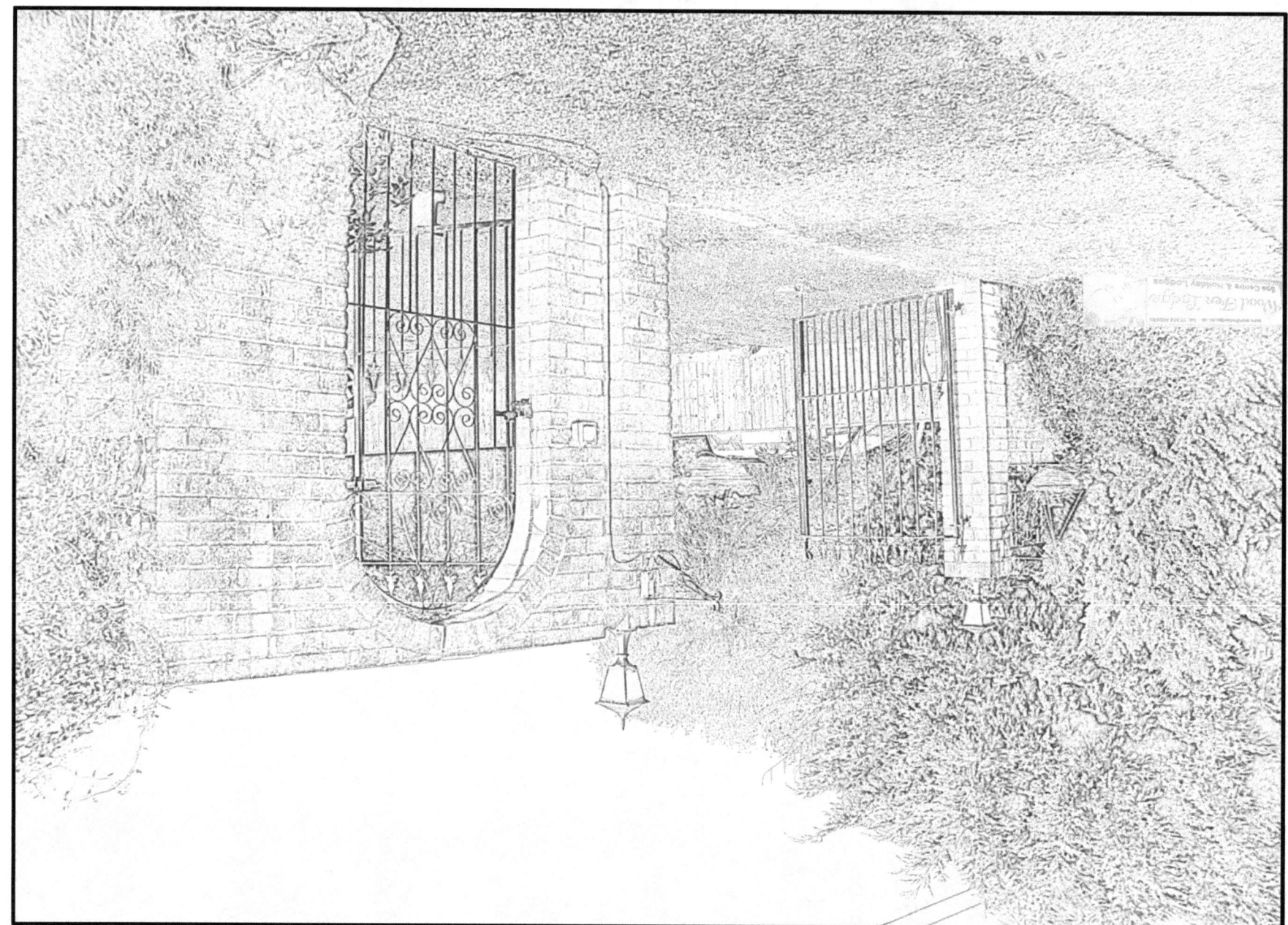

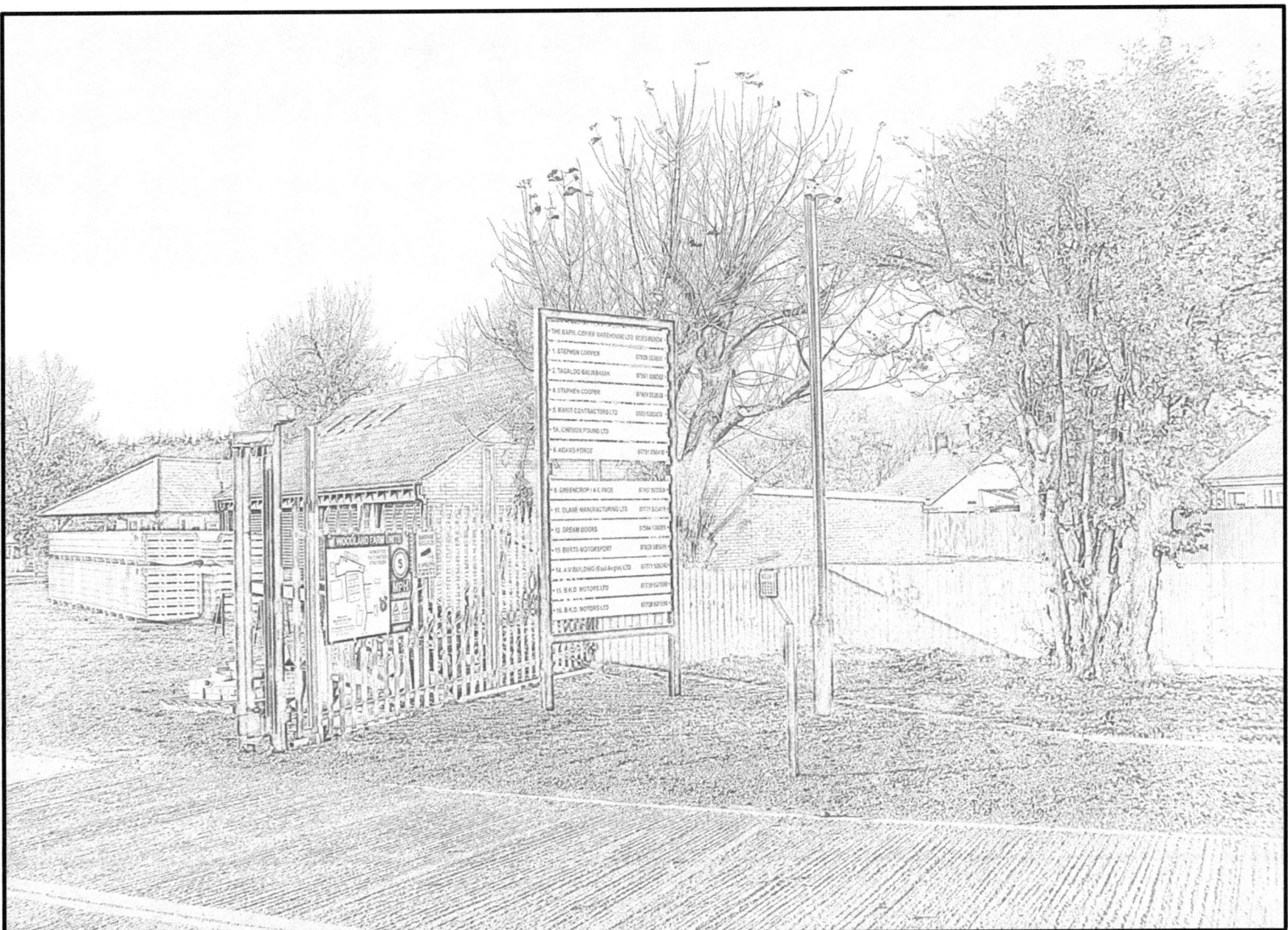

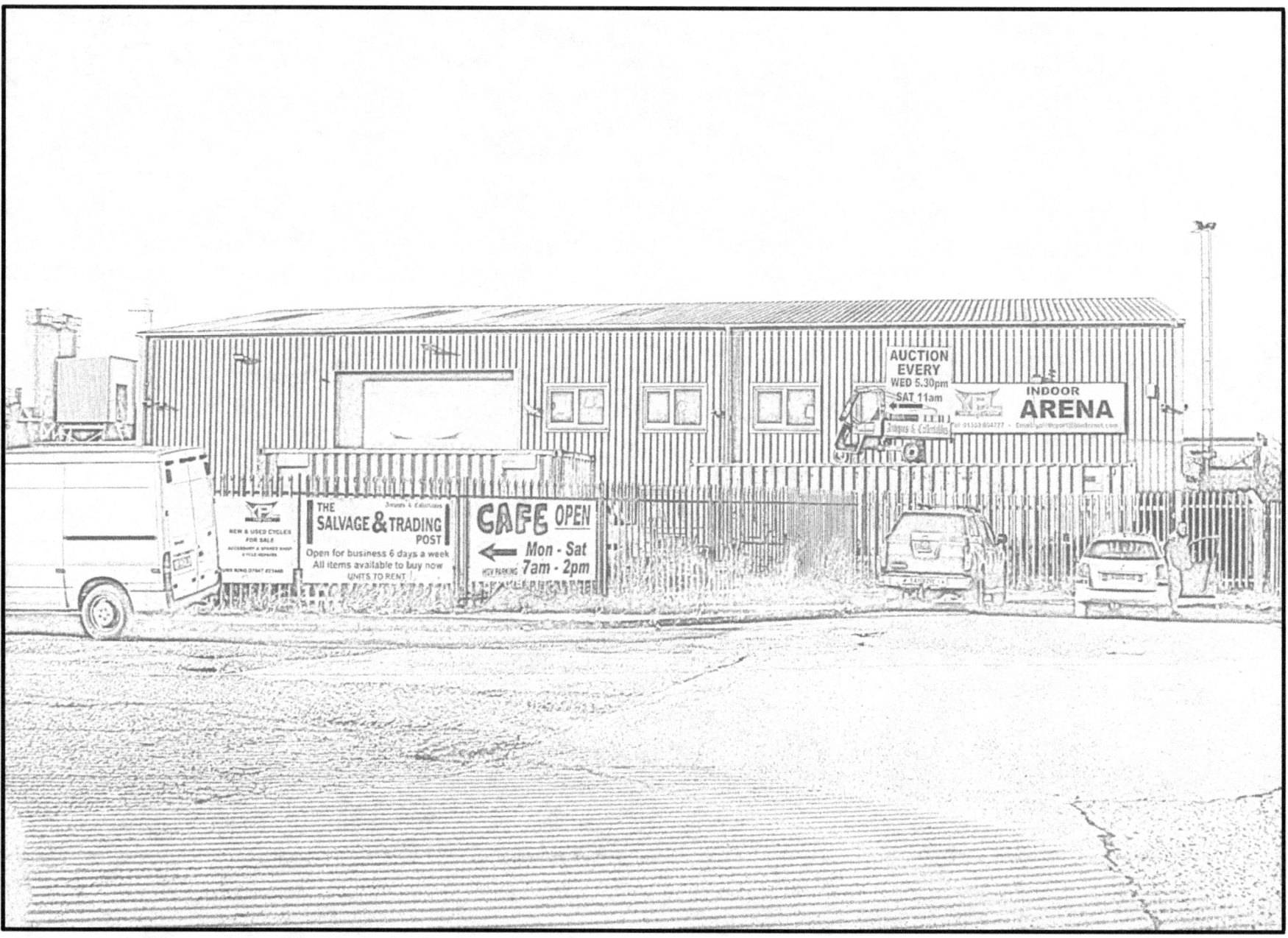

Section 3

- Alderton House   (01353) 862677
- Beech Court   (01733) 309194
- Branching Out   (01353) 863561
- Busy Bees Play School   (01353) 968606
- The Gables   (01353) 861935
- The Grange   (01353) 861329
- Laburnham Lodge   (01353) 860490
- Library   (0345) 0455225
- The Limes   (01353) 863194
- Littleport Community Primary School   (01353) 860235
- Methodist Church   (01353) 662426
- Millfield School   (01353) 861612
- Old Rectory   (01353) 865200
- Salvation Army   (01353) 862851
- St George's Church   (01353) 860207
- St George's Medical Centre   (01353) 864100
- St. George's Pharmacy   (01353) 861081
- The Barn and Toilet   (01353) 860449
- Village Hall   (01353) 860449
- Vine Community Church

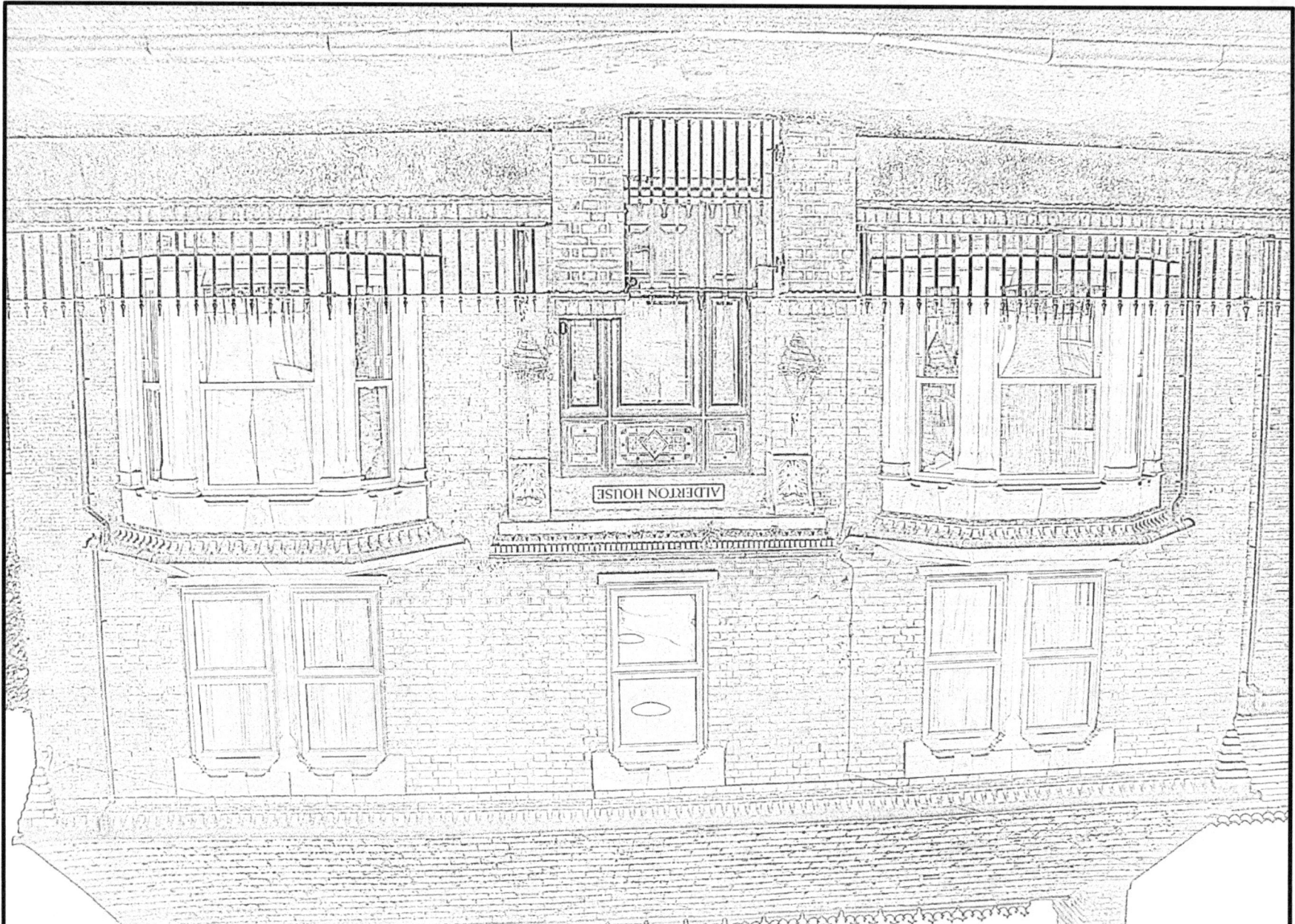

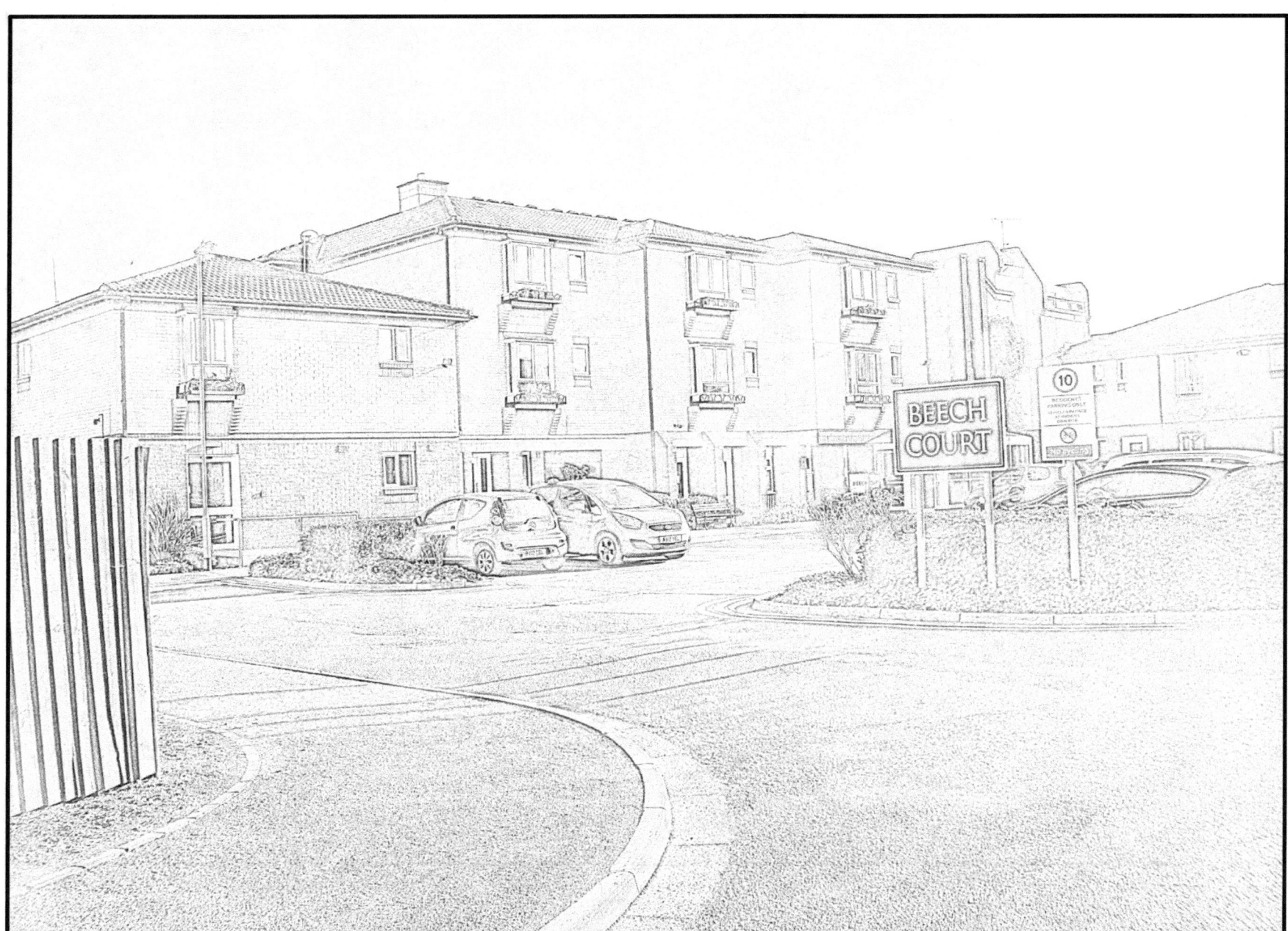

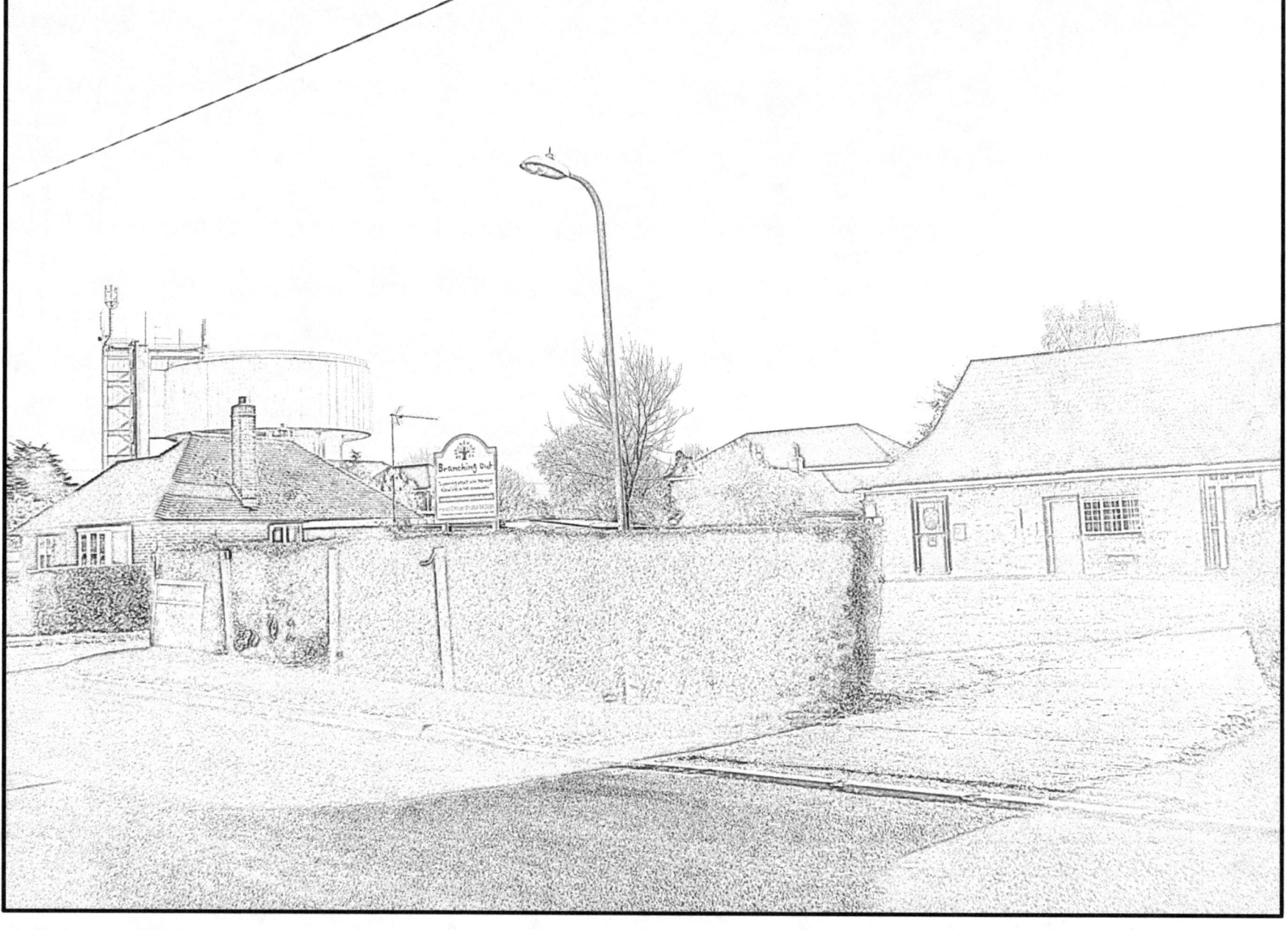

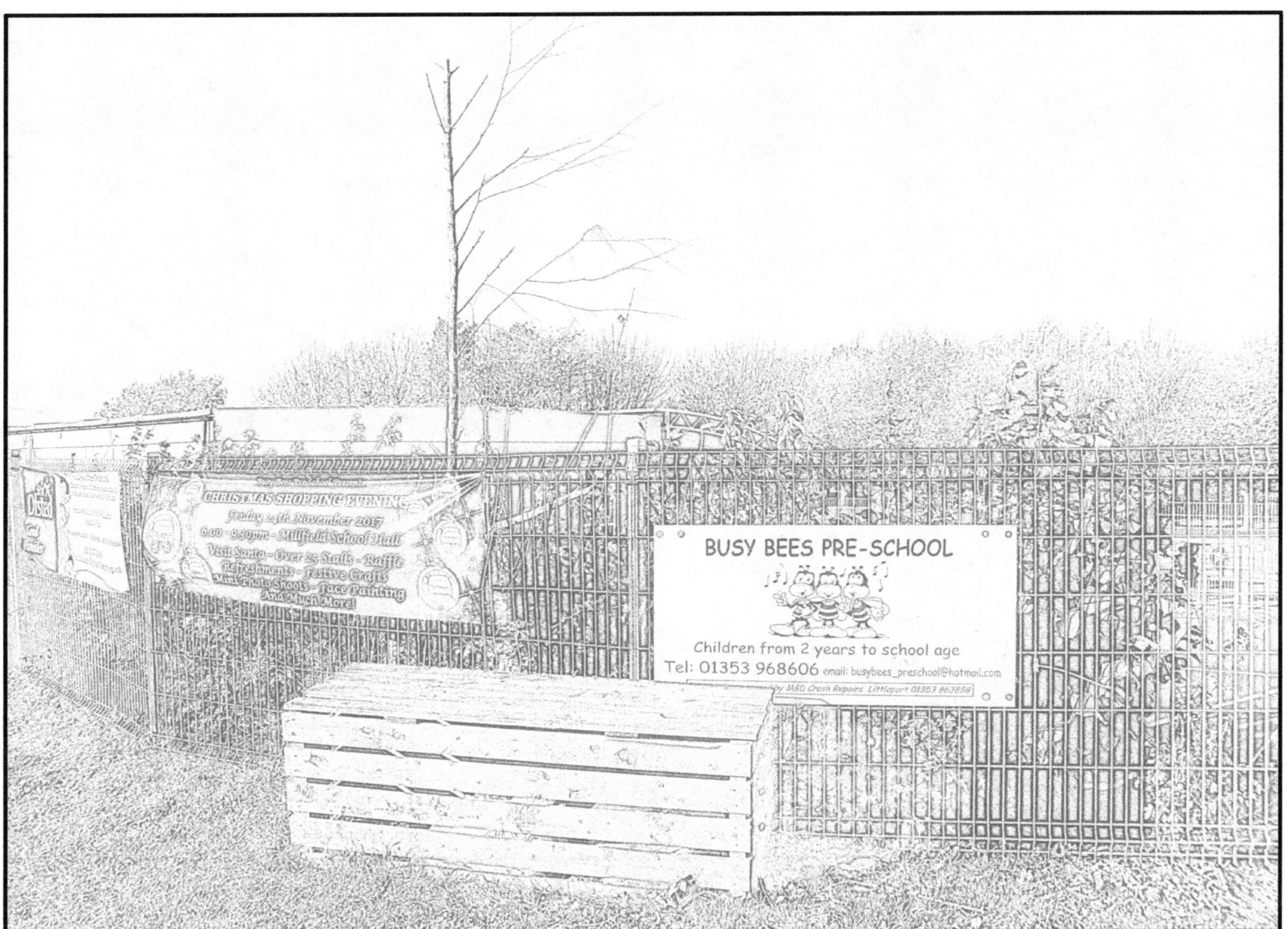

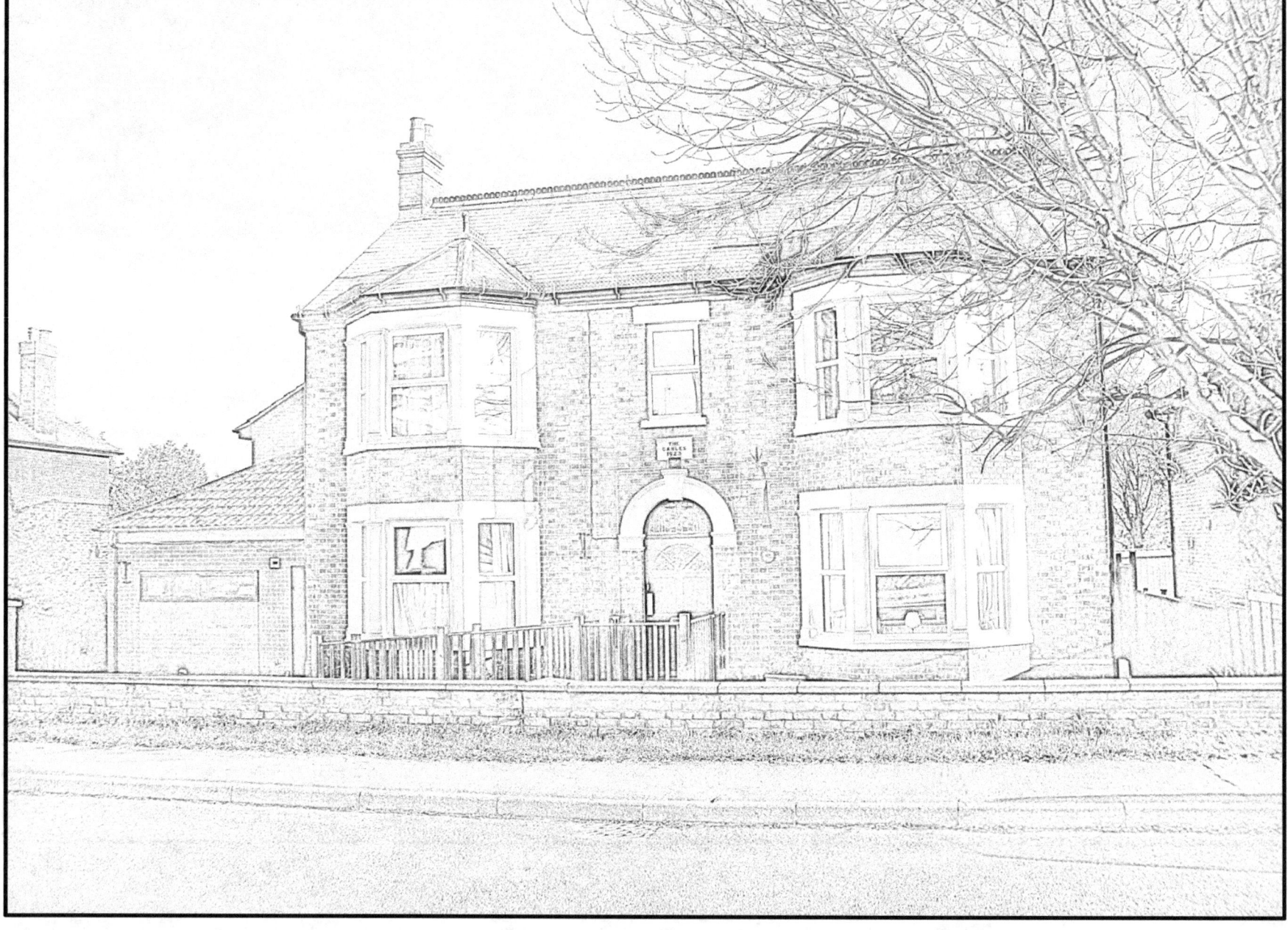

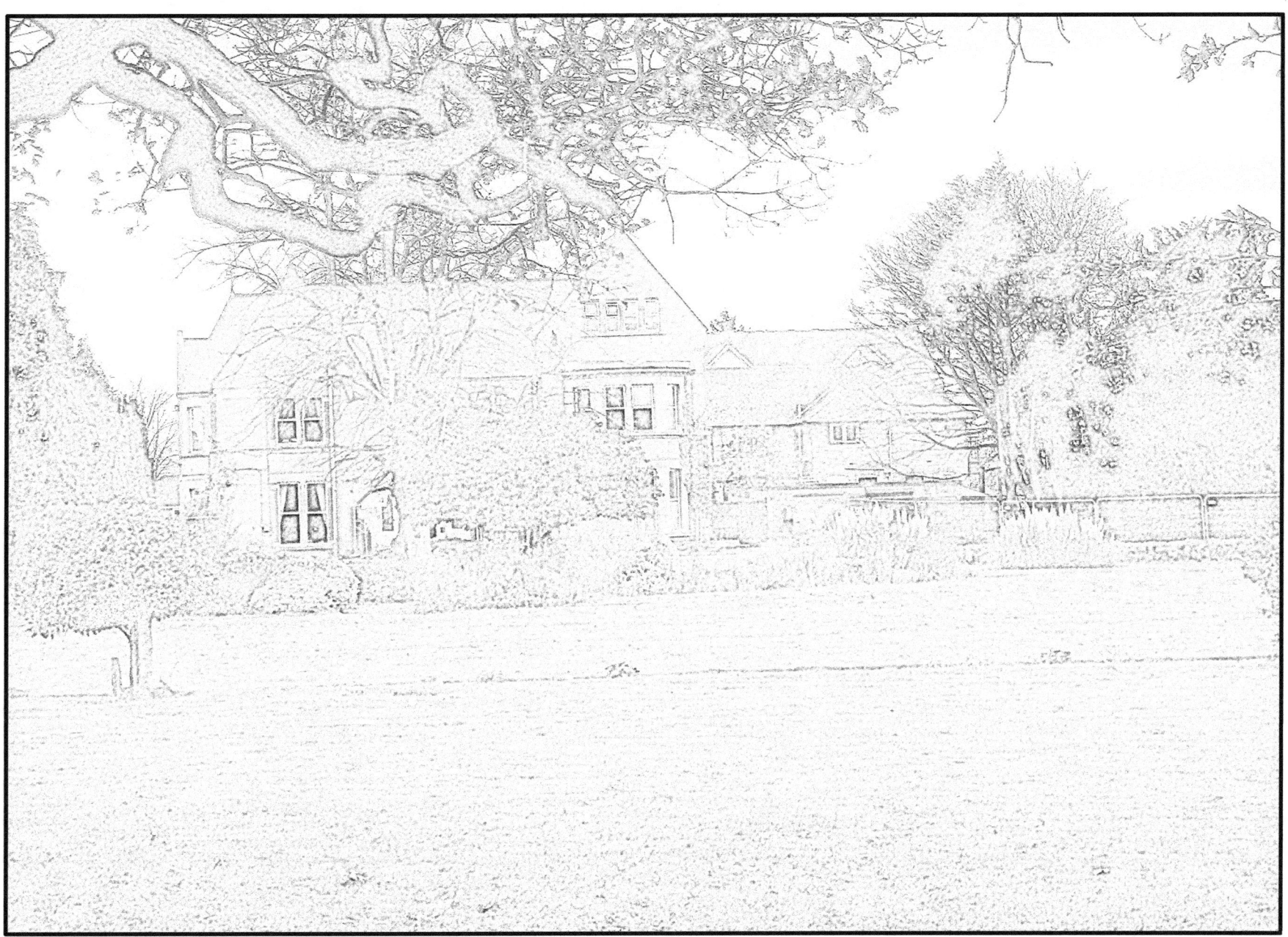

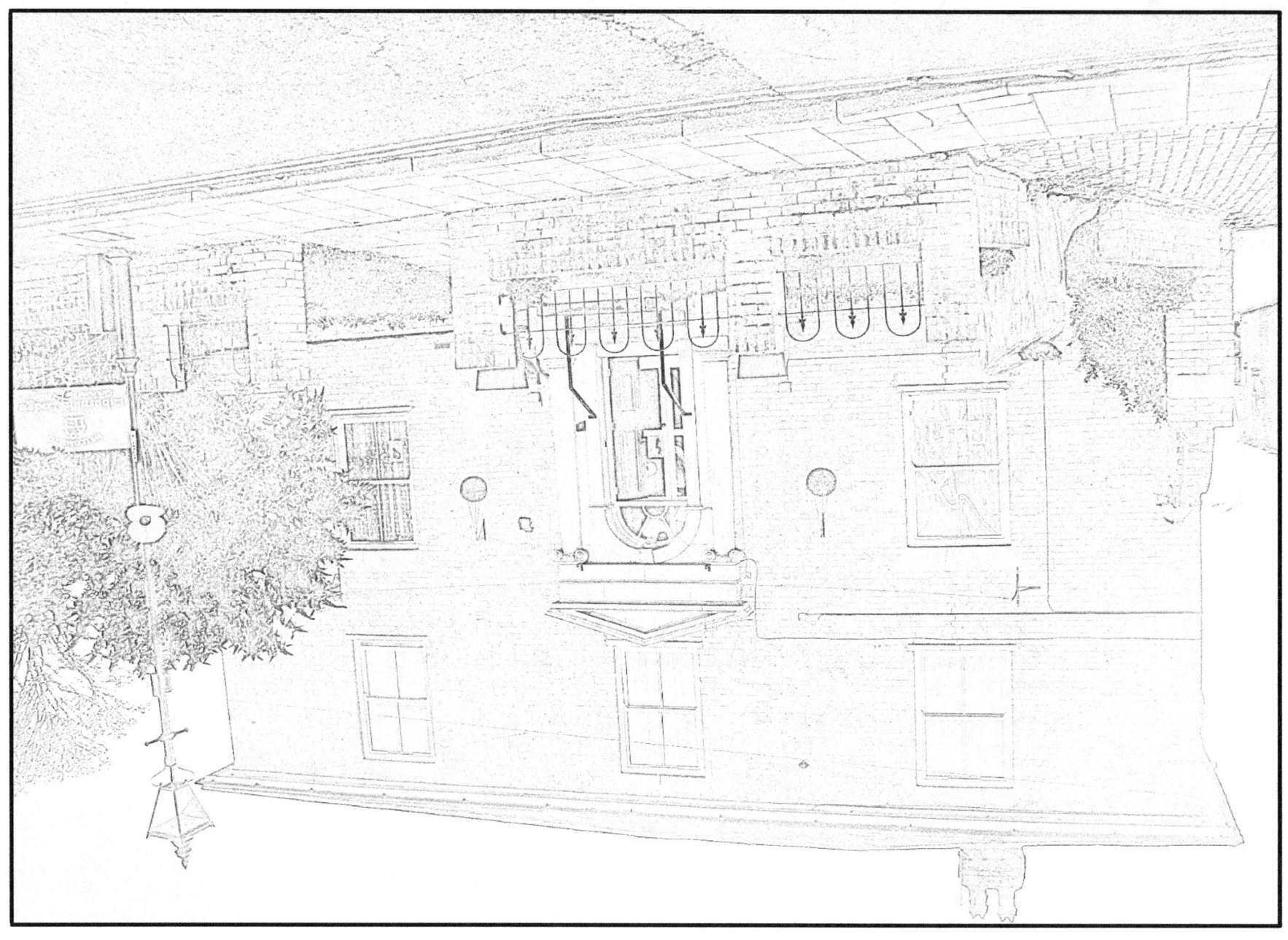

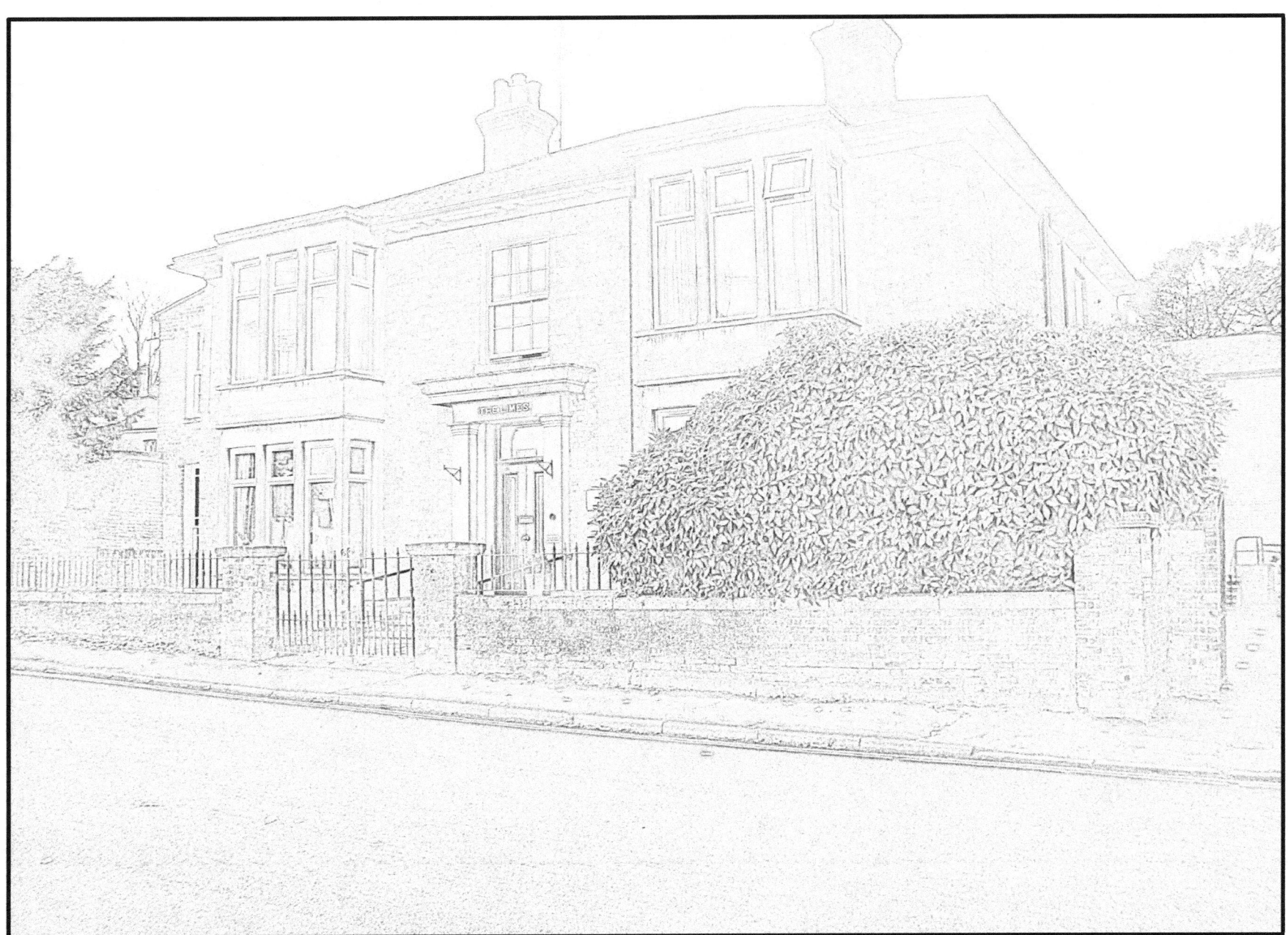

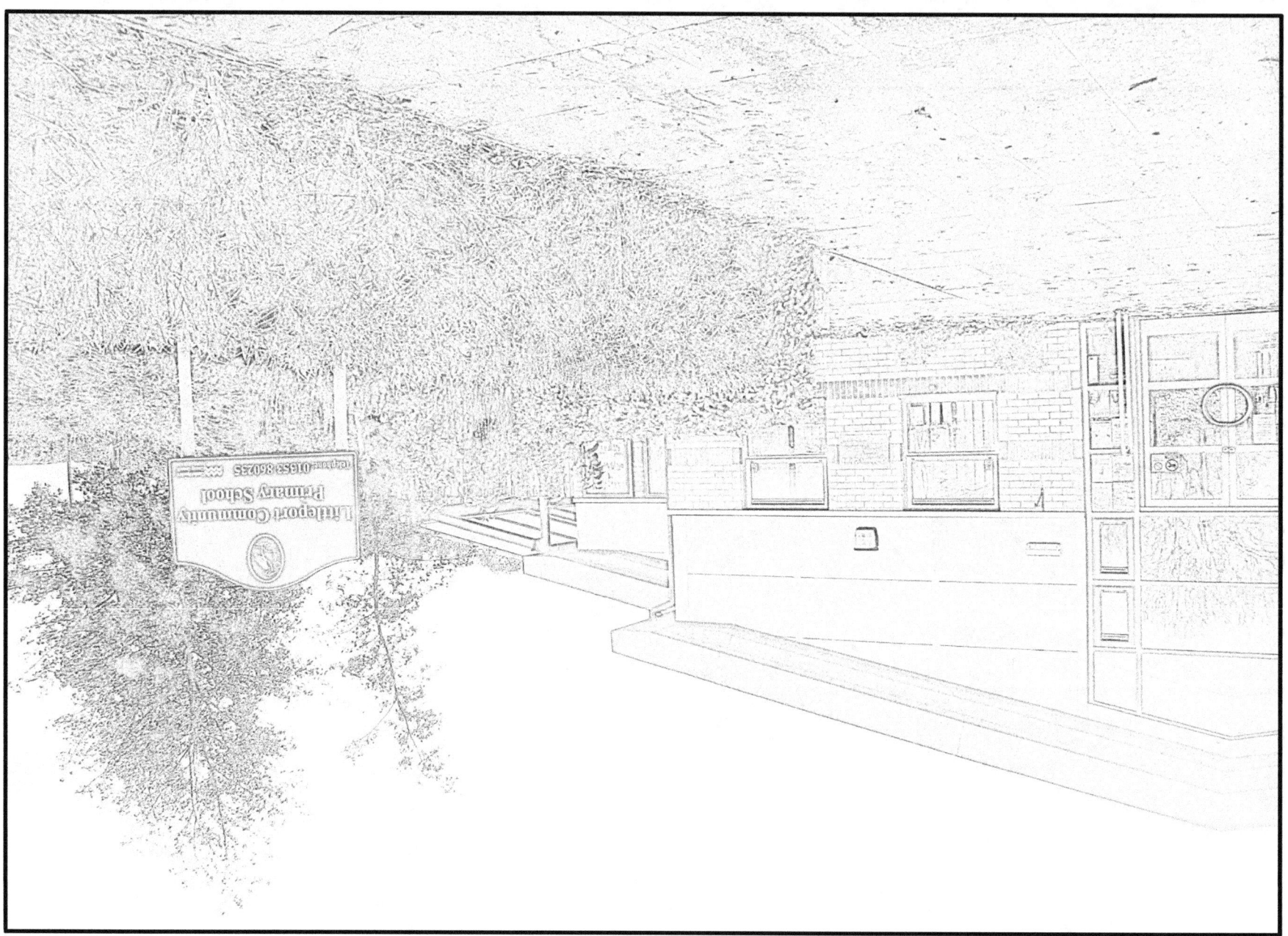

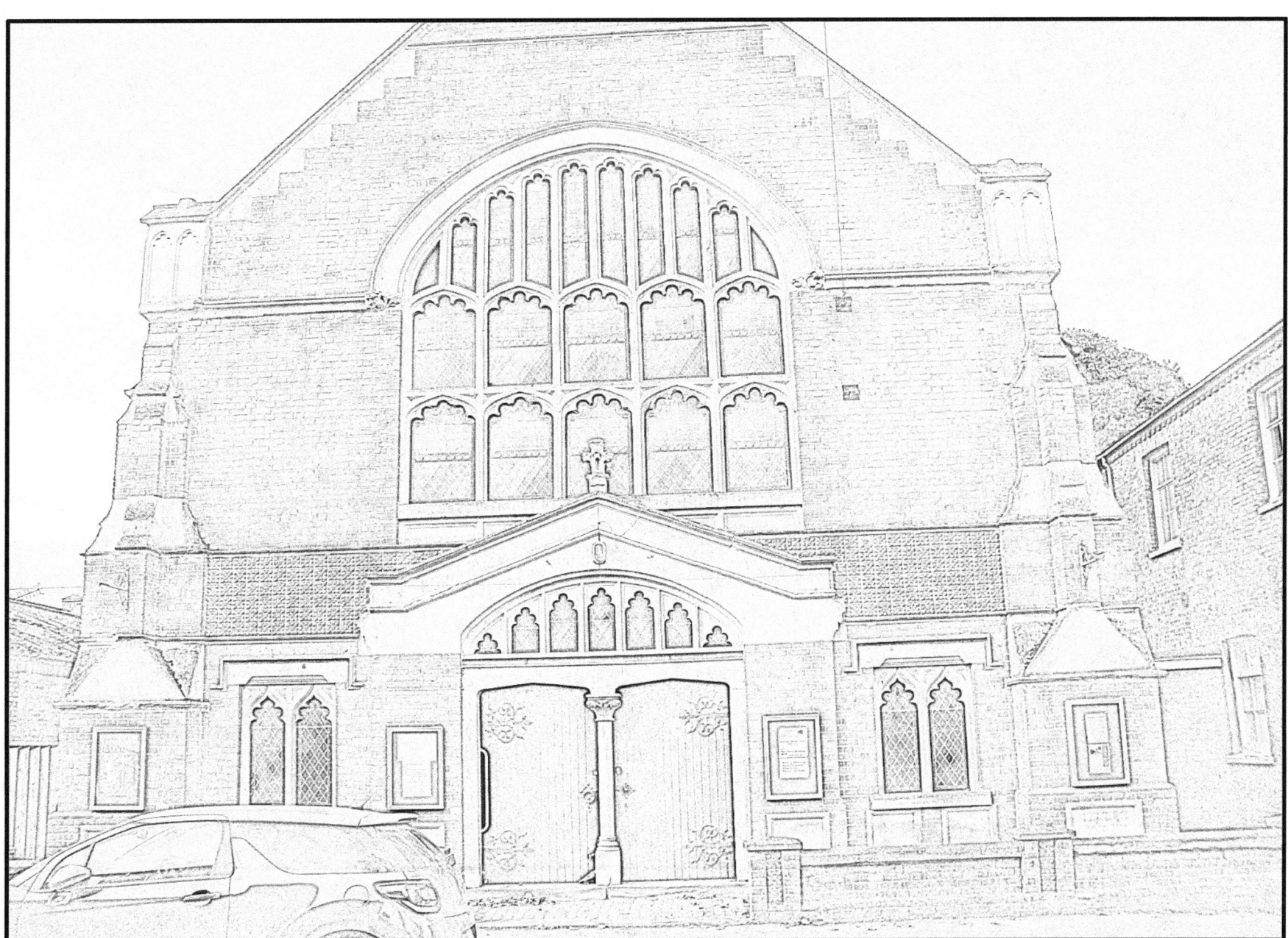

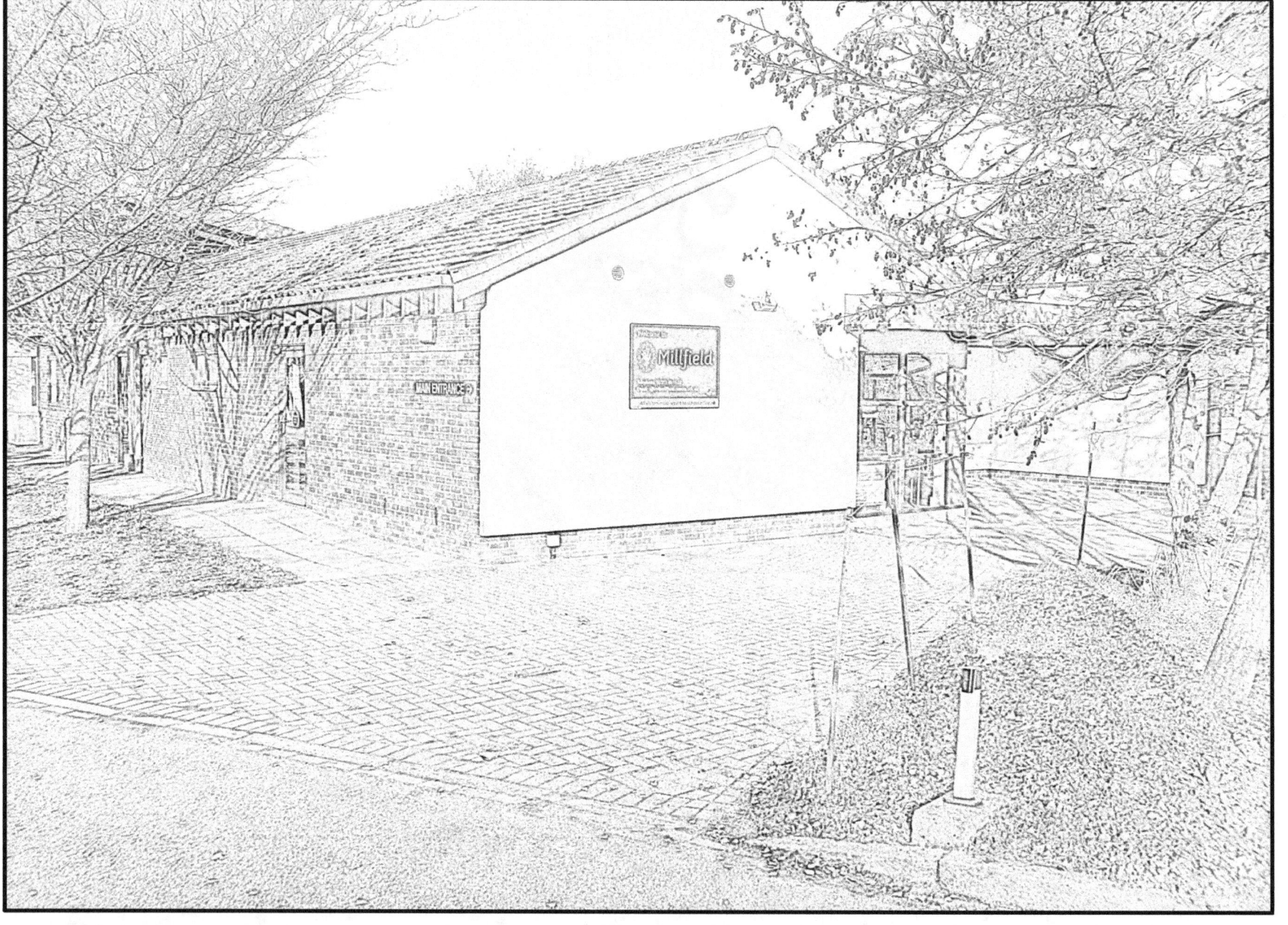

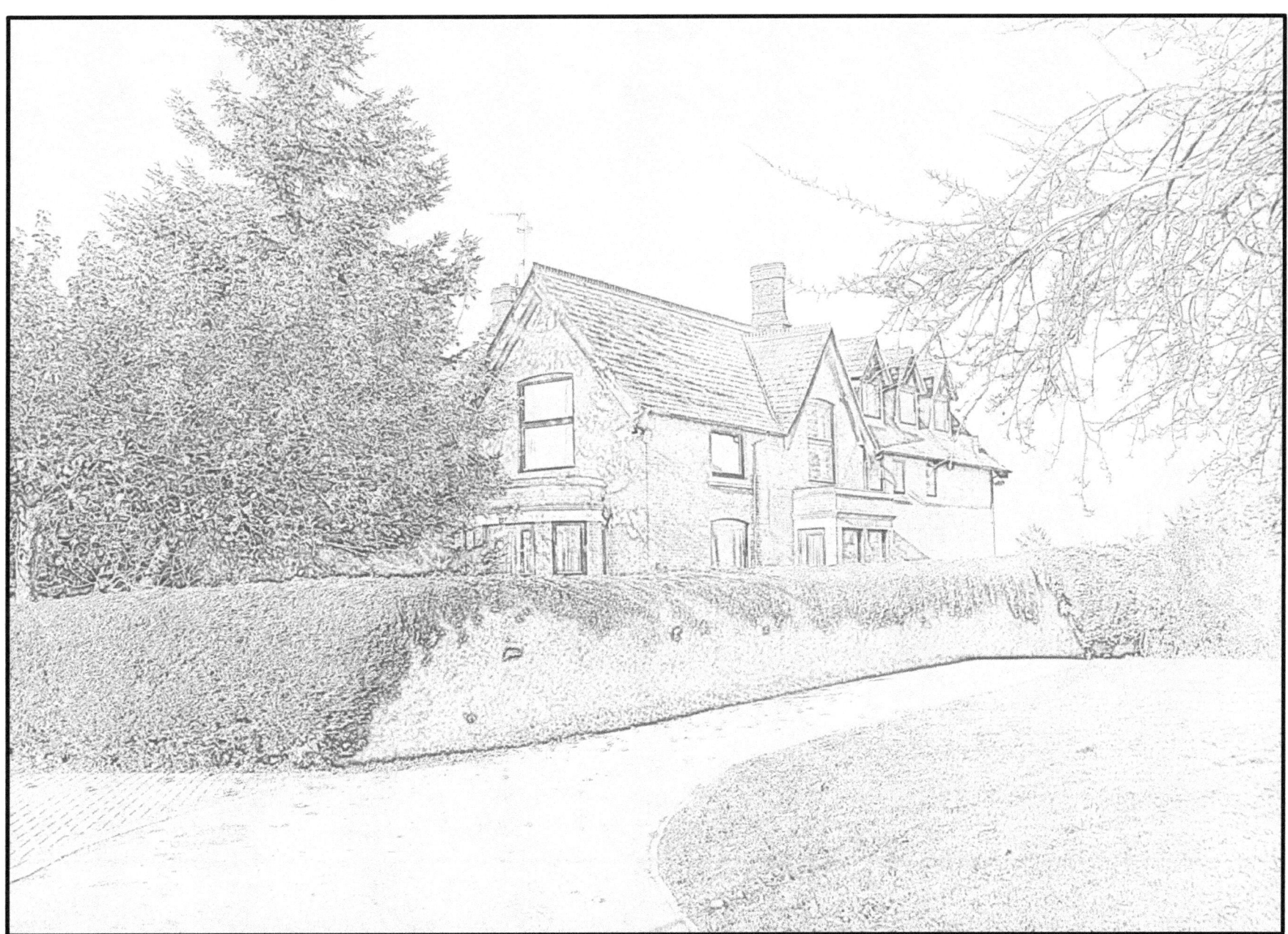

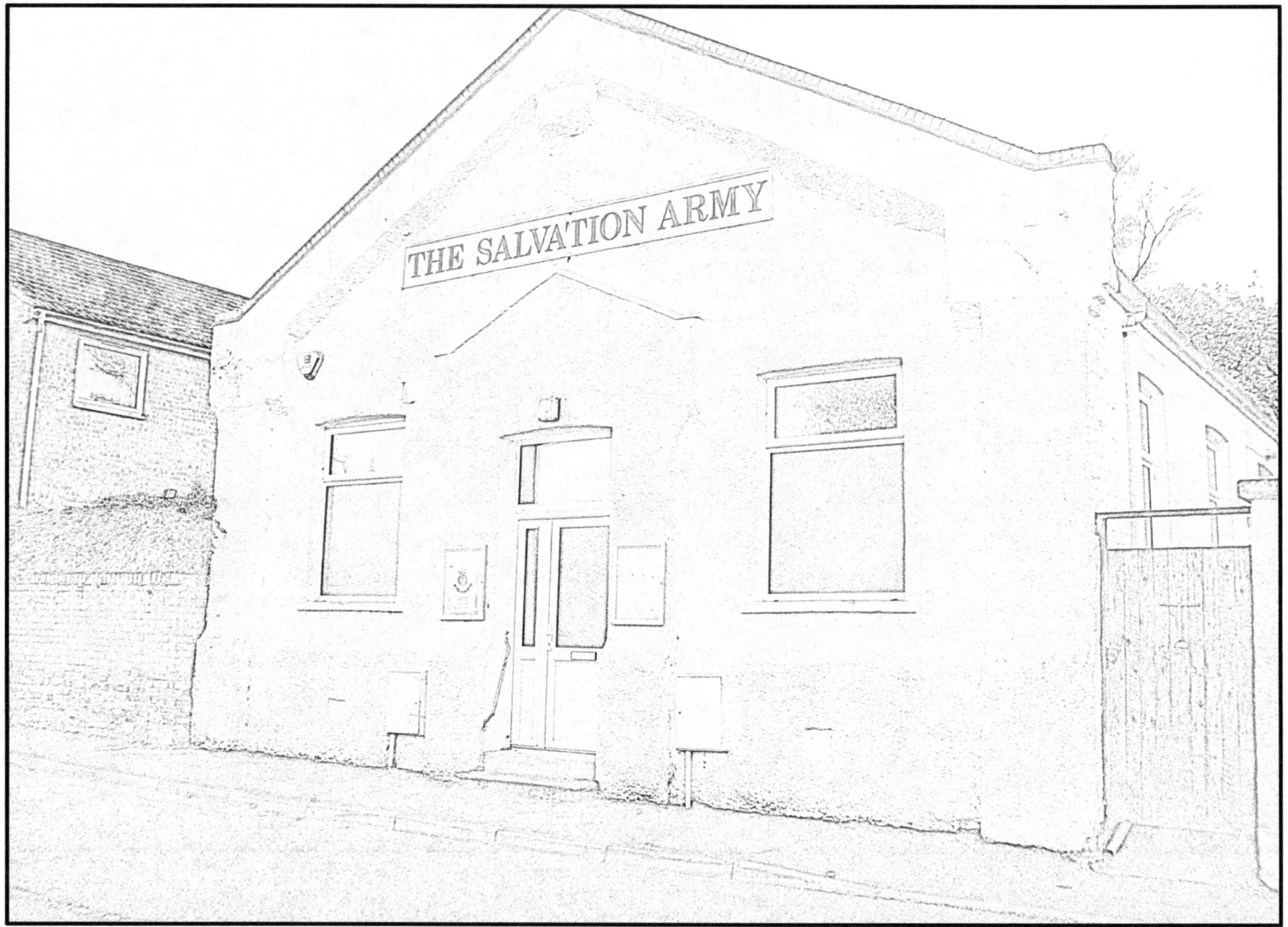

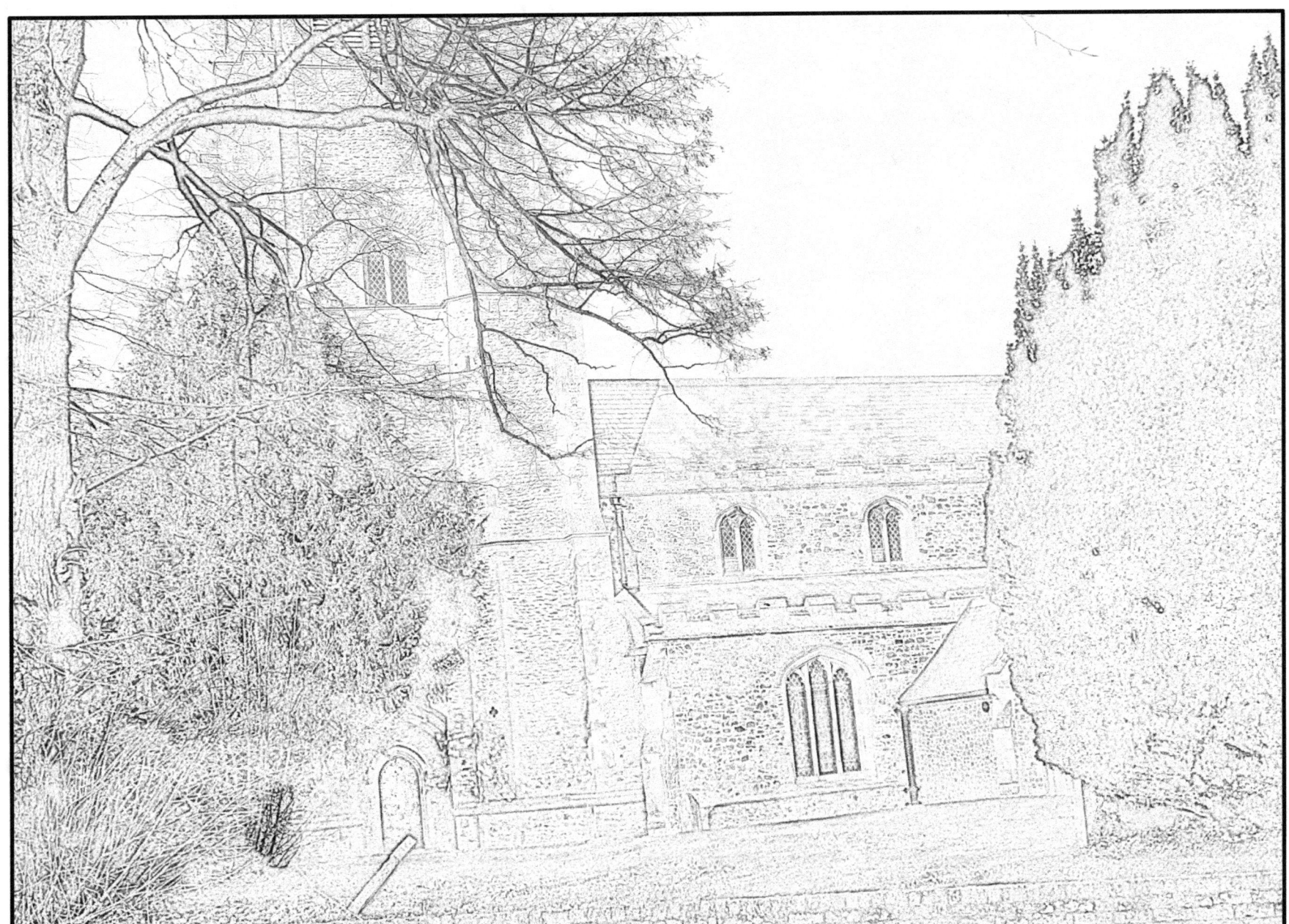

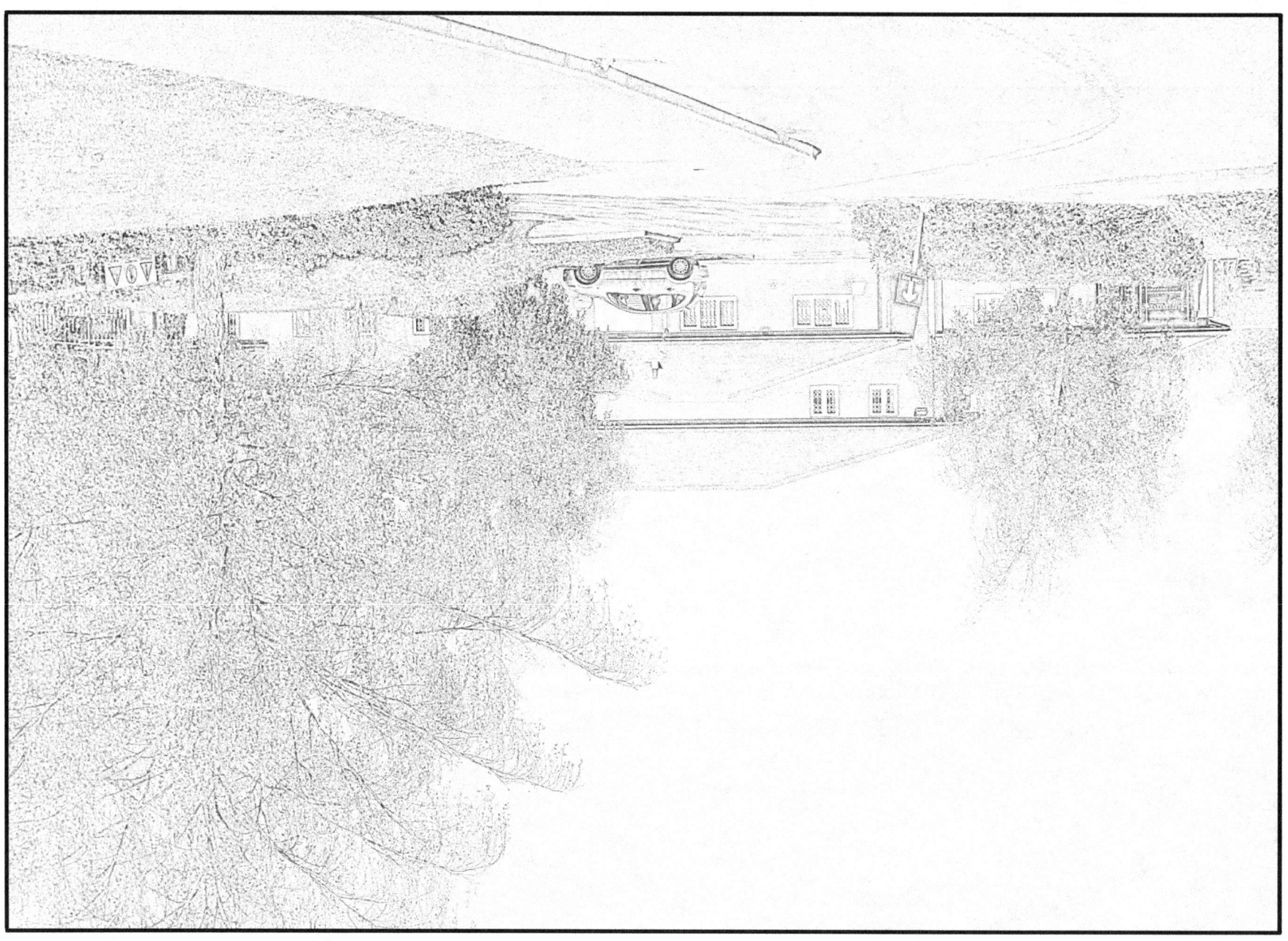

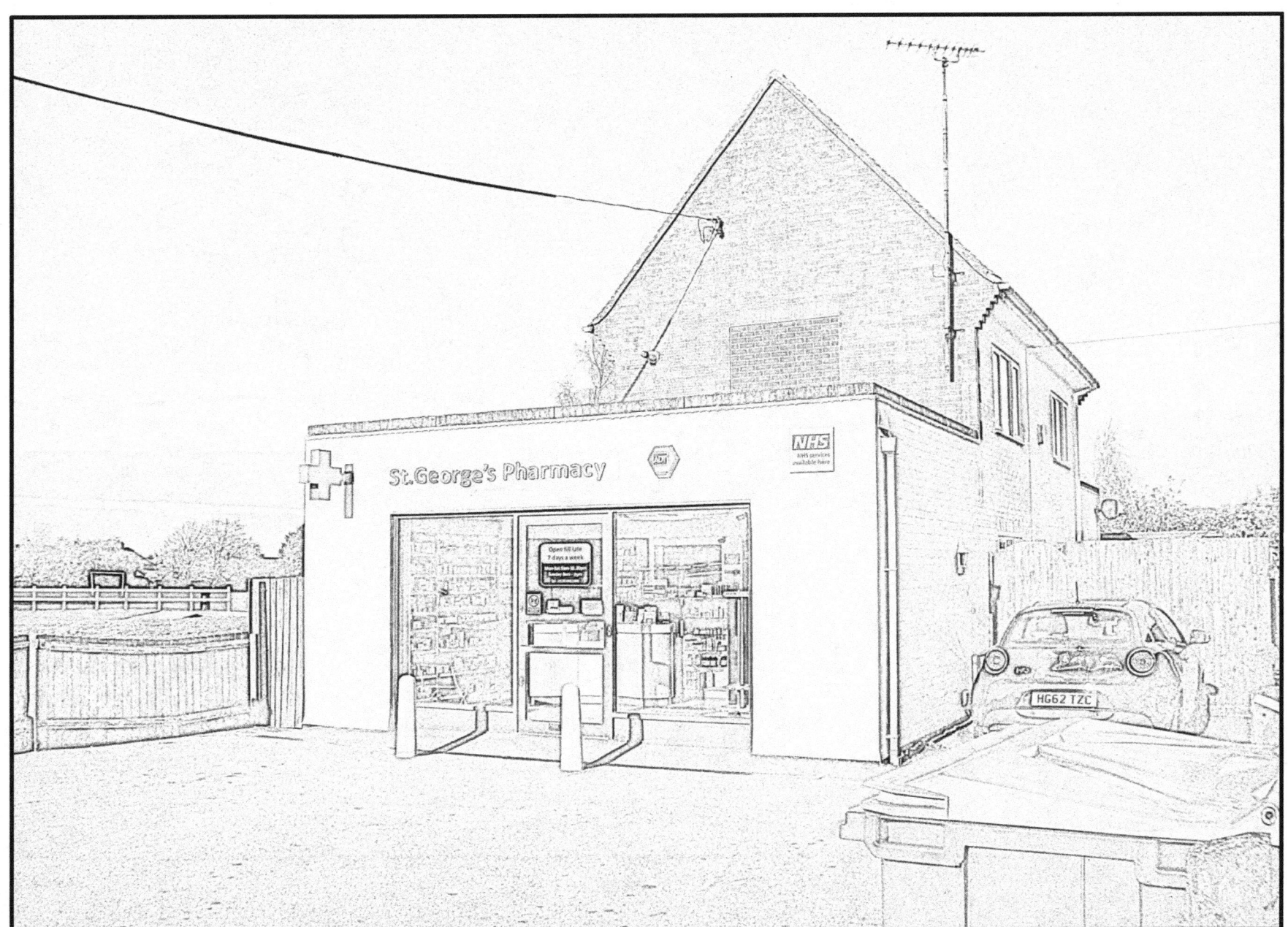

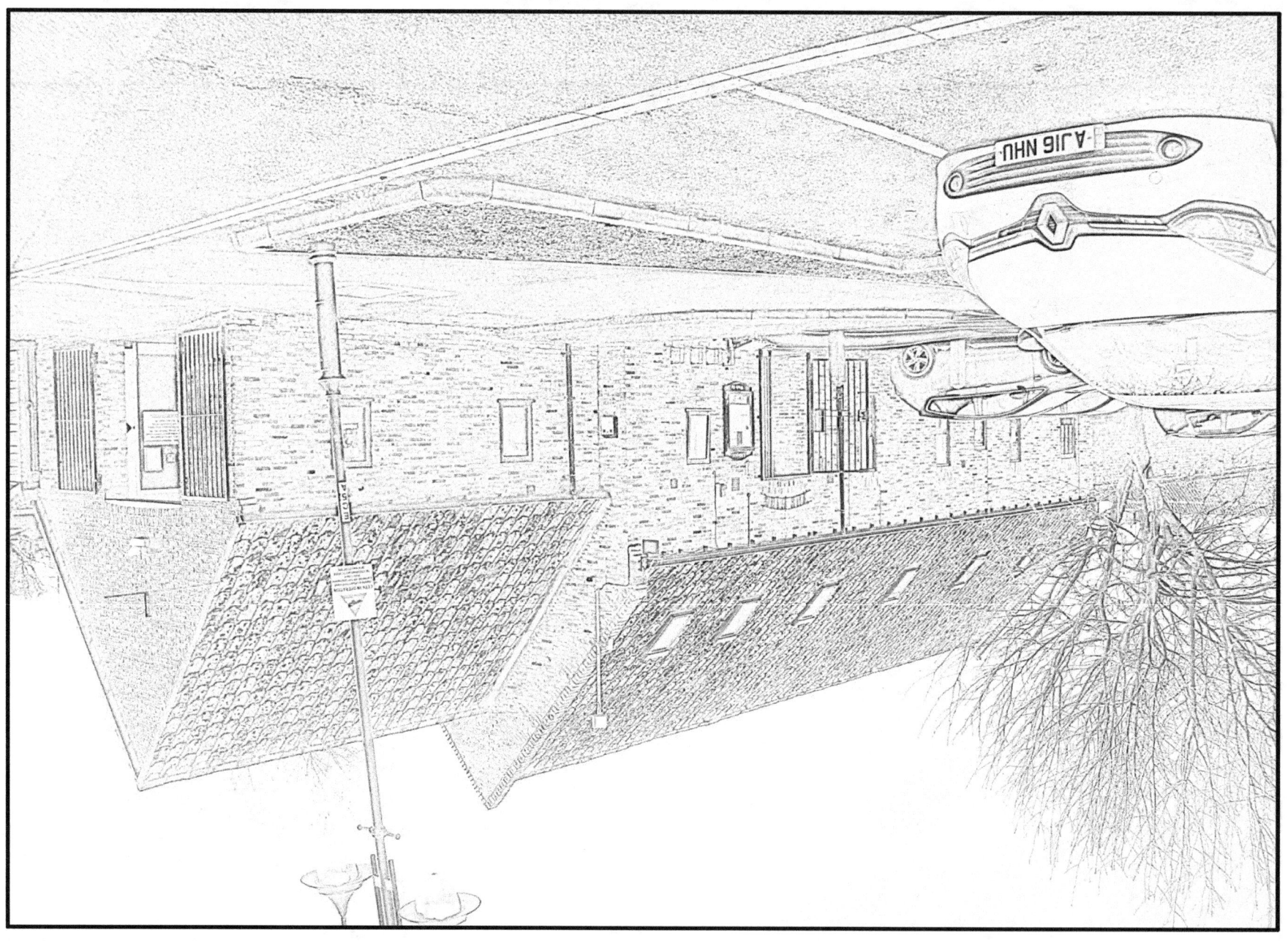

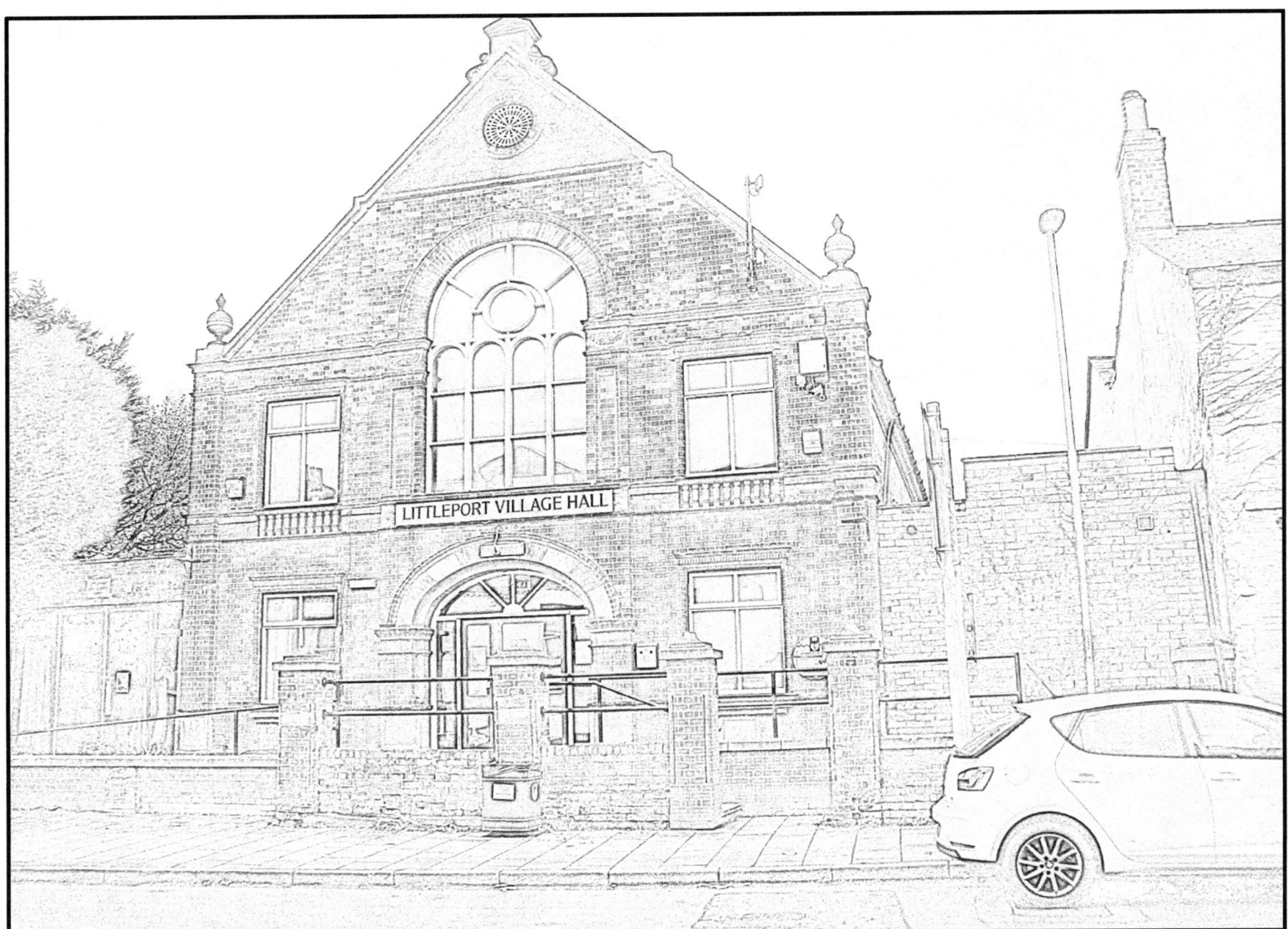

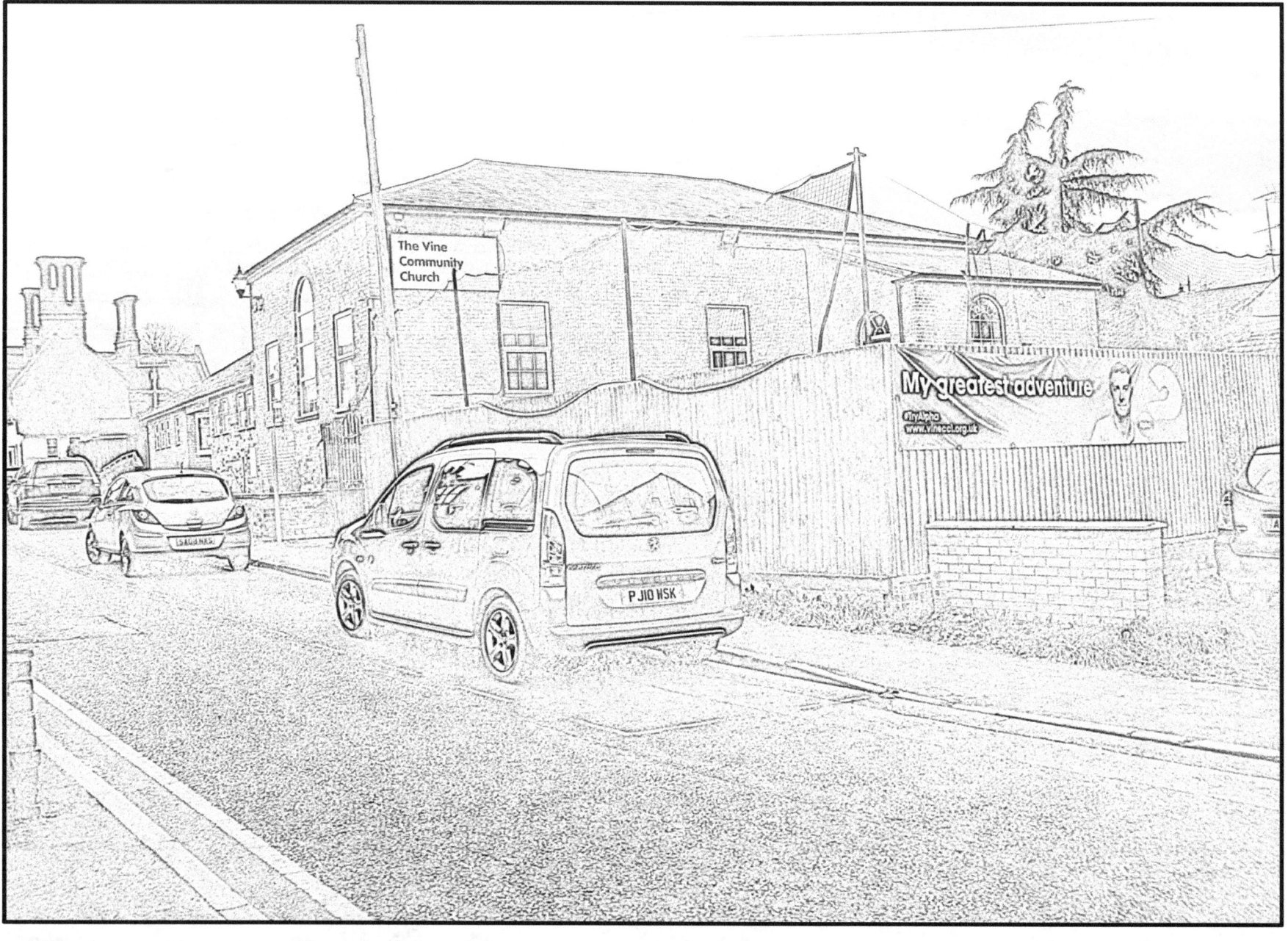

Final Word

I hope you enjoyed this book and if you wish to have something done specifically for your business or personalised for yourself, please contact me.

I live in Littleport, and can be contacted by

* telephone/text at 07780365127
* e-mail me @jean@jeanshaw.com
* Facebook - www.facebook.com/jeanshaw

To see my other books, please visit my author page at –

https://amazon.co.uk/Jean-Shaw/e/B001K8A1A0

Thank you and take care!

Jean

www.ingramcontent.com/pod-product-compliance
Lightning Source LLC
Chambersburg PA
CBHW080930170526
45158CB00008B/2238

* 9 7 8 0 9 5 5 7 7 3 6 9 3 *